2004

HUMAN RIGHTS AND MILITARY INTERVENTION

Was the bombing of Belgrade morally justified as an attempt to halt 'ethnic cleansing' in Kosovo? Should Western states have tried to prevent the slaughter in Rwanda? Are there, indeed, genuinely universal 'human rights' which could justify such interventions, or is the upholding of such rights simply the imposition of culturally specific values on other cultures? Is national sovereignty a necessary and legitimate impediment to intervention, or are we seeing the emergence of a 'new international order' in which national boundaries are less significant?

These and related ethical and political questions are addressed from a wide variety of perspectives by the contributors to this book. The answers presented form important reading for students and researchers in philosophy and in international relations, and for anyone interested in the difficult questions about whether and when other states may intervene in a country's internal affairs in order to uphold human rights.

Human Rights and
Military Intervention

Edited by
ALEXANDER MOSELEY and RICHARD NORMAN

ASHGATE

Published by
Ashgate Publishing Limited
Gower House
Croft Road
Aldershot
Hants GU11 3HR
England

Ashgate Publishing Company
Suite 420, 101 Cherry Street
Burlington, VT 05401-4405 USA

Ashgate website: http://www.ashgate.com

British Library Cataloguing in Publication Data
Human rights and military intervention
    1. Humanitarian intervention - Moral and ethical aspects
    I. Moseley, Alexander II. Norman, Richard (Richard J.)
    III. Society for Applied Philosophy
    172.4

Library of Congress Cataloging-in-Publication Data
Human rights and military intervention / edited by Alexander Moseley and Richard Norman.
    p. cm.
  In association with the Society for Applied Philosophy.
  Includes bibliographical references.
  ISBN 0-7546-0867-0 (alk. paper)
    1. Human rights. 2. Humanitarian intervention--Moral and ethical aspects. 3. Sovereignty. I. Moseley, Alexander, 1943- II. Norman, Richard (Richard, J.) III. Society for Applied Philosophy.

JC571 .H768834 2002
341.5'84--dc21

2002022546

ISBN 0 7546 0867 0

Reprinted 2004

Printed and bound in Great Britain by MPG Books Ltd, Bodmin, Cornwall

Contents

List of Contributors

Iain Brassington is presently completing his PhD in the Department of Philosophy at Birmingham on moral responsibility and innocence. His interests are in healthcare ethics and continental philosophy.

Chris Brown is Professor of International Relations at the London School of Economics, the author of *International Relations Theory: New Normative Approaches* (1992), *Understanding International Relations* (2nd edition, Palgrave, 2001), and *Sovereignty, Rights and Justice* (Polity Press, 2002), and editor (with Terry Nardin and N.J. Rengger) of *International Relations in Political Thought: Texts from the Greeks to the First World War* (Cambridge University Press, 2002).

Gideon Calder teaches philosophy at Cardiff University, and for the Open University in Wales. Recent and forthcoming publications include a co-edited collection on *Liberalism and Social Justice* (Ashgate, 2000), and a short book on Richard Rorty for the Phoenix 'Great Philosophers' series. He is currently Reviews editor for the journal *Res Publica*.

Stephen R.L. Clark is Professor of Philosophy at Liverpool University. His most recent publications include *God, Religion and Reality* (SPCK, 1998), *The Political Animal* (Routledge, 1999), and *Biology and Christian Ethics* (Cambridge University Press, 2000). He is currently working on a study of G.K. Chesterton.

Nigel Dower is Senior Lecturer in the Department of Philosophy, University of Aberdeen. He is currently Vice-President of the International Development Ethics Association. His publications include *World Ethics: the New Agenda* (Edinburgh University Press, 1998). He is co-editor of a Critical Reader on Global Citizenship to be published by Edinburgh University Press in 2002.

Heather Eisenhut is a graduate of the University of York and is presently working on an MPhil in English Literature at York on the colonial experience in East Africa.

Mark Evans is Lecturer in Politics at the University of Wales Swansea. He is the editor of the *Edinburgh Companion to Contemporary Liberalism* (2001), the author of *Liberal Justifications* (forthcoming), and has contributed numerous articles on contemporary liberalism and democracy to scholarly publications.

Paul Gilbert is Professor of Philosophy at the University of Hull. His principal publications are *Peoples, Cultures and Nations in Political Philosophy* (Edinburgh University Press, 2000), *The Philosophy of Nationalism* (Westview, 1998), *Philosophy of Mind* (with Stephen Burwood and Kathy Lennon, UCL Press, 1998), *Terrorism, Security and Nationality* (Routledge, 1994), and *Human Relationships* (Blackwell, 1991).

Brendan Howe is Assistant Professor of International Politics at Ewha Women's University, Seoul. His PhD (*Comparative Military Interventions: the Question of Legitimacy*) is a product of the Political Science Department of Trinity College, Dublin and the International Law Department of Georgetown University. Previous publications include *Southeast Asian Counter-Insurgency Techniques: the Malayan Experience* (Dublin: Alumnus, 2001), 'Can NATO Intervention in Yugoslavia be Justified by Existing International Legal Norms?' (*Irish Studies in International Affairs* vol.11, 2000), and *An Analysis of Walzer's Contributions to Debates on Domestic and International Social Organisation* (Dublin: Alumnus, 2000).

Maria Michela Marzano is Chargée de Recherche au CNRS (Centre National de la Recherche Scientifique), Paris, France. She is the author of *Norme e natura: una genealogia del corpo* (Naples, Vivarium, 2001), and *Le corps: normes et passions* (Paris, PUF, 2001).

Alexander Moseley was Assistant Professor of Economics at the University of Evansville from 1996 to 2000, and is the author of the forthcoming *A Philosophy of War* (Spring, 2002) and 'Is War a Hayekian Spontaneous Institution?' (in *Peace and Change*). He is an active contributor to the Internet Encyclopedia of Philosophy and also writes for the Foundation for an Economic Education's Ideas of Liberty.

Jamie Munn is Lecturer in International Politics at the University of the West of England, where he teaches critical international political theory, humanitarianism and nationalism. He is currently completing two manuscripts, on *Kosovo and the Myths of Nationalism* (forthcoming 2002) and *Concepts of Culture and Identity in Humanitarian Crises* (forthcoming 2003).

Richard Norman is Professor of Moral Philosophy at the University of Kent, and Chair of the Society for Applied Philosophy. His books include *Ethics, Killing and War* (Cambridge University Press, 1995), and he has previously edited *Ethics and the Market* for Ashgate.

Donal O'Reardon is currently completing his PhD thesis in the School of Hebrew, Biblical and Theological Studies at Trinity College Dublin on the subject of the place of theological ethics in contemporary moral discourse.

Paul Robinson is a lecturer in security studies at the University of Hull, and the author of various works on military history and contemporary security. He has also served as an officer in both the British and Canadian armies.

Philip Ross is senior lecturer in social sciences at York St. John College of the University of Leeds. Previous publications include *De-Privatizing Morality* (Ashgate, 1994), 'Utility, Subjectivism and Moral Ontology' (in *Journal of Applied Philosophy*, vol.11), 'The Self and Compulsory Treatment' in S.D. Edwards, *Philosophical Issues in Nursing* (Macmillan, 1998), and 'The Third Way, the Radical Centre and New Labour' in K. Knauer and S. Murray, *Britishness and Change in Narrating the Nation* (Katowice, 2000).

Preface

The chapters of this book originated as papers presented to the conference of the Society for Applied Philosophy in May 2001. We should like to record our thanks to Stephen Burwood, who was responsible for the practical organization of the conference, and to the contributors for allowing their papers to be published and for their cooperation in the preparation of the book.

Our special thanks go also to Alison Priest-Karolinski and Aisling Halligan for their skill and patience in preparing the typescript for publication.

Introduction

Alexander Moseley and Richard Norman

There is a long intellectual and moral tradition that encourages people to assist their neighbour in need: ethicists are familiar with the exercises that stem from the parable of the Good Samaritan. But alongside the humanitarian ethic exists the just war tradition, and the two doctrines and their implications simultaneously coincide and clash in modern interventions. They may coincide, for example, when aid workers need military protection; they may clash when military intervention creates a humanitarian crisis.

However, responses to the humanitarian plea for assistance, or for justice for an oppressed people, rarely escape criticism. On one level, the obstacle of political sovereignty stands in the way of international assistance and intervention - states possess territorial inviolability enshrined in UN conventions. On a deeper level, a lack of moral recognition undermines attempts to assist foreigners: on the one hand, when a people in need are considered so morally remote as to be not worth considering, then assistance is rarely forthcoming; while on the other hand, interventions that do take place are often criticized either as self-interested or for being inconsistent or morally asymmetrical - that is, interventions take place in some situations but not others with similar conditions. NATO intervened against Serbian oppression in Kosovo, but not against Russian oppression in the seceding Chechen republic.

Nonetheless, the parable of the Good Samaritan reverberates through Western thinking. Shakespeare's Shylock presents the classic literary expression of the ideas of a common humanity and humanitarian concern,[1] whilst the plight of many peoples in the last century has persistently dogged the collective conscience of the West: Armenians (1915), Jews (1933-45), Ukrainians (1929-33), Cambodians (1975-79); and especially in the past ten years the devastations wreaked upon Rwanda (1994) and Yugoslavia (1992-99).

The twentieth century produced 160 million victims of war, genocide, and torture, generated by state directives against civilians and foreigners. The international bodies and conventions drawn up to arrest what F.J.P.

Veale termed 'the advance to barbarism'[2] seemed impotent as the forces of hate were unleashed around the world. Against pleas from humanists and humanitarians for peace and good will to all men,[3] international law has upheld the rights of states to exist as inviolable entities. The great eighteenth century jurist, Christian Wolff, put it succinctly: 'no ruler of a state has a right to interfere in the government of another, nor is this a matter subject to his judgment.'[4] This principle is now enshrined in UN Article 2(7), but the UN has also enacted a convention 'to prevent and to punish' genocide as 'a crime under international law'.[5]

The chapters of this book explore the case for military intervention across state borders for humanitarian purposes, and the possible tensions between the military action and the humanitarian objectives. In this Introduction we shall summarize recent historical events which have brought these issues into sharp focus, and we shall then identify the ethical questions which subsequent chapters will raise and discuss.

The Historical Record

Following a problematic intervention supported by the United Nations in the Belgian Congo in the 1960s, the 1970s and 1980s were characterized by UN non-intervention; the interventions that took place (India into Bangladesh in 1971, Vietnam in Cambodia and Tanzania in Uganda both in 1979) were undertaken independently of the UN. By the late 1980s the mood began to change towards deploying UN peacekeepers in trouble-spots,[6] and as the Cold War ended, the promise of a New International Order loomed in which those able to do so would act to protect those struggling for freedom. In the aftermath of the Cold War, it was increasingly recognized that behind the curtain afforded by inviolable national status, various states had been pursuing policies inimical to international conventions and declarations. Against the universalism of rights, perpetrators of violence, displacement, oppression, torture, and war defended their actions on relativist grounds, employing the language and politics of local affairs and internal disputes; and they have decried the universalists as new imperialists who seek to intervene where they possess no jurisdiction or moral right. In restating the humanitarian claim, however, Vaclav Havel commented: 'no decent person can stand by and watch the systematic state-directed murder of other people.'[7]

In the early 1990s the UN advanced a more pro-interventionist philosophy. It created 'safe havens' in northern and southern Iraq to protect Kurds and Shiite Muslims respectively following the end of the Gulf War

(1991). It intervened in Somalia to enforce the peace and defend aid supplies.[8] It applied an arms embargo on Yugoslavia in 1991 and in 1992 permitted the sending of a Protection Force to create safe havens around Srebrenica and Sarajevo. Its record was, however, questionable, and deaths of US soldiers in Somalia raised doubts, at least from an American and European perspective, about the costs of humanitarian intervention. So in 1994 the rising deaths in Rwanda were ignored.

Hatred between the Hutus and Tutsis[9] was not new: mutual resentment went back generations with exploitation of one group by the other and outbreaks of massacres in pre- and post-colonial times. The end of German and then Belgian colonial rule saw the traditionally dominant Tutsis overthrown; many were killed in the late 1950s[10] and 1960s by the Hutus. In 1990 a dissident group of exiled Tutsis (the Rwanda Patriotic Front or FPR) led an invasion force from neighbouring Uganda. The ruling President, General Habyarimana, sought peace through a broad based coalition government that would draw upon the Tutsi FPR party. He was opposed by Hutu extremists, and after his death in 1994, when his plane was shot down by extremist Hutus, the blame was thrown on the Tutsis.

In the following months both Hutus and Tutsis fled a bloodbath in which several hundred thousand Tutsis (and moderate Hutus) were indiscriminately killed by the Interahamwe ('those who attack together'). In July the Tutsi FPR took control of the capital, Kigali, which prompted a swift departure of two million Hutus to neighbouring Zaire (now the Democratic Republic of the Congo): an unprecedented modern massacre turned into a massive refugee crisis. The FPR forged a coalition government under a Hutu President, Pasteur Bizimungu, that promised a safe return for the refugees, but the speed and extent of the massacres raised many questions concerning the role of the UN.

In 1994 the United Nations fielded 2,500 men in Rwanda. Ten Belgian troops were killed at the beginning of the massacre, but the UN troops were ordered not to use force to save victims. Instead the troops were subsequently withdrawn. The Clinton administration in the United States could not proffer support to any foreign military intervention - it was reeling from the recent and disastrous attempt to intervene in Somalian affairs in which 18 American soldiers were killed in Mogadishu. Yet the obvious unfolding genocidal campaign should have flagged the United Nations Convention on the Prevention and Punishment of the Crime of Genocide, which had come into effect in 1951. According to the convention, a genocidal state loses its rights to inviolability and thus opens itself up to a justifiable armed intervention - a positive duty that falls upon UN members. But in 1994, US State Department officials avoided using the term 'genocide' to describe what was happening, in order to evade any obligation to intervene militarily; the Security Council of the UN followed suit.[11]

But the West's guilt was not just of omission - it was also of commission. It had recently elected the Hutu government onto the Security Council. France supported the regime and together with Armscour of South Africa supplied the regime with weapons. The UN Secretary General refused to intervene in the affair, despite evidence of escalating deaths.[12] Eventually troops and police, mainly from Africa, were sent as part of a humanitarian aid package, and in the aftermath of war the hard task of forging reconciliation and justice began: the International Criminal Tribunal for Rwanda was set up by a UN Resolution in 1994, and so far it has sentenced 500 and 100,000 remain in prison.[13] But the deaths of 800,000 people will remain a contentious reminder of the case for humanitarian intervention.

The perception of political and moral failings on the part of the UN in Rwanda was reinforced by the massacres taking place within Europe when UN safety zones failed to protect thousands of civilians driven from their homes. The symbolic collapse of the Berlin Wall and the ending of the Cold War had brought to the fore hitherto restrained tensions in Yugoslavia, again whipped up by a propaganda machine. Religious and ethnic differences had subsisted for years under President Tito, who had kept a lid on bubbling nationalism and had balanced the differing groups with some success. Following his death the various ethnic groups struggled to assert their own power and eventually were to seek independence.

The election of two nationalistic presidents, in Serbia (Milosević in 1989) and in Croatia (Tudjman in 1990), was soon followed by rising tensions and clashes between Serbs and Croats in Krajina. Slovenia seceded from federal Yugoslavia, which prompted Tudjman to declare Croatian independence. Both nations gained European Community recognition, but the recently popularly re-elected Milosević invaded Croatia. After months of stalemate UN Peacekeepers were brought in and the Yugoslav army withdrew.

Events in Bosnia attracted Milosević's attention. Serb Autonomous Regions were declared, on the pretext of defending Serbians resident in Bosnia, and when Bosnia seceded from Yugoslavia, war broke out. The citizens of Sarajevo stopped attempts by Serb paramilitaries to take over the capital - both on the day of the referendum and on the day Europe acknowledged Bosnia's independence. After the failure of this attempted coup d'état, Bosnian Serbs besieged Sarajevo, bombarding the city with mortar and artillery. Serb forces began terrorizing Bosnian Muslims and

Croats, forcing women into rape camps, destroying homes, and firing upon surrendering civilians.[14] The UN responded by setting up no-fly zones, in which four Serbian jets were shot down, and by bombing Serb positions around the stricken towns. But massacres continued on the ground.

In August 1992 refugees pouring into Croatia were halted by the UN. It did not wish to been seen as abetting the Serbian ethnic cleansing of Bosnia, so the refugees were turned back. As Serb forces gained control over more territory, Milosević claimed that they were fighting in a civil war - i.e., a Yugoslavian internal affair that should not warrant external intervention. Croat President Tudjman then joined in to support independent Bosnian-Croat enclaves: Bosnian Muslims were under attack from both Serbia and Croatia, and both groups implemented terror tactics and ethnic cleansing against the Muslims.

Once again trouble began when UN troops were instructed not to use force. Secure enclaves were created but they were bombarded by Serbs, who captured two of them in 1995: Srebrenica and Zepa.[15] The attempted flight to 'safer' havens left 8,000 Bosnians massacred, many executed and hastily buried in mass graves that the War Crimes Tribunal staff have been unearthing since then.

Against a background of growing criticism that the UN had refused to intervene - and more specifically to commit troops on the ground - when it mattered most, NATO unilaterally intervened in the growing Kosovo problem. In 1998 atrocities by Serbs against Kosovar Albanians were being reported. In response to this, a guerrilla campaign on the part of the Kosovo Liberation Army began to claim world attention. The KLA's legitimacy was however often questioned, which implied that if the UN were to support the Kosovars, any alliance with the KLA could become problematic. Reports of a massacre of Kosovars at Racak increased the tension in the area and against NATO warnings and on-going peace negotiations Milosević ordered Serbian troops and tanks to the Kosovo border. Serbia rejected plans for Kosovar autonomy and in March 1999 NATO struck at Serbian positions and at the capital, Belgrade. The NATO military action was not authorized by the UN, but earlier UN resolutions had criticized the human rights violations in Kosovo and NATO invoked these to legitimate its action. The bombing campaign eventually forced Serbia to accept the deployment of NATO ground troops in Kosovo. Although it had not sanctioned the military action, the UN channelled humanitarian aid to displaced Kosovo refugees and began to investigate war crimes in the conflict. However, the liberation of Kosovo and the withdrawal of Serbian troops was followed by brutal reprisals against Serbs. In October 2000 the head of the Serbian state, Milosević, was ousted from power and subsequently was arrested, extradited to the Hague, and indicted for war crimes.[16]

While NATO acted unilaterally in Kosovo, the UN has had more success in its support of East Timor's secession from Indonesia. Following Indonesia's invasion in 1975, upwards of 200,000 people, roughly a third of the population of East Timor, were killed. In 1999 a referendum in favour of independence created a violent backlash by Indonesian sponsored militia until calm was restored when Australian UN peacekeeping troops were deployed. Two years later, East Timor elected a Constituent Assembly that is presently writing its constitution in preparation for full independence in 2002.

While the UN is looked to for solutions to international problems, in many war-torn zones local communities attempt to forge their own solutions, or, as in the Israel-Palestine conflict or in Northern Ireland, the United States is turned to or unilaterally offers assistance in negotiation. Nonetheless, the UN is active in, amongst others: the Congo (sustaining a ceasefire between the warring groups and committing 5000 military personnel); monitoring a ceasefire between Ethiopia and Eritrea with 4000 troops; Georgia, promoting humanitarian aid and observing a delicate military situation; and the Golan heights between Syria and Israel with 1000 military personnel. In total the UN deploys 47,451 military personnel and police, and 12,742 civilian personnel in 15 programmes, costing over $3bn for 2001.[17] Yet other hot zones remain outside the UN's present political remit.

The Ethical Questions

These historical cases all raise the same fundamental question for the ethics of international relations: is it permissible for states, or groups of states, to intervene militarily in the territory of another state with the aim of protecting the human rights of members of that state? This question can in turn be broken down into a number of sub-questions, each of which is the focus of a section of this book.

Are there genuinely universal human rights? Those who attempt to justify 'humanitarian' intervention claim that this is more than simply the use of military force by states in pursuit of their own national interests. The appeal to human rights is an attempt to invoke universal values. They must be more than the parochial values of a particular community or a particular culture, if they are to render military intervention legitimate from the point of view of the international community. Are there any such values, or does the imposition of so-called 'human rights' on a particular community amount to no more than 'rights-imperialism'? Perhaps it is just the old imperialism under a new name. The question is especially pressing if we are at all persuaded by those philosophers, who argue that all ethical values are culturally embedded. The chapters of Part I explore this tension between universalism and particularism. They ask whether it is possible to base human rights on a universal human nature so that they can be seen as more than just the values of liberal societies, and whether this can be made consistent with the recognition that such rights must be given substance and meaning within particular cultures. Questions are also raised about the range of these 'humanitarian' values. Our historical cases are ones where it was argued that intervention was justifiable to prevent genocide, but what about rights to certain kinds of basic liberties, or women's rights to autonomy and equality - would it be justifiable to impose these in opposition to long-standing cultural traditions?

Is military action a morally acceptable form of intervention? Even if it can be established that there are universal human rights which we should seek to protect in societies other than our own, it does not follow that military intervention is the appropriate means of doing so. Military intervention is problematic because it is itself especially liable to involve violations of human rights. The chapters in Part II explore the possible conflict between humanitarianism and military intervention. They suggest that although the two are not necessarily incompatible, the nature of modern warfare may well make it in practice an inappropriate instrument of humanitarian intervention, and a cosmopolitan concern for the global protection of human rights may be better expressed through other forms of action.

Can military intervention be justified selectively, or must it be consistently undertaken either in all comparable cases or in none? Many critics of NATO's intervention in Yugoslavia argued that it was morally suspect because, although NATO governments attempted to justify it in terms of the protection of human rights, they had not similarly intervened in other cases where human rights were being violated. This inconsistency, they argued, revealed as hypocritical the alleged concern for the human rights of Kosovar Albanians, and thus undermined the justification for intervention. The chapters in Part III respond to this criticism. The fact that we cannot intervene to prevent every violation of human rights, or even to prevent every case of genocide, is, they suggest, no reason why we should not intervene where we can, even if the choice of when to do so is determined by pragmatic considerations or by the accidents of geography. The traditional ethical concept of 'imperfect obligations' is, in chapter 8, refined to provide a possible way of thinking about the inescapable element of selectivity in humanitarian morality.

Is military intervention in defence of human rights an illegitimate violation of the sovereignty of nation states? The idea of sovereignty has until recently been central to mainstream thinking about what makes a war a *just* war. The modern international system of sovereign states is sometimes referred to as the 'Westphalian System', after the Treaty of Westphalia in 1648 which first established the modern political framework of sovereign states in western Europe. If the idea of the sovereignty of nation states is fundamental to the international political order, this may be taken to imply that all wars of intervention are an illegitimate violation of sovereignty, and that the only kind of war which can count as a 'just' war is a defensive war intended to prevent or reverse the previous unjust violation of sovereignty committed by an act of invasion or aggression. Michael Walzer's book *Just and Unjust Wars*, first published in 1977, is an extremely influential re-working of the traditional theory of 'just war', built around the idea that the fundamental rights of states are the rights of territorial integrity and political sovereignty, and that it is the protection of these rights, by military force if necessary, that makes possible the flourishing of political communities and their exercise of collective self-determination. Although Walzer's theory allows for the legitimacy of wars of intervention in extreme cases, these are by their nature exceptional. In Part IV questions are raised about this conception of the international order. Is it really historically accurate to invoke the so-called Westphalian Order to rule out military intervention in the affairs of other states? Does Walzer's theoretical structure of political communities and the rights of states provide a sufficiently cogent moral underpinning to rule out wars of intervention?

These questions are further complicated if a proposed military intervention to protect the human rights of a minority within a state can also be seen as intervention to assist a minority which is attempting to secede from the state and to constitute itself as an independent political community with its own state. The case of military intervention in Kosovo had this kind of ambiguity. Here the questions and issues raised in Part I about the status of human rights again come into play. If the significance of human rights depends in part on how they are understood in a particular political community, then the question of whether to intervene in order to protect them may become inseparable from the question of what boundaries can best identify a state jurisdiction capable of embedding human rights.

If the traditional picture of an international order based on sovereign nation states is questionable, what alternative conception of the international order might be preferable? In recent years politicians, including a previous President of the United States and the present British Prime Minister, have spoken of a 'new international order'. Is there such a thing, and if so, what is it? These questions are considered in Part V, and they require us to raise even more fundamental questions about the nature of human communities. Whom are we to regard as fellow-members of our moral community? Are moral communities ('communities of concern') constituted by political boundaries, or are political communities themselves an expression of more fundamental moral communities? If the latter, then is it plausible to see the moral community as global and all-embracing? Both of the authors in Part V invoke Aristotle's conception of a political community as a community of shared values to suggest that in the modern world such a community may exist at the global level. This takes us back to Part I and the question, posed there, of whether universalist values exist - but now with the suggestion that an international order may need to rest on something more extensive than the idea of human rights.

Are there, then, other universal human values which might be invoked to justify humanitarian intervention? If it is permissible to intervene militarily to defend human rights and liberties, what about other things which are perhaps equally fundamental in giving value to human life? In Part 6, the final chapter of the book considers whether military action would be justifiable to protect works of art, for instance, and other cultural artefacts.

We began by mentioning recent historical events that have raised the philosophical and moral questions discussed in this book. A few months after the conference on which this book is based, there occurred another set of events which raised similar questions - the terrorist attacks on New York and Washington on 11th September 2001, and the war which they unleashed. Those events are likely to have further momentous implications for our understanding of the international order and of war in the modern world. We do not yet know what their effects will be, but for our present purposes we can note the ambiguities in the language used by the American and other governments to justify the military intervention in Afghanistan, which is taking place as we write. The military action has been justified in terms of America's right to defend itself against attack, and that language invokes the traditional vocabulary of 'sovereign states' and of 'just war' as a response to aggression. It does not, however, apply easily and straightforwardly to the response to an attack launched by a terrorist network rather than by another nation state. Talk of a 'war on terrorism' employs a different vocabulary - a language of human rights and of military intervention to defend such rights. We make no comment here on either justification, other than to note that the contrast between them reflects the questions discussed in this book about human rights, war, and the international order. The questions are philosophical questions, but the recent events make it abundantly clear that they are questions of *applied* philosophy.

Notes

1   'I am a Jew. Hath not a Jew eyes? hath not a Jew hands, organs, dimensions, senses, affections, passions? fed with the same food, hurt with the same weapons, subject to the same diseases, healed by the same means, warmed and cooled by the same winter and summer, as a Christian is? If you prick us, do we not bleed? if you tickle us, do we not laugh? if you poison us, do we not die? and if you wrong us, shall we not revenge? If we are like you in the rest, we will resemble you in that.' *Merchant of Venice*, 3:1.

2   From the title of his book, *Advance to Barbarism: The Development of Total Warfare from Sarajevo to Hiroshima*, The Mitre Press: London, 1968.

3   From Erasmus's *Complaint of Peace* to Kant's *Perpetual Peace* and a host of literature and poetry to match: Stephen Crane's *The Red Badge of Courage*, Erich Maria Remarque's *All Quiet on the Western Front*, and so on.

4   Christian Wolff, *Jus Gentium Methodo Scientifica Pertractatum*, Trans. Joseph Drake. Clarendon Press: Oxford, 1934. Section 258, p.132.

5   See Stephen Clark's chapter 'Genocide, Consistency and War' below.

6   1988 UN General Assembly Resolution 43/131 restated the doctrine of non-intervention but legitimatized humanitarian action in Nigeria. Cf. Chris Brown's chapter, 'Humanitarian Intervention and International Political Theory' below.

7   Quoted in Geoffrey Robertson, *Crimes Against Humanity: The Struggle for Global Justice*, Allen Lane: London, 1999, p.387.

8   For a discussion of the intervention in Somalia see Munn's chapter below.

9   Although perceived as a tribal conflict, the details of the case are more complicated. As Jonathan Glover notes, the two groups shared the same language and intermarried. The Tutsis were a ruling class and Hutus who became rich became Tutsis. The genocidal campaign 'was not a spontaneous eruption of tribal hatred, it was planned by people wanting to keep power'. Jonathan Glover, *Humanity: A Moral History of the Twentieth Century*, Jonathan Cape: London, 1999, p.121.

10 Approximately 50,000 were killed in 1959.

11 Glover, op cit., p.122.

12 Geoffrey Robertson, *Crimes Against Humanity*, p.66.

13 In January 2000 two Rwandan women began proceedings against the UN for complicity in the massacres and an independent inquiry team - headed by former Swedish Prime Minister Ingvar Carlsson - has criticized the UN's failings.

14 In Kozarac, in 1992, 2500 civilians were killed in a period of three days, some of them shelled as they surrendered.

15 A recent French National Assembly report has criticized the failure of UN policy - at the time, the French had a general in charge of UN forces, Bernard Janvier, who has been criticized for not ordering air strikes on the aggressing Serbs. *Daily Telegraph*, 30 November 2001.

16 The details of the Kosovo conflict are considered in various chapters below, including those by Clark, Brown, and Howe.

17 The UN web site has up to date information on the programmes as well as their costs and fatalities.
http://www.un.org/Depts/dpko/dpko/ops.htm

PART I
HUMAN RIGHTS

Chapter 1

Grounding Human Rights: What Difference Does It Make?

Gideon Calder

Like anything else, the language of human rights can be abused. It is frequently adduced in support of projects which, in their motivations or effects, threaten the very aspects of human life which those rights were designed to protect or enhance. It can also, less injuriously, be used in apparently self-contradictory ways. One thing noticeable about 'human rights' talk is that even those who 'officially' reject the whole idea of human rights will, when convenient, quite happily rely on it for rhetorical purposes. Here are two loosely-drawn (but, I hope, familiar enough) caricatures of positions which, from a logical point of view, seem as awkward as they are commonplace.

A Left version goes something like this. So-called 'natural rights' are, at root, an ideological construct serving the interests of a given class or social order. This position might take Marx's powerful critique of formal equality in 'On the Jewish Question' as demonstrating that the *very idea* of rights derives its force from a liberal-capitalist historical context in which human beings are treated as isolated monads whose competitive existence places limits on each other's freedom.[1] The need for rights is thus the mark of a society in which we are invited or required to see others' advancement as a threat to our own. Now there is much of worth in this critique, and we shall return to its merits in due course. What might seem problematic is that having adopted it, many will nonetheless feel free to invoke 'rights' as the presumptive basis of movements towards social justice. So they will freely laud the aims and achievements of the US civil rights movement in the 1950s and 1960s, or claim that education is a 'right', and not a privilege, or insist that the 'rights' of asylum seekers are neglected by their current confinement in detention centres on arrival in the UK. Rights, then, are allowed a tactical or pragmatic role in the bringing about of a world in which - because it will leave behind the conflicts inherent in our own - there will be no need for them.

We might explain this by arguing that it is only a peculiarly Western convention, of relatively recent heritage, that fuses 'emancipation' talk with 'human rights' talk - and that Leftist struggles merely use the current utility of the latter as a convenient prop, rather than investing them with any ongoing significance.   But at any rate, such strategic appeals sit uncomfortably with the prior diagnosis of rights talk *per se* as distracting from inequalities in the social and economic spheres. This might, by its opponents, and especially by liberals, be seen as an exercise in having things both ways at once: rights are untenable when invoked on behalf of 'bad' tendencies, but the appropriate currency of struggles deemed emancipatory.[2]

This Janus-facedness is just as much a characteristic of an equally predominant attitude of the contemporary Right, especially in its communitarian moments. From this angle - of which, again, I'll draw a conveniently simplistic cartoon - the proliferation of rights talk (be it invoked on behalf of underpaid women, or hunted foxes, or cultural minorities) is symptomatic of a general corrosion of the moral fibre of Western civilization. The values of self-reliance and individual enterprise which have (say) 'made our country great' will be compromised and undone by the pernicious cultural influence of the idea that we are 'owed', as individuals, given benefits or status. The effect of this idea is to blind us to those other values - of custom and tradition - which, though not measurable on individualistic terms, are chief providers of our moral bearings. The very substance of such values will be the first casualty of the liberalization of attitudes towards them.   And at a theoretical level, the appeal to rights must necessarily abstract from the concrete, local forms of life which allow us a conception of others and of our duties towards them. Rights are thus a fiction, both socially pernicious and philosophically untenable.[3]

Note, though, how this position too will switch back on itself in certain contexts. Thus the current (as I write) military offensive in Afghanistan is billed by the Right as a war on behalf of 'democracy' and 'individual rights' - the most significant achievements of those liberal strains about which conservatives are otherwise so nervous - against the forces of international terrorism.[4] Similarly, the foetus may be presented as having a 'right to life' which overrides all other considerations in debates about the rights and wrongs of abortion - or British citizens as having a 'right to self-determination' under threat from the incursions of the European Union.

Is this, in fact, inconsistent? A communitarian rejoinder to the charge might be that if, as it happens, certain rights have grown organically to be part of the fabric of a culture's self-understandings, this itself secures their validity. Some rights work 'for us'. This does not mean that we can conceive of them as cross-culturally pertinent, or universally derivable. Again, it may be the local utility of 'rights-talk' - rather than its groundedness in anything beyond given practices - which renders it consistent with given political priorities. Proponents of both the Left and Right positions sketched here would insist that they are making no strong connection between human nature and the rights it may give rise to. Indeed, their rejection of any such connection arises from a deeper philosophical insistence. This is that *there can be no such thing* as a 'human right' if by this we mean something grounded in an account of fundamental, static, human needs, capacities or orientations. These needs, capacities and orientations will vary from one social position, or historical context, or cultural tradition, to another. It is their contextual derivation which gives them their meaning, force and substance. Recourse to universal notions of human nature as a source of principles of right treatment of others is thus both an impossible manoeuvre, and politically shallow.

There is a fairly easy step between this and another, broader implication which punctuates several of the articles in this volume. It is this: that far from being inherently emancipatory, the interrogation of, or intervention in, a given community's practices in terms of any putative notion of 'universal' human rights is an imperialistic gesture which inevitably involves the imposition of culturally specific values across the boundaries of cultural difference. This charge stems from a deeper claim: that every universalism masks a particularism. The appeal to 'human rights' in anything other than a self-avowedly pragmatic (or as Richard Rorty would call it, 'ironic') way involves not only a metaphysical extravagance, but a moral violence which entails the suppression of alternative, non-Eurocentric, priorities and forms of life. As a staple ingredient of postmodernism and cognate trends, this claim is as fashionable as - in my view - it is problematic. In what follows, I want to explore first its philosophical provenance, and then its practical application. In both respects, as I shall argue, it leads to the entrenchment of certain difficulties rather than their resolution. This in turn suggests that rather than rejecting the very idea of grounding human rights, and along with it their admissibility as a critical resource, we would do better to reconsider certain assumptions as to what a defence of such an idea might entail. That the language of human rights may be ripe for abuse, or misappropriation, does not make the underlying notion redundant. But it does require - even to identify cases of such abuse - that we maintain close critical attention to what might be required for genuinely critical, emancipatory and unhypocritical 'human rights' talk. This preliminary question, and the claim that it is indeed preliminary to discussion of the detail of human rights themselves, forms the focus of the remainder of this chapter.

A False Antithesis

Each of the rejections of the idea of human rights we have encountered has centred on a particular version of the provenance of those rights, and of their understanding. In their opposition to universalism, they tend to tie it to a stereotypically liberal articulation, according to which human rights, to have universal application, must be based on an ahistorical and atomistic conception of the individual. Atomism in this sense amounts to the claim that it is possible for human beings to go it alone: that we can be fully-fledged agents quite apart from any relation to society, or to the world.[5] On these terms, exemplified most starkly in Descartes' location of rationality in a severed realm of introspective thought, the world and others are only a secondary intrusion on an already self-sufficient subjectivity. On this basis, of course, liberals have tended to conceive of freedom negatively: in terms of my freedom, as a radically individuated subject, from external obstruction in realizing my own life-projects as I see fit.[6] Thus, political philosophers in the liberal tradition have tended to focus their attention on how to maximize the potential for each individual to realize those projects without impediment: typically, by a negative right to freedom from state interference in so doing.

The now-standard, already mentioned objection to such rights was inaugurated by Marx's objection that so conceived, they are rights of separation from others and from the community, and so invoke a monadic, egoistic paradigm of human subjectivity, 'withdrawn into himself'.[7] It has since been reinforced in C.B. MacPherson's critique of 'possessive individualism', arguing as it does that philosophers such as Hobbes and Locke have installed as self-evident aspects of human nature features which have, in fact, been fostered and encouraged by capitalist market relations.[8] The liberal-individualist treatment of rights thus mistakes a contingency (the conflicts engendered by the relations inherent in a given socio-economic formation) for a necessity, and builds from it a putatively 'neutral' picture of what is natural, or primary, about being human. The conception of the *individual* derived from this reifying move is duly *individualistic*, in a normative sense. To put this differently, the claim that rational subjectivity is something achievable in abstraction from community life in the 'real' world leads to the moral priority of individualized, rather than communal, pursuits. Methodological individualism of this kind conceives of social relations in terms of aggregations of individual wants. Since those wants will be presumed to conflict, social justice is conceived in terms of fair negotiations between those wants. Once human beings are conceived in possessive-individualist terms, the enforcement of the rights so derived will serve to entrench the unequal distribution of opportunities and resources within a capitalist society, rather than addressing the underlying structures of power which give rise to that distribution.

It seems to me that this critique is both pertinent and forceful. If human rights are 'the rights one has simply as a human being', as one defence of the liberal case puts it reasonably enough, then much will hinge on the conception of the human being which 'simply' has those rights.[9] If that conception is in key respects dependent on the hypostatization of what in fact are socio-historically contingent attributes and orientations, then those rights lose their universal purchase and application. At a deeper level, if the 'liberal individual' is itself conceived in untenably asocial terms, then the rights which it 'simply has' will be available only in the form of abstract, generalized imperatives which may be ideal fodder for university courses but of little practical application in terms of making the world a more humane place.

A topical example here might be the careful wording, noted by Phillip Cole, of the 1948 Universal Declaration of Human Rights on the issue of asylum for refugees.[10] Article 14 states: 'Everyone has the right to seek and to enjoy in other countries asylum from persecution.'[11] Yet on the part of states, there are no corresponding obligations for admission, nor for the granting of full residence rights, even towards those who are established as meeting the definition of a legitimate refugee. Even in conjunction with the 1951 Convention Relating to the Status of Refugees, rights are bestowed only upon those who have been *granted* asylum - a process entirely at the discretion of the host state. Thus, as Cole points out, despite there being, formally, a right to *seek* asylum, there is no formal offering of protection to asylum *seekers*.[12] Indeed, as is well enough known, the UK government has proceeded to strip away many of the benefits and entitlements previously granted to asylum seekers. Current practice is to assign problematic cases (asylum seekers whose claims are believed by immigration officers to be unclear, or who are deemed for whatever reason to be likely to renege on the terms of their provisional admission) to 'detention centres' - often prisons - until such time as their *bona fide* status has been proved.

The problem here, then, is with the lack of necessary purchase which any formal declaration of a given list of human rights will have at the level of concrete cases - for instance, the non-English-speaking Algerian asylum seeker who suffers malnutrition as a result of being detained in a prison where officers have not registered that he will only eat Halal meat.[13] This is not to suggest that any such formal declarations of human rights are rendered redundant in such concrete cases. Rather, it is to suggest that they are not enough in themselves to provide protection for those who are most in need. The force of the critique of formalism lies in its redirection of our attention from abstract definitions of human rights, in charters and declarations, to the concrete, material conditions under which such ideals might be realized. While justifications for, and proclamations of, human rights have proliferated, they have not come remotely close to being universally realized. That explaining this requires attention to historical, social and economic factors of which such rights, abstractly conceived, will make no mention seems to me to be fundamental to realizing their emancipatory potential. But this is not, in itself, a reason to drop the whole idea of universal rights as necessarily dependent upon the extravagance of the liberal conception of the individual.

And yet one finds exactly this response in areas of contemporary political philosophy - whether of communitarian, postmodern or other inflection - which make much of a rejection of the liberal account. Communitarians, for instance, insist that the very abstraction of 'the individual' from 'society' will always be a mistaken move. This is because we simply can't understand the individual's needs and wants in separation from its embeddedness amid the 'encumbrances' - shared understandings and values - which enable us to find an orientation for our actions and priorities in the first place. On these terms, a morally significant account of the individual is unavailable except by recourse to the particular communities within which that individual will gain moral significance. Postmodern critics will more likely reject the very idea of 'individuality', or 'humanity' as an effect of habits of intellectual discourse which have proved to be without foundation. By inflating what were in fact European values into a supposedly ahistorical conception of 'the human', Enlightenment attitudes in particular have required that we exclude, suppress or just override everything 'other' to that definition. Thus non-Europeans are in effect not quite 'fully human'. To extend the reach of 'humankind' to the point of a supposedly universal category merely extends the violence entailed in enforcing a particular conception of the human across incommensurable cultures. We should, instead, in so far as we admit a universal imperative at all, seek to avoid such generalizations at all costs and instead encourage the flourishing of a multiplicity of ways of human being without ranking them in terms of their proximity to a prior ideal.[14]

Both of these rejections of liberal universalism issue in a more or less relativistic picture in which cultural difference, or tradition, or context, provide a replacement for the misconceived and morally dangerous appeal to an unencumbered individual as paradigmatic of the human being. As such, they share with liberalism the assumption that to be universalist, a political theory must rest on an ahistorical, monadic atomized conception of the individual, for whom relations to the world and to others are incidental or secondary. Accepting *this* version of universality as the only available option, one accelerates (whether gleefully or with regret) straight down the expressway to an outright relativism in which human needs, values and entitlements can only be conceived as the effects of cultural factors which by their nature are local and specific. Once we have arrived *there*, of course, then the very invocation of 'human rights', or 'crimes against humanity', becomes at best empty rhetoric, and at worst, complicit in the imposition as the global norm of a particular (and inevitably partial) perspective on human nature and its priorities.

If the liberal conception of the human being that 'simply has' rights is the only available option, then it seems that a certain abstract formalism will characterize any appeal to universal human rights. If one supports the liberal conception then we may be committed to an approach to human rights which both presupposes intersubjective conflict and fails to address this issue at socio-economic level. But by rejecting this alternative on communitarian or postmodern grounds we are granting it sole copyright on 'human rights' talk by closing off alternative conceptions of the human being, and the ways in which it might 'have' rights.[15]

There is a deeper problem. For as we saw earlier, communitarian-minded conservatives will regard the traditions of a given community as morally worthy of protection and continuance in and of themselves, resisting their subjection to criticism by external standards. What if liberal rights are themselves a part of the fabric of convention to which one thereby has recourse, and the protection of which one will regard as imperative? To the extent that those rights have contributed to the formation of those conventions as we know them, they must be valuable. But to the extent that they are based on a fundamental misconception of the individual, they must also be mistaken. Thus it seems that - for communitarians and postmodernists alike - the claim that cultural specificity is somehow good in itself must require the relinquishing of their own core objections to the pernicious effects of liberal theorizing. To put this problem differently: either what constitutes cultural conventions makes a difference to their value, or it does not. If the former, then they are not good in themselves; their value depends on their provenance. If the latter, then the fact that 'our' conventions are based, very largely, on the influence of certain ideas of individuality which might cause problems elsewhere means that here, in our morally particular environment, they are worthy of protection.

The drift of my argument so far, then, is that if there are problems inherent in the liberal conception of human nature, then its rejection need not entail the rejection of the idea of human rights. In saying this, I do not dispute the claim, part-cited above, that 'if human rights are the rights one has simply as a human being ... then they are held "universally" by all human beings'.[16]   Quite how we might 'ground' human beings in an alternative to the liberal conception of human being is something I begin to explore towards the end of this chapter. In the meantime, I want to address the question of why this might be worth doing in the first place. Why *bother* finding a grounding for human rights?

The Need for a Grounding

There is, to be sure, a case to be made that upholding human rights requires no such grounding. This claim - that the idea that philosophical support for human rights is neither possible, nor necessary for the success of the real-life projects which would bring about the values they embody - has been directly put forward by Richard Rorty in his contribution to the 1993 Oxford Amnesty Lectures.[17]   Rorty regards the presumption that we need a grounding as an outworn philosophical conceit. As a pragmatist, he counts as irrelevant any fine-tuned philosophical dispute which does (or will) not make a difference to our practical engagement with the world or with others.[18]   The idea that there might be anything essential to being human, or distinctively human attributes, is just one such 'fifth wheel' when it comes to figuring out how to treat our fellow human beings. In particular: 'it is not clear why "respect for human dignity" - our sense that the differences between Serb and Muslim, Christian and infidel, gay and straight, male and female should not matter - must presuppose the existence of any such attribute.'[19]   On this basis, Rorty rejects the question of what he terms 'human rights foundationalism' - 'the question of whether human beings *really* have the rights enumerated in the Helsinki Declaration' - as 'not worth raising'.[20]

Why not? For strategic reasons. While 'human rights culture' is one of the more precious achievements of the present-day west, and while there is a wider and deeper concern than previously, or elsewhere, with the concerns which inform 'human rights' talk, we will not extend or enhance that culture by appeal to some or other base-level common human denominator:

> To get whites to be nicer to blacks, males to females, Serbs to Muslims, or straights to gays, to help our species link up into what [Eduardo] Rabossi calls a 'planetary community' dominated by a culture of human rights, it is of no use whatever to say, with Kant: notice that what you have in common, your humanity, is more important than these trivial differences. For the people that we are trying to convince will recognize nothing of the sort. Such people are *morally* offended by the suggestion that they should treat someone who is not kin as if he were a brother, or a nigger as if he were white, or a queer as if they were normal, or an infidel as if she were a believer. They are offended by the suggestion that they treat people whom they do not think of as human as if they were human.[21]

Rorty's point, then, is that the success and furtherance of 'human rights culture' owes nothing to the adequacy of 'human rights foundationalism'. If human rights are a project worth pursuing, then our commitment to them should require that we jettison the sorts of claim to a common humanity which will only hinder them in terms of suasive force.

We might see Rorty as providing ballast for the sorts of slippery, selective recourse to 'human rights' talk discussed at the start of this chapter. For there will be no contradiction in making purely expedient, rather than philosophically consistent, appeal to human rights in certain contexts if, in the end, this is all that *any* such appeal can *ever* amount to. And given that the appeal to human rights has served as a very effective justification for a great range of actions and achievements - from the provision of birth control to the 1989 revolutions in the eastern Europe, and from the release from prison of Nelson Mandela and a host of other political prisoners to the 1999 NATO bombing of Yugoslavia - perhaps this strategic success is the only justification required. Would we rather, as Rorty might put it, have a philosophically tight and well-coordinated account of the ontological ground of human rights, or have 'human rights' talk that *works*? Given the choice, and granting Rorty's own (as it happens, unsubstantiated) insistence that the appeal to such a grounding does not, in fact, work, it may seem that the case is closed: that grounding human rights is both intellectually futile, and pragmatically counter-productive.

It may seem that way. But consider the following claim, made by many in the wake of the 1999 NATO bombing (and considered in greater detail by Stephen Clark and Mark Evans in this volume): that the justifications proffered on behalf of the bombing were not the true reasons for its taking place.[22]   More than that: the justifications proffered were systematically *at odds* with the true reasons for its taking place. This offensive was proclaimed, by President Clinton and Prime Minister Blair among others, as a new form of humanitarian intervention. Thus Blair described it as 'a just war, based not on any territorial ambitions but on values'.[23]   These values were those of the international community: the values, it was claimed, of decency, cosmopolitanism, and human rights. But what if other, more traditional military motivations were afoot? What if the war represented an episode in what has been called 'human rights imperialism', in which powerful, partial interests such as those of the US displace the common interests of humanity precisely by the invoking of a conveniently amenable account of those latter interests as back-up for the pursuit of political and economic gain?[24]   What if the securing of those gains involved ambitions and consequences which might, from other angles, be deemed to run counter to a genuine concern for human rights?

I raise these questions not as a prelude to an in-depth perusal of possible answers to them, but rather to see how they might be dealt with on Rortian terms. The staple point of the Rortian analysis - and the one which he sees as dispensing with 'human rights foundationalism' - is a base-level moral perspectivism. Its essence is captured by Peter A. French in a discussion of how we might understand the moral universe of the average Balkan war criminal. French's conclusion is that this figure is not morally ignorant, but 'preferentially wicked'. It is 'pathetically naïve' to think that if only he 'could have been convinced that what he was doing was raping, torturing, mutilating, and murdering other human beings, he would have been caught up by the scruff of the neck by some invisible moral hand and just stop what he was doing'.[25]   Our mistake is to consider such figures as able to be morally redeemed in standard humanitarian terms. For 'they do not...have the capacities to try to bring about events that are radically different than, indeed, opposed to, those of ethnic cleansing. They are dominated by their ingrained, unchosen, ethnic bigotry....It is who they are, their form of life, and they do not have the ability to dispossess themselves of it.'[26]   On these terms, as on Rorty's, persuasion or negotiation is pointless if it is staked in terms of the vocabulary of human rights. For Balkan war criminals, ensconced as they are within their 'bigoted form of life', will simply not recognize those terms, or those rights. Believing otherwise would be like making a serious aim out of convincing a ferret that, all along, it really should have been a hamster.

What implications does this position have for the idea that we might critically gauge whether a purportedly humanitarian military intervention was, indeed, humanitarian? As I see it, they are pretty drastic. This is for two main reasons.

The first concerns a fairly straightforward problem encountered by moral perspectivism of the form which claims that there can *in principle* be no common measure between radically different 'takes' on the moral significance of a given set of actions. For perspectivists, confronted by a Balkan war criminal whose moral language is radically separate from one's own, there really is nothing that can be said in mutually recognizable terms. If such a position holds, then the postmodernist position seems to follow swiftly on: that to 'translate' the attitudes embodied in the war criminal's moral language into terms appreciable in our own would be to violate its particularity. To condemn such acts as somehow inherently wrong would be an admission of lack of understanding, and a display of insensitivity to context. This will, of course, also apply from the reverse angle. To condemn the NATO perspective from the point of view of the Balkan war criminal would be equally, and simply, mistaken. It would be to presume that the NATO hierarchy and those on the receiving end of its bombing were members of the same moral universe, partakers in a common 'form of life'. For outright perspectivists, they are simply not. The upshot of all this is that, from an epistemic point of view, there will be no *general* means of distinguishing between a genuinely humanitarian intervention and one for which the language of humanitarianism is serving as a convenient, cynical prop. For these will be equally unfathomable from the point of view of those who, as Rorty and French claim, will not and cannot recognize the force of humanitarian claims in the first place. Thus there is no answer to the question 'Was this war humanitarian?', because the question itself is unaskable.

To this criticism of perspectivism, it might be responded: Well, maybe, but to draw such a conclusion is just to presume that you must include every available perspective in order to address the question. It is to try to be 'universalist' towards the range of different perspectives, to include them all. We need not do this - and in fact, it misses the perspectivist's point. We do not ask serial killers for a definition of murder, nor practitioners of clitoridectomy for definitive views of women's rights. No-one *seriously* thinks that all views of such issues are somehow on a par.[27] The point is merely (again) a pragmatic one: time spent trying to persuade the war criminal that our views are 'right' and his 'wrong' by virtue of some essential 'way human beings are' is pointless. It would be better spent on telling the sort of 'long, sad, sentimental story' which Rorty takes as having inculcated, over the centuries, a heightened ability in the 'rich, safe, powerful' western democracies to include more and more 'subhuman' strangers amongst those whom we count as 'one of us'.[28] Worries as to the *truth* of such stories are beside their point. It is their *effects* which count towards the furtherance of 'human rights culture'.

But this brings me to a second deficit of this account in terms of the critical grasp it might afford. For on these terms, the question of the humanitarian nature of the NATO bombing is ceded by default to its practitioners. The bombing has, on the terms of the spokespeople for 'human rights culture' who defended it, been counted a success. The Kosovan refugees who fled the bombing as it began (and the intensified programme of 'ethnic cleansing' begun simultaneously by Serb forces) have mostly, we are told, returned home. Slobodan Milosević is on trial for war crimes, as NATO had promised all along.[29] Now if there can be no distinction - and hence no discrepancy - between 'real' humanitarian aims (those based on claims on what human beings are 'really' like) and their articulation in the serendipitously predominant 'human rights culture', then we are left with a situation in which, fairly straightforwardly, 'right' has been determined by 'might'. In other words, to the extent that the bombing succeeded in its aims, and to the extent that those aims were *purportedly* humanitarian, this must count as a successful humanitarian military intervention. In its effects, it counted towards the furtherance of 'human rights culture', as defined by those with the power to enforce their definition against others. The problem here is that if what human rights *really* are is beside the point of their invocation, then this would appear to be the end of the story. Propagandic efficacy would be the sole available measure.

On these terms, again, the question 'Was this war (really) humanitarian?' is ruled out of court, except as a call to examine the success of a military operation deemed, by majority opinion in the places which mattered most to its success, to be humanitarian. Rorty's 'human rights culture' is a relentlessly self-confirming enterprise: its own asserted definitions of humanitarian ventures are insured against valid challenge as long as they are strongly and persuasively enough asserted. On these terms, a self-professedly military venture with strong public support is, almost by definition, humanitarian *if it says it is*. Notice here that what is lost in this redescription of the nature and scope of human rights is not just the possibility that a successful, widely-supported 'humanitarian' mission might be morally wrong. Also unintelligible on this basis is the possibility that those adversely affected by such actions might themselves have been 'wronged' in the process. For if we are, of necessity, bound to constrict the range of 'humanity' to those whom we regard as being 'one of us', then those who have, in different places and at different times, fallen *outside* that range (blacks, women, Muslims, gays, or infidels, to use some of Rorty's own examples) do not, by definition, count as human. So conceived, those outside the current parameters of 'human rights culture' cannot be violated unless those within decide that they have been. They are put in the position of the asylum seekers who, although they have a right to 'asylum', do not have a right to be an asylum seeker. In Rorty's version of things, nobody has a 'right' to be included in the category of humanity.

Beyond its morally unsettling implications, there is (for all Rorty's attempts to evade such issues) an underlying philosophical problem in the construction of this case. It is roughly this. Even if we grant Rorty's (as I said, unsubstantiated) empirical case that we cannot, in fact, find a common language in which to raise issues of human rights abuse with those of other cultures, what actually follows? For Rorty, it seems to be that this rules out *in principle* the very possibility of there being 'distinctively human' characteristics from which we might derive any moral principles for action. In other words, it rules out the possibility of there being such an ontological grounding for human rights of which we may not, as it happens, have so far gained an adequate grasp. The fact, as he sees it, that there *is* no such grounding means that we *ought* not to seek one. I suspect that the constrictions which his own position places on key aspects of critical inquiry - for instance, the ruling out of any possible discerning of whether purportedly humanitarian ventures are *really* such - points in itself to the need for such a grounding. Unless, that is, we are to grant the crudely consequentialist thesis that there really are no moral constraints on what may be done in combat save the end (of the furthering of 'human rights culture') which must here be taken as the only available moral index. If *that* is the case, then the very point of human rights talk as putting constraints on what may or may not be done, by way of killing or violating others, in the process of realizing aims conceived on the perpetrators' terms to be just has been finally and irretrievably jettisoned.[30] Without a grounding, such constraints, if they exist at all in 'human rights culture', will simply be malleable and adaptable according to current, and perhaps unrelated, political imperatives.

The Scope for a Grounding

If the attempt to maintain the force of 'human rights' talk without the need for a grounding fails, this does not, in itself, tell us much about how we might find such a grounding. Is there indeed a worthwhile distinction to be had between false, or merely formal and so empty, claims to human universality and 'genuine' alternatives?

On this note, let us reconsider the claim, common to the two selective usages of 'human rights' talk mentioned earlier on, that it is in fact historical context which provides for the nature and scope of whatever we deem as 'natural' rights. MacPherson's claim, for instance, is that Hobbes and Locke, in positing certain 'natural' rights which exist prior to our association in political societies, are in fact installing as 'essential' attributes and priorities those which are specific to a given form of political society. Thus, such 'natural' rights are really the artificial concoctions of theorists who have in mind the defence of a given social order. The communitarian critique has a slightly different emphasis: that rights arise only in the context of such a given social order, and so cannot, in principle, precede it, or pertain to other communities. There are no rights attaching to human beings *qua* human beings; if we can speak of rights at all, it can only be in terms of their arising within a particular tradition of moral discourse.

And even then, if one adopts the view of Alasdair MacIntyre, they are impossible to assert with any degree of self-evidence. As he observes: 'In the United Nations declaration of human rights of 1949 [*sic*] what has since become the normal UN practice of not giving good reasons for *any* assertions whatsoever is pursued with great rigor.'[31] This is true enough: there are no justifications for the list of rights there asserted. This is characteristically the case with even the strongest defences of the most politically consequential forms of rights. Robert Nozick, in beginning his defence of market freedoms in *Anarchy, State and Utopia*, famously begins thus: 'Individuals have rights, and there are things no person or group may do to them (without violating their rights).'[32] Equally famously, Nozick proceeds to provide no substantial back-up whatsoever for this claim - an absence which suggests that there may be no non-circular way of providing such back-up. Combine this with the fact that, as we have seen, even those most conspicuously in need of the protection which rights might afford - like asylum seekers - must rely on their positive conferral by some given governmental agency in order for those rights to *amount* to anything beyond an empty abstraction, and the prospects for meaningful, coherent and effective 'human rights' talk might seem irrevocably bleak. All that the arguments of the previous section may have amounted to is the conclusion that *if* we choose to invest any emancipatory or protective potential in 'human rights' talk, *then* they require a more secure grounding than Rorty will allow. It may be that, in fact, they are beyond retrieval.

It seems to me that this conclusion would be a mistake. Take the criticisms of Marx, MacPherson and others of the liberal conception of the individual, and the rights to which this gives rise. One might see them as dynamiting the very idea of 'rights talk' *per se*. But we might, alternatively, see them as deriving from a *partial* account of human nature rules which are supposed to apply to all people at all times. To concede that there is no such thing as human nature on the basis of a rejection of the liberal account of it would, in itself, be to take an unnecessary step into a void in which we refuse to recognize *any* human need - nourishment, housing, clothing, fuel, medical care, educational provision, meaningful work, freedom of thought and expression - as being held in common by all members of our species.[33] Perhaps this list is thin, and rather unhelpful in itself in terms of signalling the means by which we might bring about such provision for every human being. But it is no less radical for that. In the present world conjuncture, where, both globally and within the richer countries, gaps between rich and poor are steadily widening, the idea that we might achieve any such levels of basic equality is as ambitious as it is, arguably, necessary for the long-term survival of the world's diversity of cultures.

And this is where the radical force of 'human rights' talk comes in. To dispense with the very idea of human rights, little more than fifty years after the UN Declaration, might give the impression that the rights listed in that declaration had been, as much as they will ever be, achieved. This seems to me either complacent, or jejunely optimistic. To reject the idea that *any* human rights might follow from such basic human needs listed above (and doubtless, there will be those who would dispute that even these are 'basically' human) is to run a similar risk of complacency. For that is all that rights, at root, need mean: that on the basis of some core features of what it is like to be a human being, we have an entitlement to be treated as human, and a responsibility to treat others as such.

This need not require that we can already know in advance, and so delimit, every last context or interpretive twist of the application of human rights. Neither need it require that a full and final list of those rights is available in advance. For it need not be the case that the idea of universality is conceived on liberal terms. If the problem, in practical terms, of that particular account is that of necessity the formal rights arrived at abstract from the concrete contexts in which they will apply, then, for universalism to be retained, it will be necessary to seek a version which pays due heed to the material circumstances in which the aims of 'human rights' talk might be realized.   This in turn will require an alternative account of the human subject from that typically relied upon in liberal-individualist discourse.   Rather than abstracting the subject from the world in which we, of necessity, find ourselves and make our way, such an alternative account might concentrate on the relationality of subjectivity - in practical terms, to the objective world and to the others interaction with whom is integral, rather than incidental, to the realization of our potential for rational and fulfilled selfhood.   That these relations are, in their cashing-out, in some senses contingent upon circumstances need not, *pace* communitarianism, lead us to conclude that our moral selfhood is reducible to such circumstances.   That the human rights derived from such a grounding in human nature will in some senses be provisional - in the sense that there may be hitherto unforeseen aspects of equality and liberty to which our present horizons provide insufficient access - need not compromise the ethical basis upon which equality and liberty can be installed as aims.

There has been space here only for a sketch of the possibilities for reconceiving how we might ground human rights along lines which avoid the shortcomings of a liberal account.   What I hope to have shown is that, for all the difficulties involved in conceiving and applying human rights, the state of the world is not such that we can safely dispense with such a project altogether.   If human rights matter, then the possibility of their being grounded does indeed, both theoretically and practically speaking, make a difference.

Notes

1   See Karl Marx, 'On the Jewish Question', in *Selected Writings*, ed. David McLellan (Oxford: Oxford University Press, 1977), pp.39-62.

2   It might also be seen as concentrating exclusively on the wrongs done *to* individuals (especially those of a given subjugated group) rather than the wrongs done by individuals, of any such group, in their personal or political dealings. For a discussion of why this represents an unfortunate deficit in much of Left thinking see Kate Soper, 'Socialism and Personal Morality', in David McLellan and Sean Sayers (eds), *Socialism and Morality* (Houndmills: Macmillan, 1990), pp.100-115.

3   Alasdair MacIntyre, *After Virtue*, 2nd edn. (London: Duckworth, 1985), pp. 66-70.

4   That the bombings of Afghanistan begun in October 2001 were a response to an attack on 'democracy', 'civilization' and 'freedom' was a constantly reiterated motif in the speeches of George W. Bush and Tony Blair as they sought to build an international alliance against 'international terrorism' in the weeks after the attack on the World Trade Centre on 11 September 2001. That this alliance included countries - China and

Israel among them - among those most often cited by Amnesty International as violating the human rights of their own citizens was not dwelled upon in the process of its forging. The possibility of distinguishing between such strategic usage of human rights rhetoric and more consistent applications is, as I argue here, crucial to a sufficiently critical understanding of what we're talking about when we talk about human rights.

5   I borrow here from Charles Taylor's definition in 'The Nature and Scope of Distributive Justice', in his *Philosophy and the Human Sciences: Philosophical Papers, II* (Cambridge: Cambridge University Press, 1985), p.292.

6   Here I invoke Isaiah Berlin's influential distinction between negative liberty (as freedom *from* obstruction) and positive liberty (as freedom *to* realize my potential) – see 'Two Concepts of Liberty', in his *Four Essays on Liberty* (Oxford: Oxford University Press, 1969).

7   Marx, 'On the Jewish Question', pp.52-53.

8   See C.B. MacPherson, *The Political Theory of Possessive Individualism: Hobbes to Locke* (Oxford: Oxford University Press, 1960).

9   Rhoda E. Howard and Jack Donnelly, 'Liberalism and Human Rights: A Necessary Connection', in Micheline R. Ishay (ed.), *The Human Rights Reader* (New York and London: Routledge, 1997), p.268.

10   Phillip Cole, *Philosophies of Exclusion: Liberal Political Theory and Immigration* (Edinburgh: Edinburgh University Press, 2000), pp.36-38.

11   'United Nations Universal Declaration of Human Rights' (1948), in Ishay (ed.), *The Human Rights Reader*, p.409.

12   Cole, *Philosophies of Exclusion*, p.37.

13   The case in point here concerns an asylum seeker detained in Cardiff prison during the summer of 2001. In fact, a group of 47 such detainees were eventually led to go on hunger strike in protest against their treatment.

14   This position is the upshot of Jean-François Lyotard's meditations on the possibility of a postmodernist conception of justice. See Lyotard and Jean-Loup Thébaud, *Just Gaming*, trans. Wlad Godzich (Manchester: Manchester University Press, 1985), esp. pp.59, 100.

15   I freely acknowledge that these cartoon pictures of alternative positions will gloss over many of the subtleties of their respective articulations. Taking John Rawls as the pre-eminent contemporary representative of the liberal tradition, it is clear that in the thirty years since *A Theory of Justice* (Oxford: Oxford University Press, 1991) he has amended and qualified his methodology in response to communitarian and other criticisms. He no longer, for instance, takes his theory to rely on 'claims to universal truth' based on 'presumptions about the essential nature and identity of persons', but rather as drawing upon 'intuitive ideas embedded in the political institutions of a constitutional democratic regime' - 'Justice as Fairness: Political not Metaphysical', *Philosophy and Public Affairs* 14 (1985), pp.223-225. That Rawls' recent attempt to articulate a liberal conception of justice in terms of international law - in *The Law of Peoples* (Cambridge, Mass.: Harvard University Press, 1999) - will still meet with communitarian objections is the subject of Donal O'Reardon's chapter in this volume. That Rawls' previous work nonetheless shares presuppositions with its communitarian and postmodern counterparts is a claim made at greater length in my 'Liberalism without Universalism?', in Bob Brecher, Jo Halliday and Klára Kolinska (eds), *Nationalism and Racism in the Liberal Order* (Aldershot etc: Ashgate, 1998), pp.140-159.

16   Howard and Donnelly, 'Liberalism and Human Rights', p.409.

17   Richard Rorty, 'Human Rights, Rationality, and Sentimentality', in his *Truth and Progress: Philosophical Papers, Volume 3* (Cambridge: Cambridge University Press, 1998), pp.167-185. References are to this edition. The piece was originally published in Stephen Shute and Susan Hurley (eds.), *On Human Rights: The Oxford Amnesty Lectures 1993* (New York: Basic Books, 1993), pp.111-134. It also appears in The Belgrade Circle (eds), *The Politics of Human Rights* (London and New York: Verso, 1999), pp.67-83.

18   I will not attempt to do full justice here to the dimensions of Rorty's sustained and eloquent criticisms of the ambitions of philosophers in this regard. Especially pertinent here is the case he makes in *Contingency, Irony, and Solidarity* (Cambridge: Cambridge University Press, 1989) for an 'ironic' liberalism which recognizes that the core beliefs on which it depends are the products of 'time and chance' rather than of uncovered 'truths' about human nature.

19   Rorty, 'Human Rights, Rationality, and Sentimentality', p.171.

20   Ibid., p.170.

21   Ibid., p.178. Earlier in the lecture (p.167), Rorty cites the example of a Serbian guard who, in the Bosnian conflicts of the early 1990s, had driven over, in his lorry, rows of Muslim prisoners awaiting interrogation. He did not, on the evidence of a journalist's report, see himself as violating human rights. Rorty's gloss on this is that in the lorry driver's own eyes he has done this not to fellow human beings, but to *Muslims* - has not been inhuman, but is discriminating between true humans and pseudo-humans.

22   The same claim is just as appropriate in the context of the bombings of Afghanistan commenced in October 2001 - a campaign to which there are equally valid objections on the grounds of hypocrisy and double-handedness. But since the US justification for this offensive centred on self-defence, and of 'ridding the world of terrorism', rather than the defence of the human rights of a particular grouping (even while 'humanitarian' and pro-democracy aims featured heavily in the accompanying propaganda) I consider this less directly relevant to the particular point at stake here.

23   Tony Blair, 'Doctrine of International Community', speech given to the Economic Club of Chicago, 22 April 1999, www.fco.gov.uk.

24   For a discussion of this charge see Ellen Meiskins Wood, 'Kosovo and the New Imperialism', in Tariq Ali (ed.), *Masters of the Universe? Nato's Balkan Crusade* (London and New York: Verso, 2000), pp.190-200.

25   Peter A. French, 'Unchosen Evil and Moral Responsibility', in Aleksandar Jokic (ed.), *War Crimes and Collective Wrongdoing* (Oxford: Blackwell, 2001), p.39.

26   Ibid., p.41.

27   As Rorty himself has put it, if 'relativism' is 'the view that every belief on a certain topic, or perhaps on *any* topic, is as good as any other', then '[n]obody holds this view'. Rorty, *Consequences of Pragmatism* (Minneapolis: University of Minnesota Press, 1982), p.166. He's right, I think. But whether his own position, even so, deprives us of the means by which we could convince someone who *did* hold this view that they were wrong, is another question altogether. It's probably clear enough that I suspect the answer to this is 'yes', but this is largely for meta-philosophical reasons which it is not possible to go into here.

28   Rorty, 'Human Rights, Rationality, and Sentimentality', p.185.

29   These claims were made in Downing Street briefings to assuage growing public doubts about the legitimacy and efficacy of the Afghan bombings in late 2001. See for example, *The Guardian*, 29 October 2001.

30   For a discussion of why such very basic rights against being killed or violated are, however problematic to delimit, crucial to the coherence of self-professedly

emancipatory struggles, see Norman Geras, *Discourses of Extremity* (London and New York: Verso, 1990), pp.21-58.

31   Alasdair MacIntyre, *After Virtue*, 2nd edn. (London: Duckworth, 1985), p.69.
32   Robert Nozick, *Anarchy, State and Utopia* (Oxford: Blackwell, 1974), p.ix.
33   This list is partly borrowed from Geras, *Discourses of Extremity*, p.8.

Chapter 2

Theorizing International Rights:
Two Perspectives Considered

Donal O'Reardon

Introduction

The moral vocabulary of the west is saturated with rights terminology. Daily, we are confronted with expressions such as 'the right to choose', 'the right to political asylum', 'the right to march' and so on. Usually, these are defended and justified, either tacitly or explicitly, through appeal to a tradition of 'human rights'. However, it is not always clear what advocates of different right-based arguments *mean* by 'human rights' and hence not at all clear that different rights claims are comparable given that their respective bases may differ in crucial areas. In short, failing an explication of the theoretical underpinnings to different (and sometimes competing) 'rights' claims, rights-based arguments are doomed to pass each other in the night, receiving a sympathetic hearing from those whose intuitions they already articulate, and a hostile reception from those whose outlook is challenged. Some digging is therefore required if rights-talk in the public sphere is to be more than the accepted lexicon of prejudice.

It is my argument that the discourse of 'International Rights' also reflects this impasse. 'International Rights' extends the responsibilities and entitlements of the citizens of rights-affirming states to the international context of the duties and requirements of states and their citizens to each other. That is, it represents the development of rights-claims to the global level. This phenomenon has two features: First, it makes claims concerning the status of the person *regardless* of their cultural, ethnic, religious or national background. In other words, it makes universal claims *vis à vis* the dignity of the person *per se*. We often find this feature of international rights emphasized in discussions concerning particular 'prisoners of conscience' for example. Here the primary relationship is between the state or states on the one hand and a particular person on the other. The second feature of international rights concerns the obligations and reasonable expectations of states towards each other. Here the primary actors are not understood as 'state-person' as in the first case but 'state-state'. Obviously these two cases blend as intervention by some states into another is often justified on the basis that the individual rights *of members of a particular group* are being endangered. This at least was the justification offered for intervention in Kosovo in 1999. However, it is also found in arguments for humanitarian intervention in cases of natural disaster: a people's entitlements to food and shelter are endangered and *we* should do something about it. While interconnected, the two discourses are distinct and, significantly, the latter discourse predates the former. While the question of right relationship between states can be charted from Thucydides and before to Machiavelli's fingerprints on modern international relations in the currently prominent realist school, we can confidently trace the idea of affording universal attributes to persons back to Kant.[1] Thus, one might argue that in the history of philosophy, intellectual energies went first into defending the status of the state, and secondly of the person.

Whichever side of international rights we choose to emphasize, be it our duties to persons unknown outside our state or to whole peoples in other states, it is my contention that the above-mentioned problem remains. Put starkly: unless we grasp what we mean by human rights, that is, unless we explore and explicate the motives, assumptions and sources that go to inform why persons endorse rights-based claims and offer their own view in this vocabulary on an international stage, our controversies are here to stay. How can we expect to successfully engage with and exchange ideas if we are not clear on our own and others' assumptions? (I suspect that there is something in the generic *feel* of rights-talk in the public square that encourages this conceptual forgetfulness, as it were, but I do not have time to explore that here.)

My aim in this chapter is to make good this claim. I will attempt to do this by comparing two discourses of international rights with very different assumptions. The first perspective I call the 'Kantian' approach and take the American philosopher John Rawls' *The Law of Peoples* as a working example. Here universal claims are generated and defended by appeal to a conception of the reasonable secured and expressed through Rawls' constructs of the original position and the overlapping consensus.[2] The second approach I term 'contextualist' and use the moral and political philosophy of the Canadian philosopher Charles Taylor as a working example.[3] Here universal claims are made on the basis of attributes that are common to all persons and deemed worthy of protection. Such claims are justified by appeal to what persons consider valuable in existence. I want to examine how the assumptions of each perspective are constitutive of how they interpret and hence respond to questions of international rights violations through appeal to a concrete case. The example that I use is the genocide in Rwanda that occurred between April and July of 1994. I will argue that the Kantian approach fails to properly grasp such an atrocity as is evidenced by the practical response of the international community both during and after the genocide. I will further argue that this failure is symptomatic of its approach and that something like a contextualist outlook best serves the ends and aims of the discourse of international rights as I understand it.

A Kantian Approach to International Rights: John Rawls

No one with even a passing acquaintance of the shape of moral and political philosophy in the twentieth century can fail to have noticed Rawls. Quite simply he represents what I believe to be the most powerful voice in English speaking moral philosophy in modern times. Though there has been debate about how far and in what way, Rawls' approach is distinctively Kantian.[4] He understands his constructs of the 'original position' with its accompanying 'veil of ignorance' (in which representative parties of more than one generation are denied all but crucial information in order to fairly bargain with others on principles of justice) as a model of the moral point of view.[5] His approach, he argues, is 'implicit…in Kant's ethics' (*TJ* 140/1, 252). Furthermore, taking Kant's famous distinction, made in the course of *The Metaphysics of Morals*, between the Doctrine of Right, or *Rechtslehre* ('the sum of all laws for which an external law giving is possible'[6]), and the Doctrine of Virtue, or *Tugendlehre*, ('the doctrine of those duties that do not come under external laws'[7]), Rawls is an advocate of the former over the latter. Put in the parlance of contemporary moral and political philosophy Rawls, like Kant, gives 'the right' precedence over 'the good'. While he attributes to all citizens 'two moral powers' of a capacity for a sense of justice and a capacity for a conception of the good (*LoP* 92; see also *TJ* 12, 505, 561; *PL* 19, 81), the 'reasonable' frames the 'rational' (*CP* 317, 319). That is, for Rawls, political philosophy should concern itself with the question of how citizens should act towards one another with the aim of ensuring reasonable behaviour on both sides, and forget the quest for making sense out of existence, pondering what is worthy of pursuit in life or addressing life's great irresolvables. His brand of philosophical liberalism is thus 'political, not metaphysical'.

In prioritizing the 'reasonable' over the 'rational', it is Rawls' intention that political philosophy, properly done, would secure an 'overlapping consensus' of '*reasonable* comprehensive doctrines'.[8] However, of crucial importance to our discussion here is how Rawls conceives of the term 'reasonable'. For Rawls a 'reasonable' comprehensive doctrine is one that would 'endorse some form of liberty of conscience and freedom of thought' (*PL* 61), that is 'a constitutional and democratic regime and its companion idea of legitimate law' (*CP* 574; see also *PL* xviii; *LoP* 87).[9] Thus, Rawls fashions his conception of the reasonable from an *already existing* ideal of how the public culture of a constitutional democracy should operate. So a comprehensive doctrine is deemed reasonable to the extent that it can endorse a regime of a liberal democracy. In short, Rawls offers a pragmatic (political) conception of the reasonable over any more ontological[10] or metaphysical definition.[11]

Taking liberal democracy as the criterion of adequacy for the reasonableness of a comprehensive doctrine is the linchpin of Rawls' approach to international rights. First, Rawls characterizes societies according to the extent to which their social institutions approximate the workings of a liberal constitutional democracy. Hence, he offers the categories of 'reasonable liberal peoples' (*LoP* 4, 35ff), 'decent hierarchical peoples' (*LoP* 4, 62ff), 'outlaw states', 'societies burdened by unfavourable conditions' and 'benevolent absolutisms' (*LoP* 4, 63, 89ff). Rawls stresses that he is not expounding a hierarchy with liberal democracy at the top, but it is hard to avoid this conclusion when he argues that other societies, on seeing the benefits of a liberal regime, will move towards it over time (*LoP* 61/2). In short, Rawls' criterion of the 'reasonable', which takes as its basis the public culture of a liberal constitutional democracy, greatly influences how he conceives of and conceptualizes other social orders: the closer they are to liberal democracy, the better. What is lacking in this account, and what is lacking in his conception of the reasonable, is an argument concerning the justification of a liberal constitutional democracy. Both his ideal of the reasonable and his categorization of societies are made by reference to the benchmark of liberal democracy, however this position requires a prior explanation of why liberal democracy is paradigmatic. This Rawls does not offer. Why choose liberal democracy as one's benchmark? In failing to supply an answer to this question, Rawls leaves himself open to the charge of relativism[12] or, put another way, what separates his own work and that of Richard Rorty is a question of breadth or even style but not of approach.

The second feature of Rawls' emphasis on liberal democracy that I wish to draw attention to concerns his understanding of the value and place of human rights in the international context. Consider Rawls' account of the importance of human rights in any of the above-mentioned societies:

> 1. Their fulfilment is a necessary condition of the decency of a society's political institutions and of its legal order.
> 2. Their fulfilment is sufficient to exclude justified and forceful intervention by other peoples, for example, by diplomatic and economic sanctions, or in grave cases by military force.
> 3. They set a limit to the pluralism among peoples. (*LoP* 80)

Recall that above I argued that Rawls offers a 'pragmatic' rather than 'ontological' conception of the reasonable. The problem with the above invocation of human rights is that it sounds very pragmatic, that is, he extols human rights in their capacity of *defending the stability of liberal democracy rather than a justification of it in the first place*. Obviously, this recalls my first point on relativism, that is, why the protection of a liberal democracy is *sui generis* worthy. However, it also opens up two further problems with Rawls' approach to international rights, namely his emphasis on stability and the question as to whether his whole approach is not viciously circular.

Rawls' idea of an overlapping consensus (in which holders of 'reasonable' comprehensive doctrines achieve agreement on a political conception of justice which is endorsed by each *from within* their various comprehensive doctrines)[13] and his idea of public reason (in which citizens debate constitutional essentials using only arguments couched in terminology and employing methods of reasoning, deduction, inference and so on that are agreed to by all and, as far as possible, *not* the language of their comprehensive doctrine)[14] open up these questions further. Both ideas aim at securing a rational consensus by persons who are 'reasonable' (as defined in accordance with the precepts of liberal democracy) on matters that are essential to the public realm. Both aim to achieve this by excluding certain arguments and issues (religious and metaphysical for example) from the debate except when such arguments can be offered in the terminology of public reason. This emphasis on allowing only reasonable arguments into public debate has prompted some critics to charge Rawls with desiccating the character of public debate in favour of a dubious stability.[15] In other words, why should arguments and issues that fall outside his liberal democratic conception of the reasonable be excluded simply for the sake of achieving the stability of his brand of liberal democracy? This emphasis on stability in accordance with a liberal democratic conception of the reasonable has, it seems, spilled over into his understanding of the role and function of human rights in the international context. They are invoked so that public institutions can properly function, so that a just society may not be subject to foreign invasion, and to limit the diversification of its people by outside influence. Nowhere in the above three points does Rawls argue that human rights on an international level are worthy of protection *per se* regardless of their effect on the stability of the social order. They are invoked instrumentally as it were, rather than as an end in themselves.

It is at this point that the circularity question arises. Rawls' model of liberal democracy is taken as the criterion of the reasonable, and he orders societies in accordance with this model. In addition, as we have just seen, only those arguments that are *already consonant with its precepts* are admitted into public debate; thus his model of public reasoning becomes a viciously circular, self-justifying project. His use of human rights in the international context demonstrates precisely this point. In *The Law of Peoples* he argues that human rights 'cannot be rejected as peculiarly liberal or special to the western tradition. They are not politically parochial' (*LoP* 65). Later though he justifies intervention into other non-liberal and non-decent states 'as a consequence of liberalism and decency' (*LoP* 81), that is, by reference to an argument made *from within* his own political conception of the ideal relationship between states. Just as his emphasis on stability in his political liberalism spills over into his writings on international rights, so the problem of circularity that arises in the same context runs over when his liberalism is applied on the international level.

There seems to be little room for manoeuvre here. Though his intensions are undeniably honourable, and at first sight it seems unnecessary or unappealing to question a moral theory whose sole function is to extend basic rights to all, Rawls' method is flawed. His conception of international rights is a self-referential one. It excludes all arguments not in keeping with *his* conception of liberal democracy in the name of social stability rather than on any more worthy grounds. As such, as I will argue later on, it is not equipped to grasp the subtleties of moral controversy on a global level.

A Contextualist Approach to International Rights: Charles Taylor

Charles Taylor offers a very different understanding of international rights to the approach of Rawls. I cannot hope to outline all the differences between them here, however of direct relevance to my discussion is that, while Rawls takes the task of moral and political philosophy to be an explication of the *Rechtslehre* and thus affords the reasonable precedence over the rational, or the right priority over the good, Taylor takes just the opposite approach. It is Taylor's contention that one cannot engage in moral theory without taking account of what persons deem valuable and worthy of pursuit in existence, that is, without considering their conception of the good. Hence, for Taylor, 'the good is always primary to the right...the good is what, in its articulation, gives the point of the rules which define the right',[16] 'any theory which aims to make the right primary really reposes on such a notion of the good'.[17] For Taylor then, the good supplies the meaning of and motivation for acting upon the deliverances of the right.

The practical upshot of this for Taylor is that universalist discourses such as human rights cannot proceed without considering what attributes of moral personality persons *deem worthy* of protection, hence it cannot proceed in a fashion isolated from local or 'contextual' needs and concerns and it must take proper account of these concerns in order to establish the appropriate scope of such universalist discourses.

> We could easily decide - a view I would defend - that the universal attribution of moral personality is valid and lays obligations on us we cannot ignore; but that there are also other moral ideals and goals...which cannot be easily coordinated with universalism, and can even enter into conflict with it. To decide *a priori* what the bounds of the moral are is just to obfuscate the question whether and to what degree this is so, and to make it incapable of being coherently stated.[18]

In addition while, in numerous places in his writings, Taylor affirms the validity of universal rights discourse,[19] he views it as *a mode of expression* of respect for certain traits or characteristics that we *already* consider valuable:

> The intuition that men have the right to life, to freedom, to the unmolested profession of their own convictions, to the exercise of their moral or religious beliefs, *is but another facet of the intuition that the life-form characterized by these specifically human capacities commands our respect.*[20]

Put another way, for Taylor, rights-talk represents one articulation[21] of our prior and primary evaluations of worth, evaluations that are greatly determined by the languages of description and assessment we have inherited from our local context. Hence, while Rawls formally attributes to his citizens the above-mentioned 'two moral powers' irrespective of their background assumptions and evaluations, Taylor is reticent as to what such an attribution could *mean* (and hence what moral evaluations it might produce) independent of grasping the persons' 'contextual' self-understandings and evaluations of worth, as these *explain* the appeal of the right. Furthermore, while Rawls argues that human rights are 'not politically parochial' (see section two above), Taylor happily characterizes them as a defining achievement of *western* culture[22] that forms a constitutive element of its participants' self-understanding.

A two-fold approach thus characterizes Taylor's method when considering human rights. On the one hand, he espouses the value of certain universalist claims, while on the other he argues that their universalism is a function of their being endorsed at the level of the good and he remains circumspect as to their precise scope or domain. Put another way, Taylor adopts a simultaneously historical and systematic attitude to human rights discourse, seeing them as specifically western in origin but with broader application to other cultures subject to the caveat that local mores and claims have an essential (albeit unspecified) role in establishing them and in determining their range of application.

It is in this question of the application of human rights to the international context that the specific differences between Taylor and Rawls, and the general differences between a contextualist and Kantian approach to international rights, are most salient. In section two I noted Rawls' categorization of social orders in accordance, I argued, with the degree to which they approximate the public culture of a liberal democracy. In evaluating the moral content of alien political orders, Taylor on the other hand adopts a Gadamerian method in which, unlike Rawls, no pre-established criterion is employed but instead a 'fusion of horizons'[23] is envisioned between the two cultures[24] during which the appropriate scope and application of rights-discourse would become apparent. That is to say, Taylor leaves open the question of what one might learn from and have to offer to alien cultures, neither assuming their *a priori* merit,[25] nor condemning them out of hand subject to a criterion established independent of the cultural encounter.

Taylor employs his conception of practical reasoning to explain how one might learn something of value and worth from an alien culture. Briefly, Taylor holds that one is moved to embrace a new viewpoint when one discerns in it an epistemological gain[26] or an 'error reducing move'[27] from one's previous position. That is, when the new analysis has superior explanatory potential to the one held before, then it merits appropriation.[28] Note that in this process, for Taylor, the agent's own worldview and conception of what is of value in life is indispensable to the process. For

Taylor, as for Gadamer, critical engagement with and appropriation of an alien analysis cannot obtain independent of the engager bringing his/her presuppositions and ideals to the process. The discourse of 'International Rights' then represents a tentative extension of one's most deeply held evaluations into other cultures. The possibility of their revision and correction is as open as their proving rationally superior to whatever worldviews they encounter. International Rights discourse is one dimension of an ongoing and fallible inter-cultural process of engagement and self-discovery.

For Rawls on the other hand, certain liberties, when established, are taken off the moral and political agenda 'once and for all'.[29] Their pre-eminence is a function of the priority of the reasonable over the rational, they establish the criterion by which alien social orders can be categorized and they are in no way to be revised or have their range of application determined by local custom or mores. Indeed the reverse is the case; for Rawls, the criterion for the reasonableness of a specific comprehensive doctrine is precisely that they could endorse such values from within the doctrine. While the charge of relativism and circularity may be laid at Rawls' door, it is hard to escape the impression that Taylor's approach leaves him with little to say to a regime that steadfastly refuses to endorse human rights. How may he respond to a political order that claims the discourse of human rights represents no 'epistemological gain' or 'error reducing move' to them?

Of course, this question is simply a subset of a perennial debate in the history of ideas concerning the appropriate relationship between the theoretically universal and the historically particular. It is this issue that lay at the heart of medieval debates on nominalism and universals,[30] it arose again in Hegel's critic of what he saw as Kant's ahistorical and formalist ethics,[31] was revisited in the last century in Habermas' exchange with Gadamer[32] and again in the so-called 'liberalism/communitarianism' exchange of the last twenty years or so.[33] Before moving into my final section where I propose, by way of a concrete example, to outline a possible method for international rights discourse that attempts to mediate this tension, it might be valuable to note that the differences between the Kantian and contextualist approaches to international rights are not as hard and fast as the tensions between the above-cited schools of thought might tempt us to think. For one thing, Rawls argues in the course of *Political Liberalism* that when considering political values one must distinguish 'the order of deduction from the order of support',[34] that is, how we arrive at the deliverances of the right from how we endorse them. I have already noted that Rawls envisions his idea of an overlapping consensus as one in which persons' conception of the good endorses a claim pertaining to the right. Paul Weithman, in arguing in defence of Rawls' approach,[35] suggests that in Rawls' moral theory the good can retain motivational priority while the right retains justificatory priority.[36] For his part, Taylor still holds out the prospect of a universal rights discourse arguing only for a robust position for claims pertaining to the good in this discourse. From this, one might conclude that what separates the two theorists (on this issue anyway) is not their *intention* but their preferred method.

The Rwandan Genocide as a Failure of International Rights

The genocide in Rwanda that took place between April 6th and July 7th 1994 and claimed the lives of an estimated eight hundred thousand people represents the most intense period of killing in the twentieth century.[37] Planned over a number of years and executed with the active cooperation of civil society, the depth and intensity of its savagery beggars belief.[38] I visited Rwanda in November 1995 and, even now, nearly six years later, I find it impossible to adequately describe the sights with which I was confronted, or to convey the palpable sense of fear, violation, betrayal and loss that enveloped Rwanda in the aftermath of its genocide. Moreover, I am suspicious of resurrecting them in this context for fear that I do the story an injustice or that I be misunderstood as replacing conceptual rigour with dramatic content for cynical motives. In this context it will have to suffice to say that the evidence of a multitude of horrific acts, perpetrated on a national scale with international assistance, was all too apparent. In this context, the Walter Benjamin/Max Horkheimer debate on 'anamnesic solidarity' with the victims of history takes on a chilling resonance.[39]

However, it is precisely the description-defying character of the Rwandan genocide that lays the ground for the argument I want to make here. Consider a situation in which what we call civilized society breaks down to the extent that every social stratum is implicated both in planning and carrying out the systematic butchering of one ethic group. In Rwanda, university professors, members of religious orders and medical doctors with the rest of society have all been cited with murdering or assisting in the murder of their neighbours, colleagues, flock or peers. Consider also a situation where children (that is, persons under the age of fourteen years) were suspected of multiple murders. In July 1995 there were 187 children in jails in Rwanda, some implicated in the murder of more than one person.[40] My question in this context is whether the discourse of international rights in the Kantian mode properly grasps the depth of depravity and complexity of this situation and is thus in an appropriate position to prescribe what an adequate response may be.

Take for example the two following facets of the post-genocide discussion in Rwanda of what appropriate justice for the perpetrators might entail. First, a cultural assumption pervaded that even a child cannot be 'tricked' into doing something morally atrocious. The upshot of this was a call for the execution of those children found guilty of such acts. Obviously this violates certain deeply held convictions as to the nature of moral culpability and the primacy of human life at least in western European legal discourse. However, my point is that to properly grasp, and therefore to be in a position to adequately respond to, the possibility of children being executed, one cannot simply apply certain universals from the outside. Rather, since the call for the execution of children is a function of the worldview and conception of the good of those involved, to have any hope of understanding it and having one's own view comprehended, one must *engage* it. The Kantian view as proposed by Rawls does not allow for this possibility, arguing only that ideally all basic liberties *should* be recognized. This overlooks the depth of feeling that arose as a product of the depravity of the acts perpetrated and *is constitutive of* the avocation of execution even for children. Rawls' approach simply does not have the sensitivity to capture the issues at stake and therefore, being unable to properly comprehend it, is in no position to correctly outline a response to it.

A second feature of the post-genocide discussion in Rwanda concerning appropriate justice was its hostility towards US and EU means of dispensing it. That is, setting up war crimes tribunals in which the accused, at worst, faced the prospect of a life-sentence in a well-maintained European facility, was considered incommensurate response to the crimes committed. Again, to understand this response one has to *engage* it with the accompanying possibility, as Taylor has suggested, that *our* presuppositions are in some way altered. One motive for Rwandan hostility to western methods of dispensing justice may well have been a feeling of betrayal and abandonment by the west on the part of Rwandans. That is, the American administration's reticence in categorizing the situation as a genocide and Europe's shadowing of US policy on this front, left a lingering feeling of deep hostility and resentment: if they didn't want to help with the problem why should they be involved in the solution? Consider the causes for non-intervention between April 6th and July 7th 1994. To diagnose the situation with the universal category of 'genocide' implied certain necessary obligations on the part of the outside administrations. Either through lack of adequate incentive (the realist analysis) or through a misunderstanding of the situation as it was unfolding, the 'spontaneous-explosion-of-ethnic-hatred' analysis was the dominant one during that crucial time. However this analysis of the situation, while feeding into certain well-trodden stereotypes of 'uncivilized' Africa, is belied by even a cursory reading of the history of conflict in the area.[41] My own interpretation is that the relevant administrations wilfully misdescribed the situation, circumventing for as long as possible any responsibilities that would otherwise accrue to them. Little wonder then that Rwandans after the genocide resented western intervention with its accompanying rights terminology. (Ironically, the West's very adherence to a Kantian interpretation of the import of human rights, and of their obligations to safeguard them, issued in their hesitation to characterize the genocide in a fashion that would imply a necessary response.)

Conclusions

What I am attempting to get at in the above is an argument for a Taylor-like, contextualist approach to the formulation and application of international rights. In the case both of how to treat children found guilty of perpetrating crimes against humanity and of how the legal process in general should ensue, I conclude that neither question can be properly dealt with independently of the conception of the good of those involved. This represents a statement against a 'single-principle' approach to moral discourse, an approach that I view as a kind of philosophical equivalent to the search for a unified theory in theoretical physics. Michael Walzer eloquently expresses the idea I am trying to communicate here:

> One way to begin the philosophical enterprise - perhaps the original way - is to walk out of the cave, leave the city, climb the mountain, fashion for oneself (what can never be fashioned for ordinary men and women) an objective and universal standpoint. Then one describes the terrain of everyday life from far away, so that its particular contours and takes on a general shape. But I mean to stand in the cave, in the city, on the ground.[42]

This does not amount to the claim that persons' prejudices are determinative of the responses offered to moral atrocity. Nor is one relegated to silence by those who refuse to engage the discourse of international rights. Rather, following Taylor, this approach does maintain that their evaluations of worth and conceptions of what is meaningful in life *are constitutive of* how a situation is understood. By extension, if we are to understand *their* response and to engage *their* application of justice, we have to acknowledge this. How, moreover, can we talk of a discourse of 'International Rights' if we do not take an international overview of the bases that alien persons and cultures might employ to formulate and endorse such rights? To be true to its name, international rights must be more than western parochialism in a loud voice. If it purports to speak for an international community, it must listen to it.

With special thanks to my Mother

Notes

1   Of course the discourse of human rights has its origins in the discussions of natural rights and natural law that preceded Kant, and Kant's achievements can only be properly grasped when placed in this context. See J.B. Schneewind's *The Invention of Autonomy: A History of Modern Moral Philosophy*, Cambridge University Press, Cambridge, 1998, 58-166. My point is only that Kant's work gives classical expression to the discourse of human rights and he remains a crucial reference point and resource for it today.

2   John Rawls, *The Law of Peoples*, Harvard University Press, Cambridge, Mass. 1999, hereafter *LoP*. I will also be drawing on his *A Theory of Justice*, Harvard University Press, Cambridge Mass. 1971, hereafter *TJ*; *Political Liberalism*, Columbia University Press, New York, 1996, hereafter *PL*; and Samuel Freeman (eds.) *Collected Papers*, Harvard University Press, Cambridge Mass. 1999, hereafter *CP*. In the following I assume some familiarity with Rawls' work in general and the constructs of the 'original position' and 'overlapping consensus' in particular.

3   Unlike Rawls, Taylor has not produced a formal work on international rights, however a coherent position can be gleaned from his various writings on human rights and from his approach as a whole. See especially, 'Conditions of an Unforced Consensus on Human Rights' in Joanne R. Bauer and Daniel Bell (eds.) *The East Asian Challenge for Human Rights*, Cambridge University Press, Cambridge, 1999, 124-144.

4   See Otfried Hoeffe, 'Is Rawls' Theory of Justice Really Kantian?' in *Ratio* 26, Dec. 1984, 103-124; Arnold I. Davidson, 'Is Rawls a Kantian?' *Pacific Philosophical Quarterly* 66, 48-77.

5   See *TJ* 140/1, 148, 251ff, 584. Rawls' use of the word 'model' in this context is significant because, as he argues in *LoP* 'what is modeled is a *relation*...the relation of the parties representing citizens' (30 fn32).

6   *The Metaphysics of Morals*, trans. Mary Gregor, Cambridge University Press, Cambridge 1991, 55, (Ak 229).

7   Ibid. 185, (Ak 379).

8   For Rawls, a 'comprehensive doctrine' is one that contains ideas 'of what is of value on human life, and conceptions of personal character, as well as ideas of friendship and of familial and associational relationships, and much else that is to inform our conduct and in the limit *to our life as a whole*' (*PL* 13, emphasis added). It therefore contrasts with a 'political' doctrine which is 'worked out for a specific kind of subject, namely for political, social and economic institutions' (*PL* 11). Rawls designs his own brand of liberalism with the intention that it is a 'political' doctrine.

9   More specifically, Rawls argues that a 'reasonable' comprehensive doctrine is denoted
     by its holders subscribing to 'the criterion of reciprocity' (that is arguments offered by
     their holders to others are deemed by their holders to be the most reasonable, *PL* 17;
     LoP 14), and shared burdens of judgment (*PL* 54ff). For a summary of Rawls'
     conception of the reasonable see *CP* 613.

10   The pragmatic/ontological distinction I borrow from Robert Pippin who has suggested
     that Kant's two-world, noumenal/phenomenal distinction be read as pragmatic or
     heuristic (it assists our understanding of the import of moral claims) rather than in an
     ontological fashion (i.e. that it purports to describe the nature of reality). It is fitting
     here because while Rawls concedes that his conception of practical reason has Kantian
     associations 'political liberalism is altogether distinct from his transcendental idealism'
     (*LoP* 87). Rawls attempts to proceed in moral theory without any transcendental or
     metaphysical attachments 'beyond what is implied in the political conception itself'
     (*PL* 10), see also 'The Independence of Moral Theory' in *CP* 286-302.

11   This has been differently received in different quarters. Richard Rorty for example
     argues that this represents a decisive and welcomed shift away from a search for
     philosophical foundations and towards 'post-modern bourgeois liberalism', see 'The
     Priority of Democracy to Philosophy' in Merrill D. Peterson and Robert C. Vaughan
     (eds.) *The Virginia Statute for Religious Freedom: Its Evolution and Consequences in
     American History*, Cambridge University Press, Cambridge, 1988, 257-282. Timothy
     P. Jackson on the other hand sees it as a movement from 'liberalism as morally basic'
     (that is, an enlightenment-based morally substantive political philosophy) to 'liberalism
     as morally empty' (that is, a post-modern, normatively bereft conceptual construction),
     see 'To Bedlam and Part Way Back: John Rawls and Christian Justice', in *Faith and
     Philosophy* 8, 1991, 423-447. Both agree though that Rawls' understanding of a
     'reasonable' doctrine as outlined in *PL* represents a shift from his earlier
     'comprehensive' account of liberalism as offered in *TJ*. Rawls makes this point himself
     in *PL* xlii, 388n21.

12   See Kenneth Baynes, *The Normative Grounds of Social Criticism: Kant, Rawls and
     Habermas*, State University of New York Press, New York, 1992, 72ff, 146ff; Duncan
     B. Forrester, *Christian Justice and Public Policy*, Cambridge University Press,
     Cambridge, 1997, 115ff, 124.

13   *PL* 133-172.

14   Ibid., 212-254, *CP* 573-615 (& *LoP* 129-180).

15   See Michael Sandel, *Liberalism and the Limits of Justice*, 2nd edition, Cambridge
     University Press, Cambridge, 1998, 196ff; Donal O'Reardon 'Metaphysics and
     Normative Ethics: Partners or Antagonists?' in *Proceedings of The Irish Philosophical
     Society*, 2000 (forthcoming).

16   Charles Taylor, *Sources of the Self: The Making of Modern Identity*, Harvard
     University Press, Cambridge MA. 1989, 89.

17   Charles Taylor, 'Justice After Virtue' in John Horton and Susan Mendus (eds.) *After
     MacIntyre: Critical Perspectives on the Work of Alasdair MacIntyre*, Polity Press,
     1994, 16-43, 28.

18   On this point see 'The Diversity of Goods' in Charles Taylor, *Philosophy and the
     Human Sciences: Philosophical Papers 2*, Cambridge University Press, Cambridge,
     1985, 230-237, 233.

19   See 'Reply and re-articulation' in James Tully and Daniel M. Weinstock (eds.)
     Philosophy in an age of pluralism: The Philosophy of Charles Taylor in Question,
     Cambridge University Press, Cambridge, 1994, 213-257, 224; 'Explanation and

Practical Reason' in Charles Taylor, *Philosophical Arguments*, Harvard University Press, Cambridge MA. 1995, 34-60, 56; 1999, op. cit., 136.

20   Charles Taylor, 'Atomism' in *Philosophy and the Human Sciences*, op. cit., 187-210, 193.

21   I use the word 'articulation' in the sense that Taylor does, see for example 'Self-Interpreting Animals' in *Human Agency and Language: Philosophical Papers I*, Cambridge University Press, Cambridge, 1985, 45-76, 57, 63/4; *Sources of the Self*, op. cit. 18, 77, 92, 98ff; *Philosophical Arguments*, op. cit., 157. Michael L. Morgan describes the concept of 'articulation' in Taylor's work as 'Taylor's term of art for the process whereby the aspects of our moral world are identified, clarified and made accessible and potent for us', see 'Religion, history and moral discourse' in *Philosophy in an age of pluralism*, op. cit. 49-66, 52.

22   See *Sources of the Self* op. cit. 11/12; 1999, op cit., 125.

23   Gadamer, Hans-Georg: *Truth and Method*, 2nd revised edition, trans. by Joel Weinsheimer and Donald G. Marshall, Sheed & Ward, London, 1989; see especially 306/7, 374/5, 397, 576.

24   See *Philosophy and the Human Sciences*, op. cit. 126; 'The Politics of Recognition' in Amy Gutmann (eds.) *Multiculturalism: Examining the Politics of Recognition*, Princeton University Press, Princeton, New Jersey, 1994, 25-73, 67; *Philosophical Arguments* op. cit. 148ff; 1999, 136.

25   See 'The Politics of Recognition', op. cit., 68ff.

26   *Sources of the Self* op. cit. 72; 'Explanation and Practical Reason' in *Philosophical Arguments* op. cit. 34-60, 42; 'Comment on Jurgen Habermas' 'From Kant to Hegel and Back Again' in *The European Journal of Philosophy*, Vol.7, No.2, Aug. 1999, 158-163, 161ff.

27   'Reply to Commentators' in *Philosophy and Phenomenological Research* Vol.LIV, No.1, March 1994, 203-213, 205; 'Explanation and Practical Reason', op. cit., 51.

28   Alasdair MacIntyre advances a similar method of practical reasoning in *Whose Justice? Which Rationality?* Duckworth, London, 1988, 349ff.

29   *PL* 151n16, 161, 228.

30   See Michael Haren, *Medieval Thought: The Western Intellectual Tradition From Antiquity to the Thirteenth Century*, 2nd edition, MacMillan, London, 1992, 90-94.

31   See Allen W. Wood (eds.), G.W.F. Hegel, *Elements of the Philosophy of Right* trans. H.B. Nisbet, Cambridge University Press, Cambridge, 1991; see also Terry Pinkard, *Hegel: A Biography*, Cambridge University Press, Cambridge, 2000, 473-489.

32   For an outline of this exchange see Werner G. Jeanrond, *Theological Hermeneutics: Development and Significance*, MacMillan, London, 1991, 64-70.

33   See Stephen Mulhall and Adam Swift, *Liberals and Communitarians*, 2nd edition, Blackwell, Oxford, 1996.

34   *PL* 242n32.

35   Paul Weithman: 'Rawlsian Liberalism and the Privatisation of Religion: Three Theological Objections Considered', in *Journal of Religious Ethics* 22.1, Georgetown University Press, 1994, 3-28.

36   Ibid. 11/12.

37   For a detailed account of the causes of the Rwandan genocide see *Rwanda: Death, Despair and Defiance*, African Rights, London, 1994, 1-92, see also *Rwanda: Not so Innocent, when women become killers*, African Rights, London, 1995, 17-24.

38   See Philip Gourevitch: *We wish to inform you that tomorrow we will be killed with our families: Stories from Rwanda*, Picador, London, 1999; see also 'After the Genocide',

New Yorker, December 18, 1995 and my own 'Genocide in Rwanda' in *Intercom*, Catholic Communications Institute of Ireland, Vol.26, No.4, April 1996, 10-11.

39   The basis of this exchange is Walter Benjamin's 'Theses on the Philosophy of History', in *Illuminations*, New York, 1969. For an exposition of this text and the meaning of 'anamnesic solidarity' see Jürgen Habermas: *The Philosophical Discourse of Modernity: Twelve Lectures*, trans. Frederick G. Lawrence, MIT Press, Cambridge, MA. 1987, 11-16, see also 106ff. For an exposition of the exchange in the context of the questions it poses for fundamental theology see Helmut Puekert: *Science, Action and Fundamental Theology: Toward a Theology of Communicative Action*, trans. James Bohman, MIT Press, Cambridge MA. 1984, 206ff; 'Enlightenment and Theology as Unfinished Projects' in Don S. Browning and Francis Fiorenza (eds.) *Habermas, Modernity and Public Theology*, Crossroad, New York, 1992, 43-65.

40   *Children, Genocide and Justice*, Save the Children Federation, USA, 1995, 2.

41   Between 1959 and 1966, a series of pogroms halved the Tutsi population, forcing many to flee to neighbouring Uganda and Zaire. Habyarimana took power after an upsurge in anti-Tutsi violence in 1973 and Rwanda became a single-party state. When the regime of Milton Obote forced the expulsion of the Tutsis from Uganda in 1982/3, many joined the NRA (national resistance army) under Yowei Museveni. Many of these went on to form the RPF (Rwandese Patriotic Front) which invaded northern Rwanda from Uganda in October 1990. Fear of a Tutsi invasion sparked a propaganda machine under Habyarimana. Although he resisted it, democracy of a sort developed during this period as did the extremist Hutu party CDR. The Arusha peace agreement of 1993 ended hostilities; however, when Habyarimana's plane was shot down on April 6th 1994, a new government was immediately formed under Sindikubwabo consisting of Hutu extremists and the 100 day genocide began.

42   Michael Walzer, *Spheres of Justice: A Defence of Pluralism and Equality*, Basic Books, New York, 1983, xiv.

Chapter 3

Universalism and Cultural Specificity: Female Circumcision, Intrinsic Dignity and Human Rights

Maria Michela Marzano

At present international relations are characterized by a dialectic of two concepts: universalism, exposing what is common, and particularism, underlining what is specific. Generally, as Jose Ayala-Lasso points out, universalism is perceived as something positive, whereas particularism is interpreted as a potential obstacle to achieving common goals.[1] However, another interpretation exists according to which universalism is the uniformity of countries in line with specific concepts, while particularism is a vehicle for preserving the identity of one culture.[2]

But does cultural diversity really oppose the universality of human rights? Is it possible to reconcile universal rights and cultural specificity? How can we reconcile the enforcement of international, universal human rights standards with the protection of cultural diversity?

Most people, of all cultures, accept some validity for universal criteria: very few people would argue that torture, starvation, infanticide and slavery are to be treated at the same level as greeting customs. The question about cultural relativism is then where to draw the line and where not to, rather than whether a line is to be drawn at all. Suffice it to say that while on some questions the weight of Islamic tradition is identifiable and distinct, much of what passes for *Islam* and its associated codes and traditions is a particular, contemporary and arbitrarily formulated set of views, or local customary traditions dressed up as authoritatively 'Islamic'.[3] A good example of the latter is the practice of clitoridectomy or female circumcision which is found in parts of Africa and Arabia and which has nothing to do with Islamic doctrine.

Starting with an analysis of the practice of clitoridectomy and taking the controversy concerning female circumcision as a case study, this paper will try to bridge the gap between the view that human rights are nonexistent (according to MacIntyre, for instance, 'there is no such thing as human reason *tout court* and consequently no distinctively *human* rights'[4]) and the view of naturalistic philosophers according to which human rights are derived from a basic human nature we all share. In fact, to argue that human rights exist and have to be protected is not equivalent to denying the different cultural contexts in which human beings live and rights must be embedded.

Clitoridectomy and Female Circumcision: Judging Other Cultures

Female circumcision is an expression usually used for a wide range of physical operations upon female genitalia[5] which remain extremely common in Africa and other parts of the world.[6]

In particular, the practice called 'female circumcision' can be broken down into four basic forms that vary in degree of severity. The first, and least severe form, is the *ritualistic circumcision*; the second form is called *sunna* by the Muslims; the third is called *clitoridectomy* and it is the most common form; lastly, there is *infibulation*, which is the most severe form of the practice because virtually all the external female genitalia are removed:

> The entire area is closed up by this process leaving only a tiny opening, roughly the size of a match stick, to allow for the passing of urine and menstrual fluid. The girl's legs are then tied together - ankles, knees, and thighs - and she is immobilized for an extended period varying from fifteen to forty days, while the wound heals.[7]

This customary practice can involve the use of one or more instruments (from kitchen knives and broken glass or an old razor, to scalpels used in local health clinics) rarely sterilized. It is found in areas where there is much poverty. It is usually performed on young girls when they are just a few years old to some days just prior to their marriage, depending on the particular cultural practices of the region involved. It is, in its most severe forms, a severe mutilation of a woman's body causing pain and psycho-physical damage.[8] As Nahid Toubia, a Sudanese surgeon and expert on female genital mutilation, explicitly writes:

> The male equivalent of clitoridectomy would be the amputation of most of the penis. The male equivalent of infibulation would be the removal of all the penis, its roots of soft tissue, and part of the scrotal skin.[9]

Nevertheless, while male genital mutilation is usually rejected as a harmful and unacceptable practice, female genital mutilation is often defended. On the one hand, this operation is commonly performed by women on other females and many girls actually claim to desire it. On the other hand, such a practice is usually justified by arguments which include not only the control of female sexuality, but also the conformity to religion and to cultural tradition. As Martha Nussbaum reports,[10] the strongest argument in favour of the practice is an argument that appeals to cultural continuity. Jomo Kenyatta and others, for instance, have stressed the constitutive role played by such initiation rites in the formation of a community and the disintegrative effect of interference.[11]

At first glance, we are faced here with a radical opposition between the universality of human rights and the specificity of customs and (religious) traditions. There are at least three main international human rights which the practice of female circumcision typically seems to violate: the right to health, the right of the child, and the right to corporal and sexual integrity.[12] But how can we justify such human rights requirements? Is it possible to disapprove of and banish these operations even if they apparently respect cultural traditions? Are such practices a really essential part of some cultural traditions? Lastly, where should the line be drawn between practices we have to accept and protect as part of particularism's richness and practices we have to condemn and reject as oppressive and harmful?

Actually, as I am going to show, we are confronted here not only with a practice that no religious doctrine defends, but also with a practice which does not express the richness of cultural specificity, only social prejudices and ignorance; an operation that harms individuals by causing pain and physical damage; a custom which denies personal autonomy and violates the intrinsic dignity of women; a practice, finally, we have to reject in that it can be seen as a violation of some rights which belong to the person in that a human being is endowed with intrinsic value.

Stephen James analyses the internal cultural justification for these practices, trying to show, from the inside, how these operations are usually dysfunctional, even in the culture's own terms.[13] On the one hand, clitoridectomy and infibulation are not a way by which women can have physical and psychological benefits (as is commonly claimed), in that these operations usually result in severe pain, shock, infection, difficulty in childbirth, increased risk of sterility, increased vulnerability to the AIDS virus, psychological disturbance and emotional trauma.[14] On the other hand, these practices are not a guarantee of a woman's virginity at the time of marriage (as is also claimed), because an unmarried woman can have sexual intercourse and then be re-infibulated just prior to marriage to disguise the fact from her husband. Last, but not least, female circumcision is not part of the formal doctrine of any religion, and sixty years after Kenyatta's defence, there is widespread evidence of resistance from within the relevant cultures. Indeed, an Islamic gynaecologist, Professor Hathout has argued that 'This topic [female circumcision] may be out of place in a book on Islamic aspects [of gynaecology and obstetrics], for the practice is neither Islamic nor ordained by Islam.'[15] Moreover, the Inter-African Committee on Traditional Practices has produced a film, *Beliefs and Misbeliefs,* opposing female circumcision on the grounds of the chronic health problems associated with it, the suppression of sexuality it involves, and the myth that the operation is an Islamic practice.[16]

Now, leaving aside James's analysis and the very fact that clitoridectomy and infibulation are opposed by many organized local agencies, what I would like to stress in what follows is that respect for cultural particularism does not imply the acceptance of such harmful practices. The universality of human rights is not a way of denying the difference and the richness of local cultures and traditions, but rather it is a way of protecting persons: accepting cultural specificity does not mean accepting that persons participant in specific traditions cannot be autonomous decision-makers, persons endowed with intrinsic dignity and value. Each person, even if she/he is part of a specific community and therefore also a 'product' of this community's particular culture, is in fact worthy of respect as a human being. But in order to show all this, I need not only an analysis of specific practices (such as clitoridectomy and infibulation), but also an ontological investigation. In this sense, an ontological investigation into what it means to be a human being must be prior to both a discussion of the protection of human rights, and an analysis of customary and specific practices. On the one hand, our moral and juridical point of view is 'contingent upon what we think persons are or what it means to be a human being'.[17] On the other hand, the preservation and the justification of cultural and customary diversity does not imply the acceptance of any harmful practices - as in fact the Program for Action, which was elaborated at the Beijing Conference (1995), clearly points out: 'Any harmful aspect of certain traditional, customary or modern practices that violates the rights of women should be prohibited and eliminated.'[18] In this sense, rejecting certain practices, such as clitoridectomy and infibulation, does not imply a rejection of cultural specificity.[19] Indeed, pointing out their harmful aspects does not amount to an attack on certain cultures, but aims to acknowledge their many valuable or neutral aspects,[20] at the same time as criticizing those aspects that are harmful to women and girls.[21]

Human Rights and Dignity

There is widespread consensus that human rights are a positive legal qualification of ways of acting or of being treated that are beneficial to the holder of these rights. Controversy begins, however, when one attempts to specify the notion of rights further. Most people think, for instance, that human rights are, in some sense, justified in that they concern the intrinsic dignity of each person, but there is considerable controversy about the way they should/can be justified. Some thinkers say for instance that human rights are practices (certain ways of acting or being treated) that are usually established culturally or socially. Thus, the issue for them is not only whether the fact of social recognition and enforcement is justified, but also whether the fact of cultural diversity justifies the existence of contrasting rights in societies with different cultures or in a multicultural society. Others say that human rights are universal, in that they are grounded in the universal common human nature. Thus, the issue for them is whether universality also implies the fact that human rights are absolute and independent of social and cultural specificity. On the one hand, then, in the literature, theories of universal human rights commonly imply that there is a single human nature common to all people and that human nature may serve as the basis for a political theory which dictates what is right or wrong. On the other hand, defenders of universal human rights are frequently accused of operating with concepts which are abstract and distant from the realities of life. Human rights themselves 'have come under attack as strange, quasi-metaphysical entities, abstractions from the real world'.[22] The idea that there might be such things as human rights, valid for all people in all times and places, has often seemed implausible in the face of a wide variety of practices that are taken for granted in different parts of the world so that, according to some philosophers such as MacIntyre, the only foundation of human rights is to be found in the specific conceptions of reason which spring from within specific traditions.[23]

Nevertheless, both positions seem, at least in my opinion, problematic. On the one hand, a naturalistic position does not justify the link between the descriptive level (all human beings have the same rational nature) and the normative one (all human beings are worthy of respect). On the other hand, relativists have an understanding of human rights which is at odds with universalism. And if rights are not universal, they cannot justify interventions in the practices of other communities, nor international actions such as those by the World Health Organization (WHO), nor even the protection of people who are subjected to harmful practices.

Now, the position I want to defend before going back to the discussion of female mutilation, is that human rights are claims to which persons are entitled by virtue of being human, that is to say in virtue of their intrinsic dignity or value which is a normative property (or concept) that ontologically supervenes on their intrinsic nature. In this sense, human rights are due to all human beings by virtue of their very existence and their ontological status.

But what argument can justify the inference from 'they are persons' to 'they should be treated in such-and-such a matter'? To claim, as Kant does, that respect for inherent human dignity must be understood as the essence of human rights is to leave unanswered the critical question of why people should deserve dignity and respect. Perhaps theorists have thought the Kantian point that persons are owed dignity and respect in virtue of being rational beings so obvious that it does not require further arguments. However, rationality is neither a necessary nor a sufficient condition for being the recipient of moral concern. Nor is it sufficient simply to allude to the dignity of the person as a basic ideal so generally recognized as to require no independent support.[24] In some situations a definition is not needed; but it is not entirely satisfying to accept the idea that human dignity cannot be defined or analysed. Without understanding its meaning, we cannot easily draw specific implications for relevant conduct.

Nowadays, people are usually considered as subjects possessing qualities such as self-consciousness, reason and autonomy. This is why a person is usually described as a creature who has basic moral standing and is capable of moral concern and consideration. And this is why a person should always be respected. Of course, this does not necessarily mean that animals should not be respected; given that they are beings that, though not rational, are more than merely sentient, that is, they have enough psychological structure and complexity to count as ongoing 'subjects of life', the majority of people think they should be respected. Nevertheless the kind of moral concern they warrant is completely different from the concern people are worthy of. (See Hume's claim, in his *Inquiry Concerning the Principles of Morals*, III, I, that while humans must treat animals kindly, they are not required to treat animals in accordance with the rules of justice.)

Now, the one discernible property which sets human beings apart from other creatures, and which seems to be relevant to moral concern and respect, is usually identified with intelligence and with what flows from its possession, that is to say self-consciousness, autonomy and rationality. This is why human beings are not creatures who merely have experiences and desires. They are creatures who can accompany those things with a sense of self and can refer to items of consciousness as things which they have. Human beings can then give substantive content to the idea of themselves as having these thoughts and these desires, because they can recall past thoughts and preferences and project themselves into the future. Nevertheless, the grounding of differential status in the possession of higher functions of intelligence and agency naturally raises the question of the moral status of human beings who appear to lack those higher functions to some degree or other. In every measurable respect, in fact, humans differ in degree, and if we adopt an empirically discernible quality (or qualities) as the basis for moral worth, our resulting criterion seems to be bound to be discriminatory.

A possible solution, in my opinion, is to use the notion of supervenience in order to show how it is possible to speak of the universal dignity of each human being, without claiming the existence of a common and identical human nature.   Supervenience, in fact, is usually used to refer to the relationship between two kinds of properties that things may have, that is of a relationship between two different realms that is weaker than reductionism, but stronger than dualism. In the philosophy of mind the realms thought to stand in a supervenient relationship are the mental and the physical.[25] In moral philosophy they are the moral and the natural.[26] When speaking of the relationship between moral and natural properties, then, supervenience refers to the way in which moral properties are present in virtue of the presence of some other natural property: a thing can only possess a property of the first supervening kind (the moral one) because it has properties of the underlying kind (the natural one), but once the underlying kind is fixed, then the properties of the first kind are fixed as well. The supervening features exist only because of the underlying, or subjacent or base properties, and these are sufficient to determine how the supervening features come out. Nevertheless, at the same time, the two levels of properties are always and genuinely distinct levels. The basic idea is then that if two things are identical with respect to their base natural properties, they must also be identical with respect to the upper-level moral properties. Nevertheless, at the same time, the converse is not the case, for two things may be identical in the upper-level respect without being identical all the way down (which is referred to as 'variable realization'). This is why, for instance, two people may be equally good, but have different characters. As G.E. Moore puts the matter:

> If a thing is good (in my sense), then that it is so *follows* from the fact that it possesses certain natural intrinsic properties, which are such that from the fact that it is good it does *not* follow conversely that it has those properties.[27]

The moral property of good cannot then be reduced to any natural intrinsic property, nor to a number of different intrinsic properties. Good is not identical with each of a number of intrinsic properties, or with any conjunction or disjunction. Good is a unique kind of property, a uniqueness which can never be reduced to something else. Even if it supervenes on intrinsic properties, so that a thing which is exactly alike another that possesses intrinsic value will possess intrinsic value too, we cannot say that, if we have two objects which possess the same intrinsic value, then these two objects are exactly alike. Different groupings of base properties may give rise to the same supervenient property, and the same supervenient property may be realized in distinct individuals that have nothing in common.

Returning now to our specific subject, we can say that 'dignity' is a moral and normative property whose meaning is 'to be worthy of respect' in that it is a property that supervenes on the *intrinsic nature* of all human beings. Nevertheless, this does not imply that all human beings share exactly the same intrinsic and basic properties. All human beings have in fact the same intrinsic dignity, in that they are all human. But, at the same time, each human being is different from all others in that personhood may be realized in distinct individuals who have nothing in common. As Simone Weil writes:

> Equality is a vital need of the human soul. It consists in a cognition, at once public, general, effective and genuinely expressed in institutions and customs, that the same amount of respect and consideration is due to every being because this respect is due to the human being as such and it is not a matter of degree. It follows that the inevitable differences among men ought never to imply any difference in the degree of respect.[28]

In this way, we can give our conception of dignity an ontological basis and, at the same time, we can avoid some problems linked to the concept of the common rational nature of all human beings. Claiming that there are inevitable differences among men does not in fact mean that we lose sight of reality and of its richness, of different customs and their specificity. Saying that all human beings are worthy of respect in that 'dignity' is a moral and normative property which supervenes on intrinsic human nature does not remove all the diverse and rich aspects of reality, nor the fact that in order to know who the different persons are that we are considering, we need a moral insight into their uniqueness and into the uniqueness of their cultural traditions.

Clitoridectomy, Harm, and Personal Autonomy

What happens then in cases such as clitoridectomy and infibulation? After having shown the existence of a normative property (dignity) all human beings share even if they all differ from each other, the idea I would like to defend is that such practices are harmful and unacceptable in that they violate the intrinsic dignity and value of women, dignity and value that they have as human beings. In this sense, clitoridectomy and infibulation violate universal human rights in that they harm and offend some human beings.

Feinberg explains that the words 'harm' and 'offence' both have a normative sense, the former including in its reference any or all of a miscellany of disliked states (disgust, shame, hurt, anxiety, etc.), while the latter refers only to those states caused by the wrongful (right-violating) conduct of others.[29] He postulates that offence takes place when three criteria are present: a person is offended when she/he suffers a disliked state, attributes it to the wrongful conduct of another person and resents that person for causing that state. Nevertheless, he also asserts that offence is a less serious thing than harm and thus ignores the possibility that psychological offences might amount to physical harm, with the same serious implications. Starting then from Feinberg's analysis of harm and offence, we can now try to explain that female circumcision is a practice that harms and offends women in that it is caused by the right-violating conduct of some members of a community in which this practice is performed and, at the same time, it causes suffering and psycho-physical disliked states.

On the one hand, female genital mutilation harms women in that it has many painful consequences. It is usually performed in conditions that are dangerous and unsanitary. It is linked to extensive and in some cases lifelong health problems, even death. It denies women their sexuality by reducing or even eliminating sensibility and responses to stimulation. In the rare cases in which a woman can make the comparison, she usually reports profound regret.[30]

On the other hand, female genital mutilation offends women, in that it violates their intrinsic dignity, by denying their own autonomy. I have said that usually female circumcision is performed on young girls. This fact raises the question of how well-informed, mature, free and meaningful their consent to the operation is. A non-infibulated girl is often despised, ridiculed and referred to as *el beydourha meno* ('who wants her?') and *el beyaresha meno* ('who marries her?').[31] A girl who has not participated in the ritual is likely to be denied the possibility of marriage and is thereby foreclosed access to certain privileges in her society. Muslim men hold uncircumcised women in contempt as immoral freaks[32] (as Slack reports, the greatest insult a Muslim can issue is to call someone 'son of an uncircumcised mother').[33] Since the *choice* for the girl - assuming that she can give her consent - is between having the operation and being banished from her community, it cannot be said to be a situation promoting freedom and autonomy. Moreover, despite the apparent voluntariness of the victims involved, circumstances prove that female circumcision is mostly carried out by coercion. Clitoridectomy and infibulation are usually associated with poverty and illiteracy. This is why social acceptance and support may mean the difference between life and death and women are reluctant to question the tradition: in a certain way, women in these communities have no alternative but to go along with these practices and to consent to their daughters having the operation.[34] (The wife of the patriarch in Fauzia Kassindja's clan, for instance, told a reporter that she is opposed to the practice and would have run away - but nonetheless, she will allow her infant daughter to have the operation: 'It is not for women to give an order. I feel what happened to my body. I remember my suffering. But I cannot prevent it for my daughter.'[35])

Actually, the question of personal autonomy cannot be raised without considering the context in which decisions are made.[36] Persons do not enter life's interactions as independent and interchangeable units, and few operate according to the abstract principles of rational decision-theory. Often particular social, political and cultural events surrounding persons influence both the types of decisions that they are faced with and the sort of factors that shape their behaviour.[37] Hence, we must be careful to take into account, for instance, the role played by social background in creating the conditions necessary for a person to be autonomous. At a minimum, autonomous persons should be able to refuse the choices that reinforce social oppression.[38] Ideally, they should be able to avoid the structures of oppression altogether and pursue options that are not defined by the very values that promote their social oppression.

Moreover, if we believe, following Raz and others, that autonomy is the way a person can fulfil herself, we can say that one important argument against female circumcision is that it thwarts women's autonomy which should always be protected against the cultural compulsion of parents and community groups (including midwives, religious leaders and men).[39] As Raz explicitly claims, only an autonomous person is the author of her own life, because her life is her own making.[40] The autonomous person's life is marked not only by what it is but also by what it might have been and by the way it became what it is. A person is autonomous only if she/he has a variety of acceptable options to choose from and her life has become as it is through her choice of some of these options:

> A person who has never had any significant choice, or was not aware of it, or never exercised choice in significant matters but simply drifted through life is not an autonomous person.[41]

Where To Draw the Line

What then of the cultural relativist's challenge to human rights? Much of the attractiveness of cultural relativism is derived from its apparent anti-imperialism. It claims both that each culture has an equally valid way of life, and that moral claims coming from outside a particular culture have no validity within it. At the same time, however, all human beings have the same intrinsic and normative property, that is to say dignity, even though they all differ from each other. Furthermore, many indigenous values and practices in the Islamic world, which are compatible with the protection of universal human rights, include values and practices discernible in the religion of Islam. The Islamic scholar Majid Khadduri, for instance, identifies human dignity and equality among members of the community (without any distinctions based on race, sex or class), as Islamic concepts of human rights. And we may take this as evidence that the condemnation of the violation of human rights in Islamic countries need not necessarily, as it is argued, originate in and be imposed by *alien*, imperialistic Western cultures.[42]

It is not because of someone's order or superior decision that human rights are universal. They are universal, as we have tried to show, in the light of the equal dignity of all human beings, in which they have their primary source. This is why, even if 'to force people into the neat uniforms demanded by dogmatically believed-in schemes is almost always the road to inhumanity'[43] because there is no 'perfect whole' or 'ultimate solution' in which all things coexist, the respect of the intrinsic dignity of each person requires us to reject all harmful and offensive practices.

Having shown this, however, it would be a mistake to abstract human rights from their environment. In fact, forms of life differ. There are many ends, many moral principles. But at the same time, as Berlin states, there is not an infinite number of values and, in particular, they must fall 'within the human horizon'. Even if there are no absolute values, at any rate there exists a minimum of values without which societies could scarcely survive:

Priorities, never final and absolute, must be established. The first public obligation is to avoid extremes of suffering.[44]

In such a philosophical context, I believe it is possible to reconcile the standard of human rights with the preservation of cultural diversity, by accepting and promoting the right of all people to choose among alternatives that are equally respectful of human dignity.

But again, where should we draw the line? Through the analysis of female circumcision, we can probably say that the line has to be drawn between customary practices which respect human intrinsic dignity and therefore have to be acknowledged in their valuable and culturally rich aspects, and harmful cultural practices which seriously limit personal autonomy and do not allow human development and therefore have to be criticized and rejected. When we are confronted with extreme suffering, we are not confronted with different ends that persons may seek and still be complete persons, but we are rather confronted with oppressive practices that violate human dignity. This is why, ultimately, female circumcision has to be criticized and rejected.

As we have tried to show, female genital mutilation is unambiguously linked to the violation of human dignity: it implies not only the irreversible loss of the capability (in Nussbaum's terms) for a type of sexual functioning, as well as much body pain and suffering, but also the violation of personal autonomy and the denial of the possibility for a person to become the author of her own life, to fulfil herself and to flourish. And denying these possibilities means violating human rights in that it is the very dignity of the person that is at stake.

Table 1   Prevalence rates for FGM, World Health
Organisation, February 2001

(Available from : www.who.ch)

Country	Prevalence (%)	Year
Benin	50	1996
Burkina Faso	72	1999
Cameroon	20	1998
Central African Republic	43	1994
Chad	60	1996/97
Côte d'Ivoire	43	1994
Democratic Republic of Congo (formerly Zaire)	5	unknown
Djibouti	98	unknown
Egypt	97	1995
Eritrea	95	1995
Ethiopia	85	1984/90
Gambia	80	1985
Ghana	30	1998
Guinea	99	1999
Guinea-Bissau	50	1990
Kenya	38	1998
Liberia	60	1986
Mali	94	1996
Mauritania	25	1987
Niger	5	1998
Nigeria	25	2000
Senegal	20	1999
Sierra Leone	90	1987
Somalia	98-100	1982/93
Sudan	89	1990
Tanzania	18	1996
Togo	12	1996
Uganda	5	1995/96
Yemen	23	1997

**Table 2 Female Genital Mutilation: United Nations
Action
(Available from : www.who.ch)**

1952	UN Commission on Human Rights raises issue for first time.
1958	The Economic and Social Council (ECOSOC) in resolution 680 BII (XXVI) invites WHO to undertake study 'of persistence of customs which subject girls to ritual operations'.
1960	UN Seminar on the Participation of Women in Public Life discusses the question in Addis Ababa.
1961	The Economic and Social Council requests World Health Organization to examine the medical aspects of operations based on customs to which many women were still being subjected.
1962	WHO Executive Board widens the scope of the study to include cultural and socioeconomic background of countries involved.
1976	WHO Regional Office for Eastern Mediterranean undertook a review of the medical literature and embarked on a programme of activities.
1979	WHO Regional Office for Eastern Mediterranean in Khartoum holds seminar on the subject of Traditional Practices affecting the health of women and children. The Seminar takes a major and unprecedented step in formulating recommendations for governments to eliminate female circumcision.
1980	The World Conference of the United Nations Decade for Women, in Copenhagen, appeals to African governments and Women's Organizations to seek solutions to the problem of female circumcision and infibulation.
1981	The Association of African Women for Research and Development, under the aegis of the Economic Commission for Africa discuss FGM. WHO's Mother and Child Health Programme, in collaboration with UNICEF, offers support to governments to combat female circumcision.
1982	WHO makes a formal statement of its position regarding FGM to the UN Human Rights Commission. It expresses unequivocal opposition to medicalization of the practice in any setting, readiness to support national efforts aimed at eliminating the practice, and strongly advises health workers not to perform female circumcision under any conditions.
1984	Seminar on Traditional Practices Affecting the Health of Women and Children in Dakar condemns female circumcision as a health

	hazard and as unnecessary human suffering. The seminar also creates an Inter-African Committee (IAC) on Traditional Practices. The Commission on Human Rights recommends formation of an inter-agency working group to conduct a comprehensive study of traditional practices affecting the health of women and children.
1985	World Health Assembly resolution WHA 38.27 recognizes problem of harmful traditional practices and calls for concrete action to eliminate FGM. First session of Inter-Agency Working Group calls on governments to adopt policy measures for the elimination of FGM.
1986	Report of Inter-Agency Working Group presented to 42nd session of UN Human Rights Commission.
1987	WHO co-sponsors IAC Regional seminar on FGM and other traditional practices in Addis Ababa.
1988	WHO Regional Committee for Eastern Mediterranean adopts a resolution EM/RC35/R.9 stating that women's health must be safeguarded by ensuring the elimination of harmful practices.
1989	Safe Motherhood Conference in Niamey calls for the elimination of harmful traditional practices including FGM. WHO Regional Committee for Africa adopts resolution AFR/RC39/R.9 recommending that concerned members adopt appropriate policies and strategies to eliminate female circumcision.
1990	WHO co-sponsored IAC Regional Conference in Addis Ababa proposes change in terminology from 'Female Circumcision' to 'Female Genital Mutilation'.
1991	United Nations Seminar on Traditional Practices affecting the Health of Women and Children in Burkina Faso, recommends new terminology be used in future.
1992	WHO Technical Discussions on Women, Health and Development propose more courageous steps be taken by national and international communities to eliminate FGM. WHO position opposing medicalization of any form of female genital mutilation was reaffirmed during the Netherlands Consultancy for Maternal Health and Family Planning Congress on Female Circumcision.
1993	46th World Health Assembly passes Resolution WHA 46.18 and issues a press release on female genital mutilation. The Vienna Declaration and the Programme of Action of the

	United Nations Conference on Human Rights addresses gender-based violations which include female genital mutilation. The UN adopts the Declaration on Violence Against Women which also encompasses female genital mutilation and other traditional practices harmful to women.
1994	93rd session of WHO Executive Board adopts resolution on traditional practices harmful to the health of women and children. The Programme of Action of the International Conference on Population and Development (ICPD) includes recommendations which commit governments and communities to take urgent steps to stop the practice of female genital mutilation.
1995	The Declaration and Programme of Action of the World Summit for Social Development in Copenhagen refers to female genital mutilation, reinforcing the ICPD recommendations. The Platform for Action of the World Conference on Women in Beijing, includes a section on the girl child and urges governments, international organizations and nongovernmental groups to develop policies and programmes to eliminate all forms of discrimination against the girl child including female genital mutilation.

Notes

1 J. Ayala-Lasso, 'The Universality of Human Rights', in D. Warner (edited by), *Human Rights and Humanitarian Law. The Quest for Universality*, The Hague, Nijhoff Pub., 1997, p.87.

2 The term 'culture' is here used to refer to a large set including what people know, their store of experiences, their skills and all that each person has learnt since conception. In this sense, all cultures have some forms of repeated symbolized behaviour, or rituals, that are tied to their fundamental way of understanding the purpose of human existence.

3 For one exploration see F. Halliday, 'Relativism and Universalism in the Islamic Middle East', *Political Studies*, 43, 1995, pp.152-167.

4 S. Mendus, 'Human Rights in Political Theory', *Political Studies*, 43, 1995, pp.10-24, p. 12.

5 The practice dates back thousands of years and is reported in Egypt as early as 5th century BC (cf. H. Lightfoot-Klein, *Prisoners of Ritual. An Odyssey into Female Genital Circumcision*, New York, Harrington Park Press, 1989, p.27). According to the standardized WHO's definition of such a practice, female genital mutilation constitutes all procedures which involve partial or total removal of the external female genitalia or other injury to the female organs whether for cultural or any other non-therapeutic reasons (*Female Genital Mutilation*, Report of a WHO Technical Working Group, Geneva, 17-19 July 1995). Although not widely known, in the 1940s and 1950s, physicians in the United States and in England used this practice as a

'treatment' of hysteria, lesbianism, and female deviance (H. Lightfoot-Klein, *Prisoners of Ritual*, cit., p. 97). For major studies of female circumcision from a human rights perspective, see: K. Boulware-Miller, 'Female Circumcision: Challenges to the Practice as a Human Rights Violation', *Harvard Women's law Journal*, 8, 1985, pp.155-177; K. Brennan, 'The Influence of Cultural Relativism on International Human Rights Law: Female Circumcision as a Case Study', *Law and Inequality*, 8, 1989, pp.367-398; S.A. James, 'Reconciling International Human Rights and Cultural Relativism: The Case of Female Circumcision', *Bioethics*, 8, 1994, pp.1-26.

6   The *World Health Organisation* estimates that overall, in today's world, between 85 and 115 million women have had such operations. See Table 1, reporting WHO data (February 2001).

7   Slack, 'Female Circumcision: A Critical Appraisal', *Human Rights Quarterly*, 10, 1988, p.443. According to the World Health Organization the practice comprises any or all of the following procedures. Type I: Excision of the prepuce with or without excision of part or all of the clitoris. Type II: Excision of the prepuce and clitoris together with partial or total excision of the labia minora. Type III: Excision of part or all of the external genitalia and stitching/narrowing of the vaginal opening (infibulation). Type IV: Unclassified: includes pricking, piercing or incision of clitoris and/or labia; stretching of clitoris and/or labia; cauterization by burning of clitoris and surrounding tissues; scraping (angurya cuts) of the vaginal orifice or cutting (gishiri cuts) of the vagina; introduction of corrosive substances into the vagina to cause bleeding or herbs into the vagina with the aim of tightening or narrowing the vagina; any other procedure which falls under the definition of FGM given above. Types I and II (excision of the clitoris and labia minora) are the commonest types of female genital mutilation. They constitute up to 80% of all female genital mutilation. Type III (infibulation) is the most extreme form of FGM and constitutes approximately 15% of all procedures.

8   According to the WHO data, 'Female genital mutilation (FGM) is a deliberate procedure which causes grave damage to children and women, and which in many cases results in serious health consequences. [...] The mortality of girls and women undergoing these practices is probably high, but few records are kept and deaths due to FGM are rarely reported. Women subjected to the more severe forms of FGM are particularly likely to suffer from health complications requiring medical attention throughout their lives. Some complications such as severe bleeding and infections may occur immediately or shortly after the practice is performed; other complications may occur years after the event' (WHO, Fact sheet N 153, 1997 April. Available from www.who.ch). Medical discussions include N. Toubia 'Female Circumcision as a Public Health Issue', *New England Journal of Medicine*, 331, 1994, p.712 ff.; N. Toubia, *Female Genital Mutilation: A Call for Global Action*, New York, Women Inc., 1995; C.P. Howson (ed.), *In Her Lifetime: Female Morbidity and Mortality in Sub-Saharan Africa*, Washington, National Academy Press, 1996.

9   N. Toubia, *Female Genital Mutilation*, cit., p.9.

10   M. Nussbaum, *Sex and Social Justice*, New York, Oxford University Press, 1999.

11   Kenyatta, *Facing Mount Kenya*, London, Secker and Warburg, 1938. For a related anthropological account, see J.S. La Fontaine, *Initiation*, Manchester, Manchester University Press, 1985.

12   Cf. D.J. Harris, *Cases and Materials on International Law*, London, Sweet and Maxwell, 1984.

13   S.A. James, 'Reconciling International Human Rights and Cultural Relativism: The Case of Female Circumcision', *Bioethics*, 8, 1994, pp.1-26.

14   UNESCO, *Draft Report of the Working Group on Traditional Practices Affecting the Health of Women and Children*, 1985 (UN Doc. E/CN 4/HC 42/1985/L5).

15   Hathout, *Islamic Perspectives in Obstetrics and Gynaecology*, Cairo, Alam al-Kutub, 1988, p.102.

16   For evidence of manipulative and coercive practices by religious elites, see Mayer's study of the Islamization campaigns undertaken by the governments of Iran, Pakistan and Sudan (A. Mayer, *Islam & Human Rights Tradition and Politics*, Boulder, Westview Press, 1992, pp.30-42).

17   G.E. Lisenbard, 'Beauvoir, Ontology, and Women's Human Rights', *Hypatia*, 14, 4, 1999, pp.145-162, p.147.

18   *Covenant for the New Millennium: the Beijing Declaration and Platform for Action*. 1995. From the *Report of the Fourth World Conference on Women*, UN Doc. A/CONF 177/20, Santa Rosa, Freehand Books, p.112. Actually, the issue of female genital mutilation has been of concern to the UN and its agencies since the early 1950s (for more details, see Table 2).

19   'While the significance of national and regional particularities and various historical, cultural and religious backgrounds must be borne in mind, it is the duty of states, regardless of their political, economic and cultural systems, to promote and protect all human rights and fundamental freedom' (*Covenant for the New Millennium*, op. cit., pp. 9-10).

20   For one exploration see S. Moller Okin, 'Feminism, Women's Human Rights, and Cultural Differences', *Hypatia*, 13, 2, 1998, pp.32-52.

21   'For a Muslim country, as for all complex state societies, the most pressing human rights issue is not local cultural preferences or religious-cultural authenticity; it is the protection of individuals from a state that violates human rights, regardless of its cultural-ideological facade', R. Afshari, 'An Essay on Islamic Cultural Relativism in the Discourse of Human Rights', *Human Rights Quarterly*, 16, 1994, p.249.

22   S. Mendus, 'Human Rights in Political Theory', op. cit., p.19.
      In response, writers such as Gewirth (*Human Rights*, Chicago, University Press of Chicago, 1982) have argued for a constructivist account of human rights, one which eschews metaphysical and theological baggage, but which nevertheless aims to go beyond the purely stipulative. Such an account begins from human reason, or agency, and attempts not so much to justify as to articulate what reason implies in the real of political practice.

23   MacIntyre underscores that the individual who is the supposed carrier of rights simply does not exist. According to him, natural rights theory imagines human beings as monads prior to any interpersonal relations, lodged in no particular culture or tradition. Since there are no such individuals, if natural rights require such individuals, natural rights are chimerical indeed: 'Lacking any such social form, the making of a claim to a right would be like presenting a check for payment in a social order that lacked the institution of money' (A. MacIntyre, *After Virtue*, London, Duckworth, 1981, p.65).

24   The 'dignity of the human person' and 'human dignity' are phrases that have come to be used as an expression of a basic value accepted in a broad sense by many people. Human dignity appears in the Preamble of the Charter of the United Nations; the term 'dignity' is included in Article 1 of the Universal Declaration of Human Rights. In some subsequent instruments, we find the expression 'respect for the inherent dignity of the human person (see the International Covenant on Civil and Political Rights, the

American Convention on Human Rights, the International Covenant on Economic, Social and Cultural Rights). Nevertheless, we do not find an explicit definition of the expression: its meaning has been left to intuitive understanding, conditioned in large measure by cultural factors. See O. Schachter, 'Human Dignity as a Normative Concept', *The American Journal of International Law*, 77, 1983, pp.848-854.

25 J. Kim, *Supervenience and Mind*, Cambridge University Press, Cambridge, 1993.

26 G.E. Moore, 'The Conception of Intrinsic Value', *Philosophical Studies*, Routledge, London, 1922; R.M. Hare, 'Supervenience', *Proceedings of the Aristotelian Society* suppl. vol.58, 1984, pp.1-16; S. Blackburn, 'Supervenience Revisited', in *Exercises of Analysis*, ed. I. Hacking, Cambridge University Press, Cambridge, 1985.

27 G.E. Moore, 'A Reply to My Critics' in *The Philosophy of G. E. Moore*, P.A. Schilpp (ed.), Open Court, La Salle, 1968, p.588.

28 S. Weil, *The Need for Roots*, Routledge, London, 1978.

29 J. Feinberg, *Offence to Others*, New York, Oxford University Press, 1985.

30 Mariam Razak, for instance, was fifteen when she was cut; she had had sex with the man who is now her husband prior to that time and found it satisfying. Now, as Nussbaum reports, they both say things are difficult: Mariam compares the loss to having a terminal illness that lasts a lifetime; her husband recognizes that 'something was lost in that place ... I try to make her feel pleasure, but it doesn't work very well' (M. Nussbaum, *Sex and Social Justice*, cit., p.125).

31 Cf. A. Slack, 'Female Circumcision: A Critical Appraisal', op. cit., p.167.

32 As Kenyatta has written in his book (*Facing Mount Kenya*, op. cit., p.133), 'No proper Kikulu would dream of marrying a girl who has not been circumcised [...] this practice is regarded as the *conditio sine qua non* for the whole teaching of the tribal law, religion and morality'. To marry an uncircumcised woman is, according to the tradition, a curse. By doing so a man incurs the curse and becomes unclean. He is believed to have betrayed the tribe and needs extensive cleansing before participating in any traditional ritual or ceremony.

33 Ephigenia Gachiri (*Female Circumcision*, Nairobi, Paulines Publications, 2000, p.45) writes that a special song was composed to insult the first Gikuyu girl who married and became a mother while still uncircumcised.

34 S.K. Hellsten, 'Pluralism in Multicultural Liberal Democracy and the Justification of Female Circumcision', *Journal of Applied Philosophy*, 16, 1, 1999, pp.69-83, p.72.

35 M. Nussbaum, *Sex and Social Justice*, op. cit., p.124.

36 'Can the decision to be circumcised even when all the facts and risks are known, be considered truly voluntary when the only alternative is to be ostracised for such aberration?' (Slack, 'Female Circumcision', op. cit., p.472).

37 S. Sherwin, *The Politics of Women's Health: Exploring Agency and Autonomy*, Philadelphia, Temple University Press, 1998.

38 'Women are victims of outdated customs, attitudes and male prejudice. This results in negative attitudes of women about themselves. there are many forms of sexual oppression, but this particular one [female genital mutilation] is based on the manipulation of women's sexuality in order to assure male domination and exploitation' (Raqiya Haji Abdalla Dualch, cited in E. Dorkenoo, *Cutting the Rose: Female Genital Mutilation, the Practice and its Prevention*, London, Minority Rights Group, 1995, p. 29).

39 'The kind of pressure envisaged may take two forms; It may either be *direct* pressure from friends and family who seek to persuade or force women to undergo female genital mutilation or, alternatively, it may be *indirect* pressure to conform to deep-

rooted, internalised social expectations' (S. Sheldon and S. Wilkinson, 'Female Genital Mutilation and Cosmetic Surgery: Regulating Non-Therapeutic Body Modification', *Bioethics*, 12, 4, 1998, p.273).

40 J. Raz, 'Right-Based Moralities', in J. Waldron (ed.), *Theories of Rights*, New York, Oxford University Press, 1984.

41 J. Raz, 'Right-Based Moralities', op. cit., p.191.

42 See the important work of Ann Mayer, *Islam & Human Rights Tradition and Politics*, Boulder, Westview Press, 1992 where she stresses that 'Respect for international human rights law does not require that every culture use an identical approach, but it does require that human rights be defined and protected in a manner consonant with international principles' (p.20).

43 Berlin, *The Crooked Timber of Humanity*, Princeton, Princeton University Press, 1990, p. 19.

44 Berlin, *The Crooked Timber of Humanity*, p.17.

PART II
THE ETHICS OF
HUMANITARIAN
INTERVENTION

Chapter 4

Violent Humanitarianism - An Oxymoron?

Nigel Dower

Introduction

In a recent paper Hugo Slim raised the question: 'Is violent humanitarianism a contradiction in terms?' thus echoing a similar question raised by Adam Roberts 'Is humanitarian war an oxymoron?'[1] In the paper Slim argued that, whilst humanitarianism had its origins in the idea of restrictions on the manner of warfare (e.g. Red Cross care for prisoners), in modern times humanitarian intervention had come to be extended, first to include humanitarian intervention through aid agencies which is often associated with responses to war and armed conflict (as in Rwanda), and second more recently to include military intervention (e.g. in Kosovo) being justified as a humanitarian war. The last extension, he argued, distorted things too much and it would be more helpful if we could distinguish humanitarian intervention in aid programmes from the justification of warfare including intervention for the sake of human rights. In like manner Chris Brown has questioned whether wars can be 'humane', so calling war 'humanitarian intervention' is unfortunate, even if it is justified in terms of humanitarian reasons.[2]

This set me thinking about two sets of issues, one to do with the nature of humanitarianism itself, the other to do with the justification for violent intervention. After a brief exploration of humanitarianism I turn to a longer examination of the ethics of military intervention. Whilst I offer some arguments for the position that violent humanitarianism or humanitarian violence - I use the phrases interchangeably - is either never or very rarely justified, I see my task in this chapter as primarily that of setting out various approaches to the issue, partly in the context of different ethical theories concerning the nature of international relations.

The Logic of Humanitarianism

One line is to unpack the underlying logic of humanitarianism as follows. If humanitarianism is inspired by a *moral* concern for the well being or 'humanity' of fellow human beings *anywhere*, it constitutes an important element of a global or cosmopolitan ethic which stresses universal values and cosmopolitan responsibilities. If foreign policy is 'ethical', then it needs to be sensitive to such lines of thinking. Responding to human rights violations is clearly a case of responding to the denial of human well-being elsewhere. So if a government judged military intervention to be an effective mode of responding, then it does so on humanitarian grounds. Blair's moral commitment to the war in Kosovo would seem to be a modern version of just war thinking which finds a just cause in such a cosmopolitan objective. So violence may be justified by humanitarian objectives. So we have humanitarian violence.

The argument can be blocked in a number of different ways. The first is to question the underlying premise 'the end justifies the means', and to argue that the means should be seen as 'the ends in the making'. Second, it might be argued that, although the idea of violence being justified by a humane end is coherent, nevertheless this kind of justification cannot be applied to the actions of states because states ought to respect the sovereignty of other states. Third, it may be argued that although there may be a *justification* for military intervention by governments concerning human rights etc. in other states, that justification is not provided by the 'humanitarian' argument. 'Humanitarianism' only represents a sub-class of justifications of a globally ethical kind. Let us look at the last kind of move first, since it is more of a terminological issue than the other two arguments which are more substantive.

Humanitarian justification may then not belong to the right kind of justification applicable to military intervention by governments. (i) For instance it can be seen as distinct from both arguments concerning justice and arguments concerning the common good, both of which are applicable to government policies. Protecting the environment may be done for the global common good, but it does not as such constitute *humane* action. Justice, e.g. the justice of warding off aggression and stopping the violation of human rights, may be a justification from a global perspective, but it is not as such the basis of humanitarian action. Humanitarianism seems to involve a personal response to the suffering (or potential suffering) of other individuals, rather than a justification in terms of the public interest in some way or what the electorate want. There does not seem to be the right kind of reference to *motives* as in the case of individuals which seems necessary to the idea of humanitarian action. 'Humanity' and 'benevolence' appear to be conceptually linked. Governments are not kind or benevolent. (ii) A related more technical line of argument is that 'humanitarianism' refers to a very specific set of concerns enshrined initially in the rationale of the Red Cross movement and extended to the relief work of bodies like Oxfam and Médecins sans Frontières. Such work is concerned with the alleviation of suffering (often but not always caused by war) and more importantly is impartial and neutral. By contrast human rights law has developed on a quite separate track from humanitarian law, and reflects the fact that the protection of human rights can hardly be construed as neutral or impartial in the way the Red Cross model insists on.[3]

A reply to these initial terminological moves is as follows. Humanitarianism is more sophisticated than the above simple models suggests. (i) The implicit link with benevolence and charity as opposed to justice is misleading. If we consider 'human rights' justifications in these terms, it is clearly linked to justice and to the making of rights claims. It is odd to separate humanitarianism from human rights, since often the justification for humanitarian intervention is in terms of human rights. This is true not merely of violations of liberty and civil rights, but also of failures to meet rights to subsistence and so on. Whilst it is true that often reference to humanitarianism is about motives rather than actions themselves, it is also true that the term can refer to kinds of action themselves; and even if reference to humanitarian motives in governments may sound strange or needs reinterpretation, it is worth noting that the propriety of using the term of government action is partly a function of the fact that its action reflects the interests of citizens which are sometimes informed by humanitarian responses. (ii) As Slim shows, what is partly at issue is a conflict between a 'priestly' defence of a 'humanitarian' paradigm by established organizations like the Red Cross and a more 'prophetic' reminder of the root idea of 'humanity' and what range of responses - including ones cast in human rights terms - are appropriate. Neutrality may for all sorts of pragmatic reasons be valuable to some organizations, but there is nothing in the idea of humanitarianism to imply the need not to take sides; indeed in some conflicts, not to take sides in favour of those who suffer would itself be a failure of humanitarian response.

If we accept that an activity or intervention could be 'humanitarian' in view of its 'end' rather than the manner it is done in (such transference of the 'attribute' of ends to means seems quite natural), then humanitarian war seems conceivable (though not perhaps 'humane' war where 'humane' seems to apply directly to the manner of the means).

Whilst of course humanitarianism *could* be so defined as to refer only to the level of personal morality with no implication for what states should do (i.e. presupposing a radical separation of the two levels of ethical thought), it is more defensible as part of a fuller 'cosmopolitanism' with clear implications for what states should do as well. This in turn raises the question whether there is a defensible cosmopolitanism which will justify humanitarian violence. Let us now turn to this substantive issue.

Humanitarian Violence: Some Conceptual Mapping

First we need some conceptual clarification. There are three elements to humanitarian violence (or violent humanitarianism) - two explicit, one implicit. First, the implicit one is that the domain we are talking about is state action. Second, the word 'humanitarian' refers to a goal - a humane goal such as the reduction of suffering or the stopping of human rights violations. Third, the means to achieve this is violent action which I shall assume to be non-humane in respect to its involving (intentionally) the causing of suffering, death and the violation of rights. It is important to my subsequent argument that the goal and the means are stated in this fashion: a goal x is pursued by an action which is contrary to the goal x. We can state this more precisely: a goal G which has a property x in virtue of which it is a goal is pursued by a means M which intentionally destroys that property x; or, y is promoted by acting non-y-ly. Some examples: A promotes peace by acting unpeacefully. B promotes human rights by violating human rights. C promotes truth by lying. Note that the interesting cases for this formula are ones in which the goal incorporates moral values of some kind. There is nothing even *prima facie* challenging about the idea of seeking pleasure by a painful means (e.g. going to the dentist) or walking South in order to get to somewhere North (if the only available route requires this).

A series of questions can now be asked of taking a violent means in order to achieve a humanitarian goal.

Is there anything incoherent about the idea of humanitarian violence so described? Clearly not. People and states do as a matter of fact pursue the objectives of alleviating human suffering by taking violent means against those for instance who cause it. Whether they should is another matter.

Is there some *moral* incongruity in the idea of a *justified* pursuit of humanitarian violence? Again, if by moral incongruity we mean the impossibility of there being a moral theory - true or false - which provides justification, the answer is: no. Many moral theories (some of which we will look at) provide such justification.

If we mean by moral incongruity the impossibility of a justification being available from within the moral theory one endorses, then it is possible that the answer is 'yes', the theory rules out such an action as not being justifiable. By this I do not merely mean that the theory always rules out such an action as *wrong*. A simple pacifist deontology which simply said that using violence for whatever ends was always wrong would not show that justified violent humanitarianism was incoherent, merely that any claim that it was justified would be mistaken. If on the other hand the theory - no doubt often religious but not necessarily - tried to establish as part of its understanding of the nature of moral reasoning that certain kinds of action *could* not be acceptable, then we could say there was an incongruity about the very idea of justified humanitarian intervention. And this might for instance emerge from a view that moral logic requires congruence between means and ends, suggested for instance by Gandhi's remark 'the means are the ends in the making'; that is, whatever moral values are involved in one's ends, these must constrain the means taken.[4] I return to this approach later.

As a variation on the moral incongruity argument we might also have one based on our understanding of the 'state' element. Maybe justified humanitarian intervention is perfectly possible, but in the case of state action, it is not because of the peculiar character of states and their interactions. This argument to do with sovereignty (considered further below) might be seen to defeat any claim about justified intervention.

If we do not accept any of these limitations, we are left with the view that the justification of human violence by states is perfectly coherent and the question is: is it justified?

One possibility is to argue for a very strong thesis that from a deontological point of view we have a *strict* duty to intervene when human rights violations occur. I shall argue that this is implausible, and that we have to think more carefully about just what the conditions might be in which it was justifiable. The latter position is of course perfectly consistent with the possibility that in the real world there are no actual cases or at least very few in which the conditions will be satisfied.[5]

Normative International Relations Theories

It will now be useful to survey the main normative theories of international relations, with a view to seeing how they tackle the question of humanitarian violence. The three main types of position are (sceptical) realism, internationalism and cosmopolitanism. Greatly oversimplifying: the sceptical realist answers the question 'Is there an international morality?' with the answer 'no', whereas the internationalist and cosmopolitan answer the question 'yes'. However the latter two positions answer the question in rather different ways, the former stressing the existence of an autonomous 'morality of states' and a limited set of moral norms that are to be accepted, the latter stressing the idea that the moral rules that should govern states are derived from a universal morality and that what states ought to do is somewhat more extensive than is usually accepted within the internationalist framework. You will notice that the latter two are distinguished by two criteria, one to do with the *source and validation* of the morality applicable to states, the other to do with the *content* of the rules. This gives rise to other possible combinations as we shall see shortly, but as a rough and ready initial characterization of common differences of approach, it is useful at this stage.

(a) Sceptical Realism

Why might one deny that states had any moral duties towards one another? One common argument which hails from Hobbes is that in an anarchical world i.e. a world of autonomous states without a world government or 'common power' to hold them all in awe, there are no moral rules applicable because such norms are unenforceable. A variation on this is that although moral norms are in principle applicable to foreign policy, the conditions of the modern world - in particular its lack of security - mean that considerations of national self-interest systematically override such moral norms. Appeal is sometimes made to other facts like those of cultural relativism and thus to the fact that there is no common standpoint from which to construct a common global ethical framework.

Although much more needs to be said about realism and what is wrong with it, it need not detain us more here because it is not really relevant to our present concern. What I mean is that 'humanitarian intervention' from a realist point of view is itself incoherent for a rather different reason to those suggested above. Since the whole point of humanitarian violence is that a moral goal justifies violence, the realist position deprives one of a basis for having such a goal as a moral goal. It can only be a moral goal if we accept a global ethic of some kind which justifies action across borders for the sake of values elsewhere. This is what is denied. Of course a realist may accept that a government may pursue a 'humanitarian goal' by violent intervention; but such action will be interpreted as based on calculation of advantage to the country in question. In which case the 'justification' of such intervention will either be a 'smoke screen' for the pursuit of other objectives (made more acceptable if other countries accept the moral language involved) or be a way of promoting specific values in other parts of the world. Thus to many critics of American policy in the Gulf War, what was really driving the action was oil interests.[6]

(b) Internationalism

The internationalist tradition stresses the idea that there is a 'society of states' which like any other society is held together by a set of norms which if observed maintain the essential goal of that society. Whilst there are various kinds of justification which can be given for the 'morality of states' (some having a basis in a form of cosmopolitan thinking), what is important is that there is a distinct set of norms which are in practice accepted by states in their dealings with one another and which are in practice both limited compared with and distinct from the various moralities which apply to individuals in different societies. These norms can be summarized as respect for sovereignty and the primacy of non-intervention; norms to do with warfare (traditionally called the just war theory); and norms to do with honouring treaties and international agreements (*pacta sunt servanda*).

It might be thought that such a normative approach provides a very clear answer to our question: could humanitarian violence be justified? The answer is: no. The primacy of sovereignty and non-intervention, reflected for instance in UN Charter article 2.7, clearly rules out intervention with regard to the internal affairs of another country. International order and security are agreed values which are so important that, as Bull argued, we must preserve a political pluralism in the world, and not be tempted by 'solidarist' arguments.[7]

But this would be a premature interpretation. Two kinds of considerations show this. First, it is well recognized that within the dominant internationalist paradigm there is tension between on the one hand respecting sovereignty and on the other hand accepting the need to uphold and pursue humanitarian agendas. Whereas even at the time when the UN system was set up, it was still accepted that human beings were only objects of international law not subjects, by the end of the twentieth century it was becoming recognized that they had a more important status. The development of human rights law played a significant role in this. Since part of this international morality is the principle *pacta sunt servanda*, and since many international agreements impose duties on member states - including duties in connection with human rights - normative pressure from this part of the internationally agreed moral framework comes into conflict with the norms of sovereignty and non-intervention.

Much recent discussion in International Relations/International Law circles on NATO's intervention in Kosovo turns on two questions: (a) Do the rights of individuals take precedence over the rights of states? (Of interest in this regard was the speech in 1998 of the UN Secretary-General in which he said, 'Our job is to intervene ... State frontiers ... should no longer be seen as a watertight protection for war criminals or mass murderers. The fact that conflict is internal does not give the parties any right to disregard the most basic rules of human conduct.'[8]) (b) Was NATO's action, despite lack of explicit UN Security Council authorization, within the framework of international law? Nick Wheeler has recently argued that the Kosovan crisis represents a watershed in the development of thinking about the justification of intervention.[9] It is worth noting that we have come a long way from the 1970s when countries like India, Tanzania and Vietnam invaded East Pakistan, Uganda and Cambodia respectively and justified their acts as self-defence, even though the humanitarian motive was manifest in each case.

This level of debate about legitimacy in international law is important but not my main concern. Even if such legitimacy is regarded as a necessary condition of moral justification, it is hardly sufficient, and my concern is really with the moral basis which is needed alongside legal arguments. It is not in any case obvious that an action contrary to international law is necessarily morally wrong; certainly it is important that intellectual space is allowed in which someone might want to say that, since military intervention is morally justified, international law ought to be modified to allow for it, if it does not now. I say this in order to stress that, whilst many internationalists are 'restrictivists' and thus against military intervention, it is not the route for me to take, even if I am also against humanitarian intervention. A cosmopolitan defence of a position on humanitarian intervention, whatever that position is, cannot hide behind the appeal to sovereignty and existing international law in this way.

But to return to a possible defence of humanitarian intervention within the internationalist paradigm, the appeal to human rights in itself would not create a compelling case for military intervention - perhaps for various other forms of pressure but not for the use of force - but for a corresponding adjustment to the understanding of the norms governing warfare. I shall address this matter by considering the just war theory, not because I think that it is the only way of fruitfully discussing the ethics of war, but because its own complexity throws light on the issues I want to raise. The variations in the tradition also illustrate an important point, that different positions on the issue of intervention were possible in the past and are not merely a late twentieth-century phenomenon. The just war theory serves my purpose because it was an attempt to find an *ethical* justification for warfare, which is our concern here.

(c) Dilemmas Within Just War Theory

It is a familiar enough division within just war theory to distinguish two branches of it, *ius ad bellum* and *ius in bello*, the justification for going to war and the justification of how a war is to be fought. The former covers such principles as: legitimate authority, just cause, last resort, proportionality and reasonable prospect of success; the latter such principles as not making non-combatants direct objects of attack, the humane treatment of prisoners and so on.

In relation to this there is what I take to be a very important point made in Hedley Bull's article 'The Grotian conception of international society'.[10] Here he contrasts what he saw as the earlier rationale of Grotius for the 'society of states' which was firmly grounded in a universal moral order understood essentially in 'natural law' terms, with the later developments of the international society of states. In the latter that universal moral anchorage was lost, and in its place was a more pragmatic conception of states accepting the equal rights of each other based on convention and contract. Whereas in the former conception there was a universal moral law, in the latter such a framework was either denied or at least regarded as subject to sufficient disagreement that what was important was that there should be an acceptance of political pluralism.

Now the corollary of these differences of emphasis, Bull remarks, is a different reading of the norms governing war. Whereas earlier the conception of a just cause might well include the rectification of injustice or punishment, in the latter conception (given the uncertainties or disagreements about justice), the principle of respect for sovereignty became paramount and thus, as the UN charter reflects, the only international sin is aggression. Corresponding to the latter conception there was greater importance put on the rules of war; if there was no clear view that in a conflict one side was just and another unjust, there was all the more reason for each side to respect the other side. By contrast, Bull remarks, if you believe passionately that you have justice on your side such that those fighting on the other side are evil, there may be less emphasis upon the rules of war or at least upon their strict observance.

Of course strictly speaking if one accepts the just war approach, there is no reason why all the principles should not be equally accepted as necessary conditions for the justification of war, but Hedley Bull is no doubt right that there is a tension in practice between an emphasis upon a moralized conception of just causes (beyond an internationally agreed idea of injustice qua violation of sovereignty) and an emphasis upon limitations on and rules about warfare which may well be based on agreements between states rather than some deeper universal theory.

The relevance of this to humanitarian violence is this. In many ways we have moved back to the earlier Grotian conception insofar as we accept a universal moral order involving human rights; gross violations of these in other countries provide at least prima facie a 'just cause' for action. As Luban pointed out some time ago, a human rights basis for thinking about international justice and injustice confronts the UN 'non-aggression' paradigm or what Walzer called the 'legalist' paradigm.[11] A more 'solidarist' conception confronts a more 'pluralist' conception: solidarity with those who suffer elsewhere may require intervention in a way that respecting plurality and difference and leaving societies to themselves to sort out conflicts within them do not.

In many ways the numerous issues in current international relations centre on this tension between solidarity and pluralism, for which possibly one way forward is a normative account that combines them - what I have called solidarist pluralism.[12] Human rights discourse can actually be seen as a discourse which combines the two elements. Though it is sometimes seen by postmodern critics as old-fashioned hegemonic universalism in modern guise, it can I think be more plausibly seen as combining an acceptance of international responsibility for meeting the conditions of well-being anywhere (e.g. stopping violations of civil rights; meeting subsistence rights) with recognizing that local cultural conditions give rise to many different expressions of basic rights which can, within limits, be respected.

The internationalist 'morality of states' is I think more plausible if it is grounded in a universal theory, and is in other words *implicitly* a cautious form of cosmopolitanism rather than opposed to it. Whether this should be based on Grotian premises, a modern human rights theory or some other theory is another matter.[13]

However such a basis for defending the 'morality of states' paradigm is at least under modern conditions liable to undermine it *as it is usually understood,* since the implicit cosmopolitanism underlying it may well lead to a more critical approach to what states do and are. The point is that in Grotius' day conditions in Europe were such that a settled nation-state system (for which the Treaty of Westphalia of 1648 was such an important developmental moment) was so much preferable to what preceded it that the system and its rules were the best bet from a humanitarian or globally ethical point of view. But if we are returning to a moralized basis for international relations, neither the system nor its received rules are necessarily the best bet for humanity now.

So we are back to square one in terms of my initial question: is humanitarian violence justified? The internationalist tradition provides us with no clear answer. The conventionalist defence of non-intervention is seen to be inadequate, whilst a Grotian conception leads in the modern world to a more explicitly cosmopolitan defence or critique, as the case may be.

(d) Cosmopolitanism

Cosmopolitanism is at bottom a commitment to a certain view of the relationships between human beings; namely that we all belong to one global moral community. As such there are certain basic values and norms (to do with the good and with duty) common to all people, but also responsibilities we have towards one another across the world. Generally there lies behind such a view some kind of theory, worldview or what I call 'source story'; such a source-story might be a philosophical theory such as Kantianism, human rights theory, Utilitarianism, deep ecology, or a religious world view as with various forms of Buddhism or Christianity.

It should be made clear that a cosmopolitan view is not a claim that all people everywhere do accept the same values and responsibilities (any more than moral judgements made about others in one's own society imply that they accept the same moral judgements). On the other hand, given the potentially damaging criticism that the assertion of such values (especially by the powerful) may be hegemonic or culturally imperialistic, many cosmopolitans are now sensitive to this issue and take care to present their global values as those it would be reasonable to expect others to accept (even if their source stories may be significantly different). Furthermore many cosmopolitans nowadays are aware of the 'citizenship' element of 'cosmo-polites' and the challenge of creating the appropriate trans-national frameworks (e.g. in the international networks of NGOs) for expressing 'global citizenship' - a challenge which cannot be met without seeking common ground amongst actors throughout the world.

But for the purposes of this discussion I concentrate on the 'ethical' component of cosmopolitan views as something asserted by thinkers and open to critical assessment. Without pretending to do justice to the full range of cosmopolitan theories on offer, I shall discuss several in order to illustrate some general points.

(i) Utilitarianism

Utilitarianism, whatever its faults as an all-embracing theory, clearly has the merit of being global in its reach. The dictum 'everybody to count for one, nobody for more than one', whilst not the sole prerogative of utilitarianism, certainly expresses an implicitly global conception of the domain of all humans (and indeed for Bentham beyond).[14] If we accepted it, in many ways the world would be much better place, since we would need to accept something like Peter Singer's famous principle for helping alleviate distant poverty.[15] Although the standard reaction to the latter is that it demands too much, we are left with the question: well, how much are we prepared to do to alleviate ill elsewhere?

Certainly such an approach provides no principled objection to the possibility of military intervention for the sake of stopping human rights violations. Whether we could consistently support military intervention *and not do other things which we do not do* is another matter which I return to later on.

(ii) Kantianism

A Kantian approach is also clearly cosmopolitan in approach. Indeed Kant was a card-carrying cosmopolitan who certainly saw the duty to respect other persons as ends in themselves as applying globally. Kant looked forward to a federal world of republican states guaranteeing freedom and equality - the conditions of moral autonomy within states - and respecting the like aspirations of other states according to his 'articles of peace'.[16] But Kant also accepted the necessity of warfare, the right of self-defence and also capital punishment; the right of individuals not to be killed could be overridden in certain conditions consistent with respect for them as persons. Whilst so far as I know Kant never actually discussed the question whether the violation of rights in another country provides the condition in which one may attack the violators with killing force, there does not seem to be any reason why a Kantian could not accept this. On the other hand, given the deeply non-consequentialist character of Kantian ethics, there does not seem to be compelling reason why one should either.

Whilst of course there is the distinction drawn between strict duties and meritorious duties, it is not clear that military intervention is even an appropriate case of a meritorious duty. Since it would have to be an optional expression of the duty of benevolence, it is not clear why such interventions (as opposed say to intervention to give aid) would be seen as appropriate, given their problematic nature for other reasons (violating autonomy; killing people, etc.).

(iii) Human Rights

Human rights thinking has become an important discourse in the modern world and in some ways provides a middle ground between the consequentialism of utilitarianism and the deontology of Kant. Without going into the minefield of its theoretical justification (though I am inclined to think that one can be found), it is a good candidate for a cosmopolitan ethic because the very character of 'human' points to the global-ness of the conception in two respects: first, that these are rights held by all humans *qua* humans and second that the correlative duties corresponding to these rights are in principle global in reach as well. A world of hermetically sealed units in which the same rights existed in each unit is *conceivable* such that one might assert universal rights without a commitment to any sense of global community in which responsibility stretches across the community. However the general thrust behind (and indeed motivation for) human rights discourse is precisely to assert in Henry Shue's words that 'basic rights are the minimum demand of all humanity on all humanity'.[17]

If we ask 'what are the duties that correlate to rights'? a plausible answer is that given by Shue: duties not to deprive others of their rights; duties to protect from standard threats of deprivation; duties to come to the aid of the deprived. These apply equally to different types of rights whether they are rights to subsistence, security or liberty. (Such an approach rightly cuts across the traditional division between rights of action and rights of recipience.) Generally speaking one can say that the duty not to deprive is a strict duty of all agents (perhaps absolute in a strong deontological sense), the duty to protect from standard threats a collectively held duty (primarily for public organizations but backed by private citizens), and the duty to come to the aid of the deprived one that is addressed as much to individuals as to states. Since (especially from a global point of view) the amount of preventable or alleviatable deprivation far exceeds what can be reasonably expected of individuals (or even states), it is likely to be seen as a meritorious or imperfect duty (subject as Mill said to the selective choice of the agent).[18]

It may be that in some circumstances duties to come to the aid are strictly required, and that military intervention for the sake of human rights might in some cases fit this. Treaty obligations might be a case in point, though their relevance to military intervention is unclear since such action is against the wishes of the state in question. Apart from this kind of case, could there be a strict duty to intervene militarily? If not, are there circumstances in which an overwhelming case can be made for intervention, all things considered? Certainly a human rights approach which includes the duty to come to the aid of those who are deprived of what they have a right to (liberty, security or subsistence) does not rule out the possibility of military intervention being an appropriate form of such 'coming to the aid' of others.

Strict Duties?

It is striking that none of the cosmopolitan theories outlined above provides a clear case for saying either that it cannot be a duty or that it must be a duty to intervene militarily. But two deontologically simple answers might be given: first a principle like: 'the means are the ends in the making', second a principle like: 'whenever A can intervene to stop B violating the rights of C, A ought to do so.'

(a) 'The means are the ends in the making'

The first is linked of course to pacifism. I do not consider pacifism as such further, not because I think it not worth seriously considering - indeed I am attracted to it in many ways as an approach - but because it forecloses on the discussion too easily, since it has nothing specifically to say about military intervention. However I do want to explore a little more the broader principle to which it can be linked and which I have already mentioned: 'the means are the ends in the making.' This can be stated as a meta-principle: so act that the means you adopt are value-consistent with the moral values internal to the end pursued. This goes beyond a simple pacifism in two respects. First, it is not merely about the duty not to kill or about the right to life. It is about *any* core value. You should pursue justice by acting justly. Conversely, do not protect human rights by violating human rights. Do not seek peace by acting unpeacefully. Second, it is not a simple deontological principle. It is about the *pursuit of moral goals*. Such a principle might be seen as falling between the normal positions called deontology and consequentialism, in that unlike deontology it is concerned with the promotion of ends, but unlike consequentialism, the ends control the means in more elaborate ways than that of providing 'effects' in a cause-effect relationship. Though Kantians may not like this, it has a family resemblance to an important Kantian insight that the will has to be consistent with itself. Only in this case it is an internal consistency within the structure of a single willed act - a kind of inversion of the familiar claim that he who wills the end must insofar as he is rational will the means indispensably necessary to it.

Whilst I am strongly drawn to the dictum, I am well aware that stated in absolutist terms it would seem to be counter-intuitive. For one thing if one thinks that there is a right to immediate self-defence and self-preservation, there may be cases *in extremis* which entail the rightness of violating the rights of others. My position is that it should be treated as an important but non-overriding second-order moral commitment in the choice of ends. As such I would say that Gandhi's saying 'the means are the ends in the making', whilst it cannot formally rule out actions whose character is inconsistent with the end embedded in them, does create a *strong presumption* against such action being justified.

(b) Strict Duty to Intervene?

What of the other deontological claim that it is a strict duty to intervene: whenever A can intervene to stop B violating the rights of C, A ought to do so. First, I reject this as stated because it is impossible to fulfil as a principle of strict duty. The reason is simple: there is no guarantee that there will not be, and every likelihood that there will be, circumstances in which not all the situations one can respond to, taken separately, can be responded to taken collectively. Even if a Singer-like qualification is added like 'without sacrificing any comparable respect for rights', it would still be problematic in that it would share, paradoxically, the same problem as a simple consequentialist approach does: it would require us to be acting all the time.

My main problem however is that I cannot see how such a principle can be regarded as a strict principle anyway. The structure of justification for intervention is rather complex: let us grant that there is a human right not to be detained without trial; we might even characterize this as an absolute right. A government detains some citizen in this way. Does another government have a duty to intervene? It cannot be a strict duty - something it must do whatever the consequences. At best it will be a duty all things considered. We can imagine by contrast a case where legally A had a duty to intervene if B's rights are violated by C: thus within a political community this could quite standardly be a duty of governments vis-à-vis the violation of its citizens' rights. But the relations of states to one another are not like this in terms of international law. Morally the case could not be made out, since it would have to be based on some general principle, to the effect that whenever a person's right is violated by other persons, all third persons would have a duty to intervene. We do not accept this, and are right not to accept this: the structure of the moral life would be totally distorted.

The point of moral logic is this: if A has a strict duty not to do x to B (or B has an absolute right that A not do x to B), and A does x to B, others do not have a strict duty to intervene on B's behalf. Consider a parallel: A had a right to X which is not realized because of various factors such as poverty, famine or the wrongdoing of others. Do we have a strict duty to ensure that A gets what he has a right to? No. The point is that whatever the cause of the fact that A's rights are not realized - whether human wrong-doing is part of it or not - if we did not ourselves actively cause the situation, our duty to come to A's aid is not a strict duty in any of these cases. Whether we have a duty at all depends upon a whole host of factors I will mention shortly.

An example may illustrate this. A friend of mine a few years ago went to a Third World country X on a Noraid project to work on wells for a water-scarce region. The Norwegian government decided to protest against the detention of political detainees without trial in that country. Result: the Noraid project was instantly told to stop - and the prisoners remained detained. My point here is not to assess whether the Norwegian government decision was a justified calculated risk that misfired, but rather this: the duty to stop another country's government from violating the rights of some of its citizens is no more of a duty than to help realize the subsistence rights of others of its citizens through the well boring project. I am no more responsible for the human suffering I let human agents directly cause to fellow human beings than I am for the suffering I let happen to human beings through other causes, some natural, some the indirect effect of thoughtless or unjust man-made policies. In both cases 'letting' is the same: by intervention I could have (possibly) stopped the suffering.

Consistency and the Wider Picture

If then we reject the idea that it is a strict duty, might it nevertheless often be a duty-all-things-considered in many circumstances? Does the cosmopolitan acceptance that we have duties or responsibilities to promote well-being entail the correlative duty to use violence to do so? It may be thought so, but I want to suggest two general considerations which make it unlikely to have application.

(a) Consistency

The first argument is concerned with the need for consistency. I do not mean here the need for consistency in foreign policy in militarily intervening in one country if one intervenes in another. That is an important issue I do not consider here. Rather I mean consistency in the way one takes various types of justification for intervention in the broadest sense into account. Why for instance does the fact that *governments* do things which cause suffering justify intervention, but other kinds of human rights violations or realization-failure caused by or allowed by other factors (oppression, neglect, the economic system) do not.[19] If we did *everything we could* concerning the latter, then the argument for doing everything concerning the former might work. But this is not what we do or even see as something we think we should do. So why do we expend immense resources on war against government-caused human rights violations *but not on other human rights violation issues?*

Genocide is awful, but so is mass hunger. There is a problem of consistency here. If it is said 'How can we stand by and do nothing when people are murdered?', the same can be said 'How can we stand by and let countless people die from hunger and disease?' There are of course two different strategies for dealing with this kind of inconsistency: accept that we have no duty in either case, or accept that we have positive duties of intervention in both cases. In both cases I want to argue that we do not have strict duties of intervention which inter alia would mean *constant* intervention in all cases where we could intervene to protect human rights. On the other hand, I do want to argue (and have argued elsewhere) that we have significant duties to give and support increased (and more effective) aid, but still question the propriety of military intervention for 'humanitarian' reasons. The difference between the two cases rest partly on empirical consequences and partly on the structure of respective actions, e.g. the contrast between win-win strategies and win-lose strategies.

(b) The Wider Context

The example given earlier concerning Noraid illustrates my second more general point about the wider context. Whatever we do has effects on a much wider range of people than those who are the object of our interventions. Indeed the effect of the Noraid programme was the almost certain benefit for a large number of people. The effect of the Government protest was the uncertain benefit of a few. This way of putting it is a bit unfair: no doubt the Norwegian government thought that the probability of combining the two - a certain benefit to many and a possible benefit to a few - outweighed the possibility of not reaching either goal at all. But it does illustrate the more general point and that is that if one adopts a fully cosmopolitan perspective, one has to consider a wide range of effects - the likely effect on all other rights as well as many other ethical desiderata. It is worth noting that the right to peace is itself an important right which is violated by military intervention. One way of putting what I am saying is to say that the principle of proportionality has to be given a much wider interpretation than is often assumed in 'just war' justification.

It may be thought that I have now betrayed my true colours - namely that I really am merely a consequentialist, who sees decisions concerning foreign policy including decisions whether to intervene as determined by a balance of the consequences. Perhaps my consequentialism includes rights but it turns out to be a form of consequentialism in which rights are to be maximized. This is partly true, party false. I certainly do not think that governments - any more than individuals - have a duty to *maximize* the balance of good over bad. On the other hand, governments do not any more than individuals have a duty (or even a right) to engage in positive actions such as intervention if the result of such intervention is that more harm is or is likely to be caused than good *all things considered*. This is certainly so if those actions involve, as a means, violent action or other violations of rights.

There may be circumstances in which we accept that we must do the right thing, whatever the consequences: *fiat iustitia, ruat coelum*. But I cannot see how intervention fits this model. Stopping others' wrongdoing cannot be justified merely on the grounds that we have come to the aid of others whose rights are violated, whatever the consequences. *If we are intervening, it is consequences that matter* (unless we are contractually bound or obligated by special relations). Military action in Kosovo may have been justified (though I doubt it), but it certainly was not justified merely by appealing to the principle: we must stop the violation of the rights of the Kosovans. The whole impact of the strategy on the region - short-term and long-term - had to be considered.[20]

Conclusion

If we focus on the *humanitarian* element - the direct object of the operation such as the relief of suffering caused by other human beings - this may seem to justify intervention (subject to the normal just war norms about prospects of success etc.), but only because of the conjunction of three factors: (a) a misconstrual of the requirement to take action as a deontologically conceived duty; (b) a failure to attend sufficiently to the wider ramifications of the action taken; (c) a failure to recognize that if we do not think that we ought to do *all that we can* to alleviate suffering, there are generally more effective things that can be done with the resources we are willing to use.

My argument then is partly a matter of showing, in the tradition of contingent pacifism, the long-term ineffectiveness of the resort to violence. Violence leads to violence and so on. But this line of thought, like contingent pacifism, is too shallow without a deeper analysis being offered. We need a different model: (a) violations or failures to realize life rights (rights to the conditions of life, subsistence etc.) are quite as important as violations of other kinds of rights. Doing right by others is quite as important as stopping others doing wrong by them. (b) Cooperative action is better than divisive action because such actions are 'win-win' not 'win-lose'; there is a presumption in favour of actions whose means harmonize with their ends, both as something inherently preferable morally, and because this is likely to represent a far better investment of such time, resources and expertise as we are willing to give for policies directed to the improvement of human well-being. It may be thought that I remain undecided as to whether at bottom the best line is a 'contingency' argument or one that appeals to some deeper principle of morality or a feature of moral logic. Perhaps it is a mistake to think one has to choose between them.

My overall conclusion then is that humanitarian violence is not formally an oxymoron. This is partly because in the thinking of other thinkers, they could justify violence in terms of human objectives; and partly because I could not rule it out altogether. But, in the modern world, and given the rest of my way of understanding matters, the conception of humanitarian violence largely lacks application. A commitment to 'humanity' might after all induce us more to consider other forms of humanitarian intervention more consistent with the idea that 'the means are the ends in the making'.

Notes

1   Slim, H., 'An almost Intolerable Idea: paradox and ambiguity in humanitarianism's relation to violence', DSA Conference paper, November 2000; and Roberts, A., 'Humanitarian War: military intervention and human rights', *International Affairs*, no. 69, 1993.

2   Brown, C., 'A Qualified Defence of the Use of Force for Humanitarian Reasons', in Booth, K. (ed.), *The Kosovo Tragedy*, Frank Cass, 2001.

3   See Slim, H., 'Sharing a Universal Ethic: the Principle of Humanity in War', *The International Journal of Human Rights*, Vol.2, 1988.

4   Quoted in Quaker poster. The ideas are expressed in Gandhi, M. *Collected Works*, vol. 24, p.396 (reference made by Gruzalski, B., *Gandhi*, Belmont CA: Wadsworth, 2001).

5   Such a person would be rather like the contingent pacifist who thought violence might be justified in certain circumstances (even when the long-term effects of violence are factored in) but those circumstances never arise; or, to take another sub-class of violent actions involving nuclear weapons, like the 'nuclear pacifist' who thinks that whilst war with most weapons is generally justifiable, nuclear weapons are not because of their peculiar properties.

6   See e.g. Beitz, C. *Political Theory and International Relations*, 1977, and Dower, N. *World Ethics - the New Agenda*, 1998.

7   Bull, H., *The Anarchical Society*, Basingstoke, Macmillan, 1977.

8   Quoted by Tharoor, Sh., 'Humanitarian Intervention: Principles, Problems and Prospects', 5th Sydney Bailey Memorial Lecture, February 2001.

9   Wheeler, N., 'Reflections on Legality and Legitimacy of NATO's Intervention in Kosovo', in Booth, K. (ed.), *The Kosovo Tragedy*, 2001.

10   Bull, H., 'The Grotian conception of international society', in Butterfield, H. and Wight, M. (eds), *Diplomatic Investigations*, Allen and Unwin, 1966.

11   Luban, D., 'Just war and human rights', in Beitz, C. (ed.) *International Ethics*, Princeton University Press, 1985, and Walzer, M., *Just and Unjust Wars*, Penguin, 1977.

12   Dower, N., *World Ethics - the New Agenda*, Edinburgh: Edinburgh University Press, 1998.

13 If one thinks that the morality of states is grounded in conventions of states in the absence of an agreed deeper moral theory, then both the principles of respect for sovereignty (implied by legitimate authority and by the restriction of just cause to warding off aggression) and the principles for limiting warfare are seen as primarily based on what is in the interests of the state. (This is a bit like Rawls' conception of political justice as an area of overlapping consensus amongst those with different comprehensive views - only this time the bearers of different comprehensive worldviews are states or societies within states.) The advantage of this is that it provides in theory at least a strict limitation on the occasions of war and a set of rules which it must conform to. But the disadvantages are that it provides no solid basis for moral concern for the rest of the world. Even the basis for respect for individual human beings involved in conflict is somewhat contingent. This is illustrated by Mavrodes' defence of the rules of war as based on convention, which has the implication that if the other side breaks the convention, one is no longer held to it either. (Mavrodes, G.I., 'Conventions and the Morality of War', in Beitz, C.R. et al., *International Ethics*, 1985. On the other hand a morality of states grounded in a universal moral theory provides a solid basis for both concern for what happens elsewhere in the world (such as the violation of human rights and endemic poverty) and for why one should care about what is happening to the enemy soldier or civilian. It makes better sense of why all along there has been an emphasis upon the 'humanitarian' limitations on warfare (whether seen as a consequentialist concern for damage limitation or an appeal to an absolute ban on not attacking the 'innocent'). That said, precisely because the approach is grounded in a moral theory, the automatic acceptance of sovereignty or of standard established rules is questioned, and the possibility of tensions to which Bull adverts over ends and means is opened up.

14 Bentham, as quoted by J.S. Mill in *Utilitarianism* (1861), see Warnock, M. (ed.), London: Fontana, p.319, 1962.

15 Singer, P., 'Famine, Affluence and Morality', *Philosophy & Public Affairs*, Vol.1, 1972.

16 Kant, I. (1795), 'Perpetual Peace', in e.g. Reiss, H. (tr.), *Kant's Political Writings*, Cambridge University Press, 1970.

17 Shue, H., *Basic Rights: Subsistence, Affluence and US Foreign Policy*, Princeton University Press, 1996.

18 Mill, J.S. (1861), *Utilitarianism*, see Warnock, M. (ed.), London: Fontana, 1962, pp. 304-306.

19 It may be though that the following contrast is relevant: human rights violations are sometimes carried out by governments themselves; but generally poverty is either caused by natural causes or caused by individuals or groups (including economic actors) within countries - either despite or with the connivance of governments, but where governments do not actually carry out the deprivation of such subsistence or socio-economic rights. Furthermore if they did actually cause deprivation, we would be equally justified in engaging in military intervention for the sake of these subsistence rights. But if my argument is right, the contrast is irrelevant.

20 One way into understanding what I see as the impact of a fully thought out cosmopolitanism which is humanitarian in the broadest sense of taking the interests of all humans into account and not merely focusing on those of a few who suffer, is to consider what R.M. Hare said in a short not very well known essay he wrote on 'peace'

('Peace', *Applications of Moral Philosophy*, Basingstoke: Macmillan, 1972). His main theme was that if we based morality on the consideration of the equal interests of all human beings (a version of utilitarianism which he saw following from his theory of universal prescriptivity), then we would have a very strong presumption in favour of peace, and to the extent that people actually adopted such an ethic, there would be no reason to go to war. In his view the two chief sources of the breach of peace are nationalism and fanaticism - nationalism as the counting of the interests of one's own nationals as more important than those of others, fanaticism as the counting of an ideal as more important than the interests of people as such. We need not (I hope) go down the road of utilitarianism in order to gain the real insight from this analysis; that is, that if all human beings count equally, then whatever moral fabric we accept - rights, duties, virtues - it is oriented towards this fundamental consideration; and if the well being of all human beings counts and counts equally in whatever society they live, then what we do will be shaped by considerations which show, or are likely to show, that war on balance does not further such interests in general, even though it may have the interests of some as its direct object of attention.

Chapter 5

Humanitarian Intervention and the Logic of War

Paul Robinson

When questions of force are involved, moral problems become decidedly more tricky. Mark Evans and Stephen Clark suggest elsewhere in this book that some degree of inconsistency is inevitable when states opt to intervene in the affairs of other states. This is probably true, but at an intuitive level we know that there is surely a difference between inconsistently selecting to aid one group of people and not another, and inconsistently selecting to bomb one group and not another (or even choosing to aid one and bomb the other). One may argue, as some authors in this book do, that human rights transcend cultures and are so fundamental as to justify intervention to defend them. That does not necessarily, however, justify the use of *force*, rather than intervention of a more peaceful sort. There are aspects of military action which make it qualitatively different from other forms of action. Any discussion of the pros and cons of intervention must, therefore, include an analysis of the nature of military force.

An examination of the ethics of armed humanitarian intervention from the perspective of military theory casts doubt on the legitimacy of this use of force. The hurdle which democracies in pursuit of humanitarian goals must clear in order to justify force has probably been set too low. Analysts of the ethics of intervention all too often assume that the results of war are measurable and likely to be favourable. Judging military action solely in terms of the consequences, they believe that the harm it does will be less than the harm done by inaction. Yet a study of the nature of war shows that force is a chaotic phenomenon, and that its results are almost always uncontrollable and worse than expected.

This is in effect what Michael Walzer calls the 'logic of war' argument against humanitarian intervention.[1] The argument suggests that war, once started, follows a logical, almost inevitable, progression which renders it unsuitable as a tool for achieving humanitarian ends. The logic may be briefly stated as follows.

Humanitarian intervention, if opposed, is a form of war. Wars are easier to start than stop, and they tend to last longer than expected. Furthermore, the nature of war is to escalate, and interventions will therefore probably be more destructive than those starting them had originally estimated. Making matters worse, in wartime, the political or humanitarian aim tends to be supplanted by military imperatives, meaning that the actual objective is often forgotten in the pursuit of victory. Thus, instead of carrying out the short, precise humanitarian war that he or she planned, the intervenor finds himself or herself in a prolonged conflict in which the humanitarian goals are not of prime importance. One of the reasons why this happens is that the initiation of war normally provokes a violent response in the other side, the degree of which cannot be accurately assessed beforehand, and this changes the conditions which were used to calculate the intervention.

Some commentators suggest that because the nature of war has changed in the modern era this logic no longer applies, and war can now be controlled and limited. These claims are misguided. Although the above phenomena are not inevitable, they are the rule rather than the exception, and are actually more likely to occur in supposedly 'just' wars, fought by democracies for ostensibly moral purposes, than in other types of wars. In fact, democracies pursuing 'humanitarian' war are particularly likely to escalate, lose track of their aims, and find it hard to bring the war to a close.

The current trend in favour of intervention legitimizes war, and so unleashes its elemental nature and ensures an increase in suffering. In consequence, the assertion of a 'right' to humanitarian intervention should be resisted. This does not mean that force can never be used, but that there is no 'right' to intervene - rather, there must be a 'presumption against war'.

Those who assert a right to intervene in the internal affairs of other states in the name of human rights frequently refer to the death of the old international order based on the 1648 Treaty of Westphalia. This agreement supposedly made the principle of state sovereignty a fundamental basis of international relations. NATO's 1999 attack on Yugoslavia then showed that the international system had changed, and that human rights had taken precedence over sovereignty, thus making humanitarian intervention legitimate. In reality, as Chris Brown points out elsewhere in this book, the primacy attached to state sovereignty in the Westphalian system was never as rigid as is often believed, and Western states carried out numerous interventions before the twentieth century. What we are seeing today is not so much a breach of the Westphalian order as a challenge to a much more recent consensus reached after the two world wars.

Until the twentieth century, although conflict in the Western Christian world was in theory restrained by the tenets of *jus ad bellum*, in practice these did nothing to limit mankind's appetite for fighting, which was accepted as a normal part of the international order. The rules of war focused not on outlawing war, but on constraining its excesses. The emphasis was thus on *jus in bello*, rather than *jus ad bellum*. By 1945 this had changed. Two world wars taught the Western world that once war started, previously unthinkable destruction and atrocities could occur. *Jus in bello* was incapable of preventing this. Western nations came to believe that the only way to prevent the excesses of war was to outlaw the initiation of war altogether. The experience of the First World War led to various treaties and conventions which moved international law in this direction. These included the Covenant of the League of Nations, the 1924 Geneva Protocol, which defined aggression as an 'international crime', and the 1928 Kellogg-Briand Pact, whose signatories renounced war as an instrument of national policy.

This major shift in international thinking was confirmed at the Nuremburg Tribunal after the Second World War, at which German leaders were put on trial for the crime of 'planning, preparation, initiation and waging of war of aggression'. Further confirmation came in the Charter of the United Nations, and in subsequent declarations of the General Assembly of the United Nations, which defined 'aggressive war' as the use of force by one state against another for any reason other than self-defence, and stated that no political or other reasons could excuse such an act.[2] These declarations were supported by the International Court of Justice, which twice ruled that the right of intervention was a 'manifestation of a policy of force, such as has, in the past, given rise to the most serious abuses'.[3] These judgments reflected a new understanding that those who started a war were ultimately responsible for all the destruction which happened during it, even if they themselves did not carry out that destruction. Whereas previously just war theory had focused on 'opposition to injustice', now it rested on the concept of a 'presumption against war'.[4] By the late 1980s, many commentators were calling just war theory 'obsolete'.[5]

Anthony Clark Arend and Robert J. Black identify three periods in the development of the laws of war: a 'just war period' from about 300 to 1700 AD, in which people felt that recourse to war was permissible if there was a just cause; a 'positivist' period from about 1700 to 1914, in which just war theory lost support; and finally a period after 1914, in which war was outlawed except in cases of self-defence or when authorized by the League of Nations or United Nations.[6] To this we may have to add a fourth 'interventionist' period following the end of the Cold War. In this period, Western states are once again reviving just war theory and attempting to legitimize war. It is this, rather than any supposed breach of the Westphalian order, which represents the real significance of recent developments.

The assertion that states have a right to take military action to enforce Western codes of human rights on other countries has been made possible by the absence of serious military threats to the West. During the Cold War, the initiation of war was best left outlawed due to the risk of escalation into nuclear holocaust. Now, however, the balance of power so overwhelmingly favours Western states that they can safely claim a right of intervention in the full knowledge that this right will not be used against them. The incentive to keep war outlawed has diminished, while the incentive to legitimize war has increased.

In addition, the advent of 'smart' weapons has convinced Western leaders that they have found a way to control and limit the practice of war, keeping its destructive effects to a minimum and reducing 'collateral damage'. The dangerous idea that war can be fought with relatively few harmful effects has served to render it an attractive option for policy makers.

There is other evidence of a conscious or unconscious trend by the Western world to re-legitimize war. Officially, Western states no longer wage war. They do not, for instance, actually declare war on their opponents. Instead, a multitude of new types of military campaign are appearing in doctrine: humanitarian interventions, peace enforcement, and other actions defined as 'operations other than war'.[7] These operations other than war are often nothing of the sort. Some supporters of intervention maintain that there is a difference between intervention and war, because interventions are 'police actions'. Stanley Hauerwas remarks that 'it is essential to distinguish between a war and a police action. A police action means that there is a specified crime, the police go in to stop it using no more force than needed, and they do not serve as the judge and jury.'[8] In theory, Richard Miller claims, even pacifists can support wars which present themselves as 'police actions'.[9] This concept falls down, however, when the second party resists 'arrest' and fires back at the intervenor, as it is likely to do, because it will almost certainly feel that the 'police' have no jurisdiction over it. At this point any 'police action' becomes war. It is also worth noting that, contrary to Hauerwas's claim, military intervention forces act not only as the police, but increasingly also as judge, jury, and jailer. In addition, the police are not allowed to kill the neighbours of the person they are trying to arrest, and shrug off the killing as 'collateral damage'.

The distinction between 'police actions' and 'wars' seems to be one of terminology rather than of reality, an attempt to legitimize war by changing the language surrounding it. Thus, David Rieff comments that 'Humanitarian intervention is not, cannot and should not be presented as a species of crime stopping. It is warmaking ... The confusion between war and police work is morally as well as intellectually noxious.'[10] In any case, if one follows the definition by the great military theorist Karl von Clausewitz of war as 'an act of violence intended to compel our opponent to fulfil our will', all military interventions can be considered wars. Operations other than war are not something 'other than war'. They are operations of war, and as such are subject to the logic of war. It serves Western leaders to pretend otherwise. By maintaining that their wars are not wars, political and military leaders hope to control the pattern of discourse relating to military action, and so legitimize warlike conduct.

If legitimizing war served humanitarian purposes, then perhaps this would not matter, and might even be a good thing. The problem, however, is that it is extremely hard to keep war within the intended limits. The first reason for this is that wars tend to escalate. That is to say that the longer they continue, the more the level, type, geographic extent, or anticipated duration of violence increases. The list of legitimate targets grows larger; weapons and tactics previously considered illegal become commonplace; the aims of the war become more absolute. Clausewitz, who commented that war tended to totality, noted this. He wrote, 'War is an act of violence pushed to its utmost bounds; as one side dictates the law to the other, there arises a sort of reciprocal action, which logically must lead to an extreme.'[11] Richard Smoke identifies a number of reasons why warring parties may choose to escalate, the most important of which are to gain an advantage over their opponents, to avoid defeat, and to justify past losses. As wars continue, losses and costs mount, and so the stakes increase. Demands harden, and those involved become more inclined to risk.[12]

This tendency means that wars are rarely contained within the confines intended by those who started them. Political leaders do not usually launch wars in the expectation that they will be long and bloody. As a general rule, they start them in the belief that they will be short and relatively painless. They are more often wrong than right.

This does not mean that escalation is inevitable and can never be controlled. As Clausewitz noted, although in theory war tends to the extreme, in reality the absolute form of war is never reached.[13] This would appear to offer hope to those who support humanitarian intervention. If escalation can be controlled, then the violence that they have launched can be kept within reasonable boundaries. The problem is that of all types of war, those fought by democracies for altruistic reasons are precisely those which are hardest to control and most likely to escalate.

In the first place, a party intervening in a third-party conflict and using force in the process, is by that very act escalating the conflict, if only because the addition of one more combatant is a type of escalation.[14] Second, as Ken Booth says, 'Just wars justify escalation ... Because a just war demands unconditional commitment, the desire for justice and the injunction to respect proportionality are necessarily in tension ... If one's cause is "just" it seems any level of escalation can be justified.'[15] The problem with fighting wars for moral reasons is that accepting anything other than total victory means accepting an immoral result. Colin Gray notes, 'A pragmatic problem with *Moralpolitik* is that it is characteristically unyielding to suggestions for compromise. When policy success is morally defined, the stakes in the conflict become absolute. If we permit, let alone dignify by treaty, even some fraction of behaviour we have proclaimed morally intolerable, our entire policy is compromised.'[16] A.J. Coates similarly comments that, 'It is precisely the "altruistic" pursuit of warfare that generates militarism and that leads to the systematic underpinning of every limit placed upon war.'[17]

This phenomenon can be observed in NATO's 1999 intervention against Yugoslavia. NATO leaders started the war under the assumption that it would be short and that only minimal force would be required. NATO's campaign was designed in three phases: the first was to be an attack on Yugoslavia's air defence systems to clear the way for further NATO activity; the second to consist of the actual attacks on military forces in Kosovo; and the third, if it was required, was to be a more generalized attack on 'strategic' targets in the rest of Yugoslavia. But because the Yugoslavs refused to turn on their air defence radars, NATO's anti-radiation missiles could not hit them. In addition, Yugoslav forces in Kosovo proved to be very adept at camouflage and concealment. This meant that phases one and two of the campaign proved ineffective, and NATO had to escalate very rapidly to phase three. Then within phase three, the list of legitimate targets was gradually expanded. As the respected military analyst Jonathan Eyal noted, 'A strategy which was meant to allow for a careful escalation of pressure on Yugoslavia in order to produce a peace settlement became an end in itself. In the process, the list of targets was progressively enlarged and the distinction between civilian and military objectives increasingly blurred.'[18] Had the war continued any longer, it is likely that the escalation would have continued. British Prime Minister Tony Blair was pressing NATO to launch a ground invasion of Kosovo, and the international press was reporting that NATO leaders had finally accepted that this might be necessary. A ground invasion would have been immensely costly in terms of life and property, and grossly disproportionate to the original crisis in Kosovo, which had resulted in perhaps 2,000 deaths (Serbs as well as Albanians) over a period of several years. Had NATO leaders been told at the start of their operation that the only way of achieving their objectives was such an invasion, they almost certainly would have rejected it and avoided the use of force entirely. But after three months of war, an invasion was no longer unacceptable.

This example shows how, as humanitarian wars go on, the stakes increase, and the willingness of participants to make sacrifices and inflict violence on others also increases. War dehumanizes those who take part in it, densensitizes them to violence, and undermines their moral balance, so that they find acceptable what previously they would have considered unacceptable. Eventually a point is reached where the violence which intervenors are willing to use is out of all proportion to the evil which they originally intervened to stop.[19]

Not only does war tend to escalate, but as Fred Iklé has pointed out, 'Wars are easier to start than stop.'[20] Unfortunately, those who start wars rarely pay any attention to how they are going to end them. As Bruce Bade notes, people 'like to think that war termination takes care of itself. One side - ours - prevails on the battlefield and it's over.'[21] This is another reason why the legitimization of war is unwise. To use the Kosovo example again, NATO leaders clearly had no idea how their intervention was going to be terminated, beyond a vague expectation that Yugoslavia would cave in quickly.

Because wars are so difficult to stop, they tend to continue long beyond the point at which they should have been ended according to any rational criteria.[22] There are two main reasons why this is the case. One is that the losing party may find the prospect of its own surrender too painful to contemplate, and buries its head in the sand. The other is that political and military advisers are often reluctant to tell a national leader that the war is lost.[23] Whether for these reasons or any others, wars generally last longer and cause more damage than expected. They are also less effective in coercing other people than expected, because coercion only works if and when the coerced party expects to lose, and coerced parties are normally unwilling to concede this until long after they logically should have done.

There are, furthermore, good reasons to believe that 'just' wars, fought by democratic governments for supposedly altruistic reasons, are especially difficult to end. People in the Western world often believe that democracies are more peaceloving than non-democracies, and are less likely to start wars. This may be true (not all commentators agree), but one also needs to recognize that democracies are particularly bad at ending wars. As the eminent military historian Michael Howard has written, 'What is beyond contradiction is that in the era of democracy, wars may have been harder to begin but have also been very much harder to bring to an end.'[24] The same rule may be applied to 'just wars', or those fought for 'altruistic' purposes.

Theorists of war termination state that wars are ended not by the winners, but by the losers. Assuming that the loser has not actually been exterminated, a war ends when one side loses the will to fight and lays down its arms. As one analyst writes, 'War is pressed by the victor, but peace is made by the vanquished.'[25] From the point of view of humanitarian interventions, this is an important point. Those carrying out the intervention are not actually in a position to end the war that they have started, and thereby secure their humanitarian goals. Indeed, the achievement of these goals is entirely dependent on their enemy.

This is not to say that the intervening party cannot help its opponent reach the point at which he decides to stop resisting and make peace. The problem is that those fighting for moral purposes are very bad at this. As Michael Howard notes, if a peace is to be decisive, and to produce a long-lasting settlement, the defeated 'must become reconciled to their defeat by being treated, sooner or later, as partners in operating the new international order. Honour must be satisfied, unless the defeated peoples are to be massacred or reduced to perpetual slavery.'[26] But humanitarian wars specifically preclude peace settlements which permit the defeated party to exit with honour. Such wars are justified as often as not by demonizing the person against whom the intervention is targeted. Saddam Hussein is compared to Hitler, Slobodan Milosević is indicted as a war criminal, and so on. This creates severe difficulties for war termination, for one cannot allow a Hitler to retain honour. Not merely must the humanitarian win, because he cannot say that he has permitted evil to continue existing, but he must also achieve the complete political destruction of the enemy leader who was trying to stop him from achieving his goals. Indeed, with the indictment of Milosević by the International Court, and the repeated demands by the government of the United States that Saddam Hussein be removed from power, Western leaders are sending a message that those whom they defeat *must* lose their office. Thus humanitarian wars create very strong incentives for those abusing human rights to continue to resist, since further conflict is a preferable outcome, despite almost any hardships, to surrender. Looking at Milosević imprisoned in the Hague, what target of any future intervention is likely to contemplate making peace?

Another problem with humanitarian interventions is that those intervening all too often forget the humanitarian part of the operation. Clausewitz described war as a continuation of politics by other means. From this one can draw the conclusion that good military strategy is directed towards achieving the political purpose for which the war was started. The means used are those appropriate to the ends sought. In practice, this is often not the case. Wars may be started for one purpose, such as preventing a humanitarian disaster, but once started, they acquire entirely different purposes.

Fred Iklé notes that this process reflects the true nature of state policy-making. Policy is rarely made in a completely rational fashion, with action directly following coherent aims. Instead, if one refers to what political scientists call the 'bureaucratic process model', policy emerges from a complicated competition between bureaucratic organizations, each of which pursues its own, often contradictory, goals. Ensuring that the methods used to pursue humanitarian wars follow the humanitarian objectives of those who initiated it is in these circumstances extremely difficult. Iklé also states that 'When a nation becomes engaged in a major war, a new set of men and new government agencies often move into the centre of power ... the influence that comes with day-to-day decisions is transferred to the military staffs ... This shift in political influence means that the governments on both sides will be concerned primarily with their current military effort.'[27] Other commentators have made the same point. Richard Smoke states that:

> it is normal for decision-makers to set aside other policy goals ... and concentrate upon winning. Achieving victory becomes the perceived prerequisite for nearly all other policy objectives ... The conscious and unconscious identification with victory creates a psychological and political climate at the upper levels of government that is receptive to escalation options that seem to promise a quicker and more certain victory ... Organizational and bureaucratic incentives reinforce this, for in wartime it tends to be the military services (and other agencies whose mission is victory) that move to the center of the policy-making process.[28]

In short, war may be started for a clear objective, such as preventing a humanitarian catastrophe, but once it has started, that objective takes second place to achieving something called 'victory'. 'Winning' becomes more important than achieving the aims for which the war was begun. In effect, this means that humanitarian wars are impossible, because they are humanitarian only until they begin. The moment they start they become simply wars, and the objective becomes winning the war, not fulfilling the humanitarian aims. If the war is easily and quickly won, the divergence between military and other objectives will not be too great; if it is difficult, the loss of interest in the original goal will be more pronounced.

In fact, the process by which war aims are taken over by military objectives is one to which humanitarian wars are even more prone than other ones. This makes humanitarian objectives particularly ill-suited to military action. The reason for this is that such objectives are, at least in theory, altruistic. But precisely because they are not based on self-interest, the leaders pursuing these aims care less about them than they do about other aims, which do reflect genuine interests. Clausewitz was aware of the problem of matching military means to political ends, and of ensuring that the means used suited the ends sought. He concluded that, 'The more violent the excitement which precedes the War, by so much the more will it be directed to the destruction of the enemy, so much the nearer will the military and political ends coincide ... but the weaker the motives and tensions, so much the less will the natural direction of the military element - that is, force - be coincident with the direction which the political element indicates.'[29] What this means is that where the motivation is strong, it will be easier to follow a strategy which is in line with the political objectives, whereas weak motivations create poor strategy, in which the means used bear no relation to the ends sought. Since the motivation in humanitarian interventions is weak (as shown by the unwillingness of Western governments to suffer heavy casualties), Ken Booth rightly concludes that 'Just wars encourage bad strategy.'[30] This matters, because poor strategy prolongs war and makes it difficult to fulfil one's aim. Where the aim is to prevent human suffering, this means that force is being used in a way which contradicts its purpose of preventing or alleviating that suffering.[31]

Another point which needs making is that Western democracies are particularly inclined to view wars in terms of victory rather than in terms of achieving set aims. In his book, *Decisive Force: The New American Way of War*, F.G. Hoffman argues that Americans have a decidedly un-Clausewitzian view of war, in that once it starts they are not interested in the aims for which the war was started, only in 'winning'. More than that, they are only interested in winning 'big', in completely and totally crushing their opponents.[32] In a humanitarian intervention, states which view war in this way will focus on achieving 'victory' even if this jeopardizes their humanitarian objectives.

Again, NATO's intervention in Kosovo provides a clear example of this process in action. NATO's stated aim was to 'prevent a humanitarian catastrophe' in Kosovo, but its strategy - high altitude bombing of strategic targets in Yugoslavia - could never have achieved this mission. Ends and means were mismatched. Mary Kaldor has written, 'NATO's airstrikes against Serbia were much more in the tradition of warfighting. Although the goal was humanitarian intervention, the practice was conventional war ... This approach actually had counterproductive consequences ... As Gen. Wesley Clark put it "You cannot stop paramilitary murder on the ground with airstrikes".'[33] Supporters of humanitarian intervention who believe that humanitarian aims will take priority once a war has started are being naive in the extreme. Humanitarian war is not so much a theoretical 'oxymoron' (to use Nigel Dower's phrase), as a practical impossibility.

The final problem with the concept of humanitarian intervention is that it ignores the fact that war is a two-sided process. The intervenors seem to assume that those intervened against will accede passively to their demands. This rarely happens. Clausewitz points out, 'War is no activity of the will which exerts itself upon inanimate matter ... but against a living and reactive force.'[34] Those attacked are likely to resist, and once they resist the situation is changed entirely, and the fulfilment of humanitarian objectives becomes much more difficult.

Particular problems emerge when the two sides are dramatically unevenly matched. This will almost certainly be the case in any humanitarian intervention undertaken by Western powers, who have shown that in general they have no stomach for heavy casualties and will fight only those adversaries who can be overwhelmed by their massively superior force. The assumption of Western leaders in these circumstances often seems to be that their opponents will recognize their weakness and give in. Instead, their opponents may resort to what is known as 'asymmetrical warfare', which means meeting Western conventional armed forces with entirely different kinds of force. As Noam Chomsky says, 'People "react when shot at" - not by garlanding the attackers with flowers, and not where the attacker is strong, but where they are strong.'[35] Asymmetrical warfare may not ensure victory, but it does pose a very serious threat to the human values that the West proclaims that its interventions are designed to protect. For instance, Yugoslavia, when attacked by NATO, responded by expelling hundreds of thousands of Albanians from their homes. This was an asymmetric response, and it was the very thing that NATO's intervention had been designed to prevent. Had NATO leaders remembered that war is a two-way process, this tragedy might have been avoided.

The logic of war can be seen, therefore, to almost always preclude successful intervention. Some critics argue, however, that the nature of war has changed and that the logic outlined in this chapter no longer applies. James Turner Johnson claims that,

> The wars that have occurred since the end of the Cold War do not exemplify a destructiveness inexorably beyond human control, or aims that far outrun the ends of politics ... These conflicts have been limited in significant ways; none has ushered in a global holocaust or escalated to all-out use of conventional military might. In truth, the face of armed conflict since the end of the Second World War suggests that modern war is characterized by localized and limited, though sharp, conflicts ... rather than totalistic clashes.[36]

The development of smart weapons which allow accurate targeting and which minimize casualties, allied with the restraints imposed on governments during war by a free press, help to limit modern war. One commentator, Phillip Meilinger, goes so far as to say that 'in comparison with the devastating impact on civilians of coercive mechanisms such as sanctions, modern air warfare stands out as an increasingly efficient, effective, and humane tool of foreign policy.'[37]

Such views are mistaken. It is not true that the nature of war has changed, that we have finally learnt how to keep it within acceptable limits, and that we can now safely legitimize it. Underlying Johnson's statement is an assumption that war can be controlled. But recent experience suggests that this is not the case. When the Yugoslav army responded to NATO's bombing of its territory by murdering and expelling Kosovar Albanians, could NATO leaders honestly have claimed that they were controlling the process of war? The Russian Army may like to pretend that it is in control of Chechnya, but the reality is entirely different. The idea that modern conflicts are exempt from the 'logic of war' is false.

In addition, the opinions of Johnson and Meilinger are based on an exaggerated belief in the effectiveness of precision aerial bombing. Recent practice has shown that such bombing is not nearly as precise as its practitioners claim. Many bombs miss the targets, and others hit the wrong targets because the targeting information provided by Western intelligence services is far from perfect. Furthermore, air forces have only limited numbers of precision-guided missiles, and the majority of bombs that they drop continue to be so-called 'dumb' bombs. To believe in the ability of modern air forces to limit and control war is to place too much faith in the propaganda of airpower theorists.

Indeed, there are some aspects of modern war which make it particularly disturbing. Michael Walzer has said that the main thrust of the rules of war has always been to ensure that war, as much as possible, consists of 'combat between combatants'.[38] This idea was enshrined in the Saint Petersburg Declaration of 1868, which stated that 'the only legitimate object which states should endeavour to accomplish during war is to weaken the military forces of society.'[39] But much of modern strategy, especially airpower strategy, is based on what is called the 'indirect approach', which deliberately avoids 'combat between combatants'. Instead it seeks victory by striking not at any enemy's army but at his government, communications, industry, civilian morale, and so on.[40] Civilians, not the enemy military, are the main victims of this sort of strategy, since as much as possible attacks on the enemy military are avoided (they are considered too dangerous and attacks on them do not achieve a decisive effect with sufficient speed). This means that when pursuing 'humanitarian war', Western states do not attack those involved in human rights abuses, such as soldiers and policemen carrying out ethnic cleansing, but instead attack civilians who may not be responsible in any way for those abuses. Modern strategists like to say that they are not targeting civilians and are doing all they can to avoid them, but they readily admit that they are targeting civilian morale, in an effort to persuade the civil population of the enemy to pressure its government to abandon the struggle. Yet, as John Terraine notes, 'Morale is a cosmetic word. Attacking morale, whatever phrases it may be dressed up in, really means only one thing: putting the fear of death into individuals.'[41] Modern war, it appears, is no more ethical than war of any other era.

Finally, however much one may wish to believe that the Western world has mastered the art of limiting wars, one must bear in mind the words of Carl Abt: 'To the victims, the scale of warfare is always total for their own lives.'[42]

As humans, we have obligations to uphold the rights of others, and to provide aid to those in need. But this does not translate into an automatic right to use force. Those who claim such a right legitimize the waging of war. Humanitarian intervention is not a form of 'police action'. It is a form of war, and as such it is subject to the logic of war. This logic dictates that even modern limited war, once started, will escalate, and that it will tend to last longer, involve more violence, and be harder to end than those who began it expected. The aims for which the war was started will be supplanted by military objectives and the desire for 'victory'. The intrinsic nature of humanitarian wars, which includes moral certainty combined with a tendency to poor strategy, means that such wars are particularly subject to these processes. Efforts to restrain these characteristics of war by *jus in bello* have proved insufficient throughout history, and therefore, the only way to prevent the logic of war from asserting itself is to outlaw war in general. After the Second World War it appeared as if the international community had finally realized this, and had de-legitimized war. Now, however, the assertion of a right to humanitarian intervention is threatening once again to legitimize war, at least when conducted by the powerful states of the West. Their wars are meant to be tidy, limited actions, fought only for good causes. But, as Clausewitz pointed out, war inevitably has unforeseen consequences, once 'the destructive force of the element [is] set free'.[43]

Of course, the person who starts a war is not directly responsible for all the unforeseen consequences of his action, such as atrocities committed by his enemy. But indirectly, he is responsible. We now know enough about the nature of war to know in advance that such atrocities are likely to occur. It is not good enough to start a war, and then claim to be surprised by the horrors which result. Such horrors have happened often enough that there is no longer any excuse for being surprised by them. This is why the initiation of war should rightly be regarded as the most serious of all war crimes. To keep the elemental nature of war in its place, any theory which legitimizes war should be resisted. A thorough study of the nature of war indicates that the 'presumption against war' remains a sound philosophy. Because the assertion of a right to intervene undermines that presumption, it is an assertion that we should reject.

Notes

1   Michael Walzer, *Just and Unjust Wars* (London: Allen Lane, 1978), p.29.
2   Specifically, Resolution no.2131, passed in 1965, and Resolution no.2625, passed in 1970.
3   Details of these judgments and declarations can be found in Jarat Chopra, 'The Obsolescence of Intervention under International Law', in Marrianne Heiberg (ed), *Subduing Sovereignty: Sovereignty and the Right to Intervene* (London, 1994), pp.37-39.
4   The evolution of the concept of a 'presumption against war' is described in James Turner Johnson, 'The Broken Tradition', *National Interest*, vol.45, Fall 1996, pp.27-36.
5   For instance, Ingrid Detter de Lupis, *The Law of War* (Cambridge: CUP, 1987), p.127.
6   Anthony Clark Arend and Robert J. Beck, *International Law and the Use of Force: Beyond the UN Charter Paradigm* (London & New York: Routledge, 1993), p.24.
7   Peace enforcement may be defined as: 'Military operations to restore peace or establish specified conditions in an area of conflict or tension, where the parties may not consent to intervention, and may be involved in combat activities.'
8   Cited in Richard B. Miller, 'Humanitarian Intervention, Altruism, and the Limits of Casuistry', *Journal of Religious Ethics*, vol.28, no.1, Spring 2000, p.4.
9   Ibid.
10   David Rieff in 'Humanitarian Intervention: A Forum', *Nation*, vol.270, no.18, 8 May 2000, pp.21-25.

11   Karl von Clausewitz, *On War*, ed. Anatol Rapaport (London: Penguin, 1982), p.103.
12   Richard Smoke, *Controlling Escalation* (Cambridge, Mass.: Harvard University Press, 1977), pp.23-24.
13   Clausewitz, *On War*, p.118.
14   Chione Robinson, 'A Theory of War Termination for Peacekeepers', *CFC Review 2000* (Toronto: Canadian Forces College, 2000), p.88.
15   Ken Booth, 'Ten Flaws of Just Wars', in Ken Booth (ed), *The Kosovo Tragedy: The Human Rights Dimensions* (London: Frank Cass, 2001), pp.314-315.
16   Colin Gray, 'No Good Deed Shall Go Unpunished', in Ken Booth (ed), *The Kosovo Tragedy*, p.306.
17   A.J. Coates, *The Ethics of War* (Manchester: Manchester University Press, 1997), p. 42.
18   Jonathan Eyal,'Is NATO Winning?', taken from the BBC website during the Kosovo conflict, 1999.
19   In this case it is necessary to emphasize the word 'originally', that is to say the human rights violations as they existed *before* the intervention. The escalation may have been justified by the human rights violations subsequent to the intervention, but it was disproportionate to those prior to it.
20   Fred Charles Iklé, *Every War Must End* (New York and London: Columbia University Press, 1971), p.8.
21   Bruce Bade, cited in Robinson, *A Theory of War Termination*, p.82.
22   Iklé, *Every War*, p.16.
23   *Ibid*, p.98.
24   Michael Howard, 'When are Wars Decisive?', *Survival*, vol.41, no.1, Spring 1999, p. 130.
25   H.A. Calahan, *What Makes a War End?* (New York, 1944), p.18. Cited in Robinson, *A Theory of War Termination*, p.84.
26   Howard, 'When are Wars Decisive?', p.132.
27   Iklé, *Every War*, p.13.
28   Smoke, *War*, p.25.
29   Clausewitz, *On War*, pp.119-120.
30   Booth, 'Ten Flaws of Just Wars', p. 317.
31   This line of argument is supported by Charles Krauthammer, 'The Short, Unhappy Life of Humanitarian Intervention', *National Interest*, no.57, Fall 1999, pp.6-8. Opposing arguments are put forward by Elliott Abrams, 'To Fight the Good Fight', *National Interest*, no.59, Spring 2000, pp.70-77.
32   F.G. Hoffman, *Decisive Force: The New American Way of War* (Westport: Praeger, 1996).
33   Mary Kaldor in 'Humanitarian Intervention: A Forum', *Nation*, vol.270, no.18, 8 May 2000, pp.21-25.
34   Clausewitz, *On War*, p.203.
35   Noam Chomsky, *The New Military Humanism: Lessons from Kosovo* (London: Pluto, 1999), p.21.
36   Johnson, 'The Broken Tradition', p.35.
37   Phillip S. Meilinger, 'A Matter of Precision: Why Air Power May Be More Humane Than Sanctions', *Foreign Policy*, March/April 2001, p.78.
38   Walzer, *Just and Unjust Wars*, p.xxi.

39 Cited in Michael Howard, 'Constraints on Warfare', in Michael Howard, George J. Andreopoulos, and Mark R. Shulman (eds), *The Laws of War: Constraints on Warfare in the Western World* (New Haven: Yale University Press, 1994), p.6.

40 See for instance, Howard D. Balote, 'Paralyze or Pulverize? Liddell Hart, Clausewitz, and Their Influence on Air Power Theory', *Strategic Review*, no.27, Winter 1999, pp. 40-46; and Colonel John A. Warden III, *The Air Campaign: Planning for Combat* (Washington: Pergamon-Brassey's, 1989).

41 John Terraine, *The Right of the Line: The Royal Air Force in the European War, 1939-1945* (London: Hodder & Stoughton, 1985), p.261.

42 C. Abt, cited in Robinson, *A Theory of War Termination*, p.81.

43 Clausewitz, *On War*, p.370.

PART III
PROBLEMS OF SELECTIVITY
AND CONSISTENCY

Chapter 6

Genocide, Consistency and War

Stephen R.L. Clark

The Serbian War

The initial occasion for this paper was provided by the NATO campaign against Serbia in 1999.[1] Its topic is a much larger one, and not exclusively to do with war, or the Serbian War, at all. But since that war *was* the occasion, I must make some general comments first. After all, if the war was only a familiar moral and political catastrophe, it is unlikely that we could learn very much from it or from the arguments about it.

On the one hand, it is clear that NATO committed many errors of judgement, and made many mistakes in carrying out its plans. The use of depleted uranium in its anti-tank missiles, and the deliberate destruction of oil-refineries, should be banned in any reasonable reworking of the Laws of War. The politically-motivated insistence that ground-troops would not be used unless and until Serbia had already surrendered was probably a factor in prolonging the conflict. NATO's intelligence network was sometimes either incompetent or misdirected: either the Chinese Embassy was bombed in an absurd error, or it was bombed in an unadmitted, and condemnable, attempt to target Serbian leaders who might have been given refuge there. It also seems clear that the Serbian army was able to save most of its equipment from NATO, whose generals had judged it too dangerous - to NATO's pilots - to fly low enough to be sure of their targets. There may be a similar explanation for bombing civilian trains and buses, or even refugee convoys, though these are the sort of mistakes that are, unfortunately, bound to occur in any war, however well justified or conducted. We may reasonably think that compensation is owed for these without utterly condemning those immediately responsible. In other cases, condemnation - up to and including an indictment for war-crimes - might be appropriate.

On the other hand, NATO's recourse to the threat and eventual use of military violence was understandable. The Serbian Government had been terrorizing the Albanian population for years, and had flatly refused to permit any independent and sufficiently powerful force to police its unconvincing claim that Kosovar Albanians would now be spared, let alone allowed the autonomy that they had actually possessed a few years earlier. That same government, acting through its agents, had already massacred *Bosnian* Muslims, despite the presence of UN 'peace-keeping forces': the history of that calamity was fresh in the minds of European diplomats and politicians. The catastrophe that the Serbian government created in Kosovo once the bombing began was clearly planned well in advance. It was not an abrupt response to NATO's bombs. Nor is there any serious evidence, as some Serb apologists proposed, that the refugees were simply fleeing from those bombs: the suggestion is indeed a ludicrous one. The Kosovar Albanians were systematically and deliberately raped, robbed and murdered by agents of the Serbian government. Whatever the rights and wrongs of *going* to war, it rapidly became impossible to suppose that the regime which had organized this act of genocide - planned and partly enacted long before, but speeded up as soon as the campaign began - could happily be left in control of *any* part of the former Yugoslavia.[2]

In speaking of 'genocide' I have already touched on one issue of the present paper, and already made a judgement. The Convention on the Prevention and Punishment of the Crime of Genocide[3] arose from the declaration made by the General Assembly of the United Nations[4] that 'genocide is a crime under international law, contrary to the spirit and aims of the United Nations and condemned by the civilized world'. The Contracting Parties - that is, the United Nations as they then were - confirmed that 'genocide, whether committed in time of peace or in time of war, is a crime under international law which they undertake to prevent and to punish'. Genocide was defined as follows:

> Genocide means any of the following acts committed with intent to destroy, in whole or in part, a national, ethnical, racial or religious group, as such:
>
> (a) Killing members of the group;
>
> (b) Causing serious bodily or mental harm to members of the group;
>
> (c) Deliberately inflicting on the group conditions of life calculated to bring about its physical destruction in whole or in part;
>
> (d) Imposing measures intended to prevent births within the group;
>
> (e) Forcibly transferring children of the group to another group.

Critics of NATO, during the conflict, occasionally claimed that it was wrong to identify the assault on Kosovar Albanians as 'genocide', or even suggested that this charge somehow 'demeaned' the most notorious twentieth-century case of attempted genocide, namely the Jewish Holocaust. A few of them suggested that the assault was only a forgivable response to the actions of the Kosovo Liberation Army, or that - at worst - it was a pragmatic solution to the difficulties experienced in a multi-ethnic state whose ethnic groups had been encouraged to hate or distrust each other. I find these claims impossible to accept. Even if the KLA were only a bunch of terrorists, no decent government responds to terrorism by organizing the rape, murder, robbery and mass eviction of an entire civilian population. Even if ethnic groups, or nations, sometimes find it difficult to live together, enforced migration (without consent or even consultation with the neighbouring territories likely to be destabilized by this) is itself an act of war. In the Serbian case it was genocidal in intent. The government's intention was to 'destroy, in whole or in part, a national, ethnical, racial or religious group, as such', and the chosen technique involved 'killing members of the group, causing serious bodily or mental harm to members of the group, and deliberately inflicting on the group conditions of life calculated to bring about its physical destruction in whole or in part'. If excuses are found for *that* behaviour it is difficult to see why *similar* (and much better) excuses cannot be found for NATO.

It was, at the least, entirely reasonable to suppose that the Serbian Government intended and initiated a genocidal war, which all member nations of the United Nations are committed to prevent and punish. That commitment requires no further endorsement from any international agency. It was also reasonable to doubt that there was any other power than NATO capable of carrying out the necessary military intervention. NATO's critics have referred to the United Nations or to the Organization for Security and Cooperation in Europe (see http://www.osce.org/) or even to the European Union as better agencies. It is not clear why any of these organizations should have any greater authority. All three had very much less power on the ground. The security and peace of Europe (and also of the wider world) was certainly at stake. The very fact that neighbouring territories (including Montenegro, Macedonia, Greece, Slovakia, Hungary, Bulgaria and Romania) all have similar ethnic minorities, and similarly extreme nationalist movements, identifies the perils faced in South-Eastern Europe. There is a serious question, whether by going, however belatedly and sluggishly, to war, NATO did, in the event, increase the attraction of such nationalist groups. But it is difficult not to suspect that an unchallenged triumph by Serbian nationalists would have been equally encouraging, or worse. Since the NATO campaign ended, with the withdrawal of Serbian troops, a number of - mostly right wing - apologists have claimed that NATO actively *desired* to attack the Serbs (and engineered the collapse of the Rambouillet talks in order to excuse this act), that '*only a few thousand*' Kosovar Albanians were murdered rather than the tens of thousands that at one time seemed likely, and that the whole affair was, somehow, the fault of Western politicians, and not at all the fault of the Serbian Government. None of this strikes me as plausible, or even as decent.

My own judgement, therefore, is not that the NATO campaign was *right*, but only that it is difficult to see what other course of action would have been better, and that the leaders of NATO, who took the decision to go to war, need not have been wicked people. If they went to war, as some of their critics have seriously proposed, for electoral advantage, or for the dream of power, or out of ignorant malice, then indeed they acted wickedly, whatever the objective 'cause of war'.[5] If they were so caught up in their schemes as not to notice or care about the casualties, they were at least corrupted by the conduct of the war. Critics whose political consciences were forged back in the sixties and seventies are rightly alert to the corruptions, of language and the soul, involved in the use of military force. They would be right to complain - and more than complain - at depersonalizing talk of 'collateral damage', or at efforts to 'demonize' the Serbian people. But there are subtle corruptions in pursuit of peace as well. Peace seems so desirable that *any* price may seem to be worth paying to 'get people around the conference table' once again - even the price of ignoring, or trivializing, outrageous crimes. In this particular case, it seems to me, it was the *critics* of NATO's actions who were the more inclined to 'demonize' their opposition, to speak and think as if the leaders of NATO (which, after all, includes nineteen independent states whose leaders were agreed - as other statesmen also were - that Serbian behaviour could not be tolerated longer) were wicked, and the leaders of Serbia - especially Slobodan Milosević - were much misunderstood. They even chose to believe assertions that Kosovo had 'been in revolt', that there was a *Muslim* menace to European security, and that modern Serbians should all be our friends because - sixty years ago - some Serbians (along with Croats and Muslims) were allies against the Nazi Reich (which was, in turn, assisted by some Croats, along with Serbs and Muslims). These criticisms of the critics in no way suggest that it was *wrong* of them to criticize, or that the loyal subjects of NATO states should not have publicized their doubts while the war was going on. As Chesterton remarked of an earlier war, and its critics, this would be like suggesting that one should not tell one's grandmother that her nightdress is on fire. It *is* to propose that the critics were themselves mistaken: mistaken in their immediate judgement, and more seriously mistaken in their demonizing NATO.

In the dispute about the rights and wrongs of war, or of this war, both sides invoked comparisons. NATO was inclined to compare the situation to the problem posed by Hitler. In the event we went to war with Germany on the excuse of its external aggression, although we already had cause to condemn its treatment of Jews, Gypsies, homosexuals and mentally disabled people.[6] Serbian aggression has been, on Serbian terms, 'internal' - although 'ethnic cleansing', by forcing whole populations into other states, which were thereby destabilized, was itself an act of war, quite apart from the suffering inflicted on Serbia's own minority populations. A prompter response to Hitler's Germany might have helped, and modern leaders are always hopeful that they can respond in time. NATO's critics generally inquired instead why NATO had not gone to war in other, more recent situations, and drew the conclusion that NATO's reasons must be vile. Some of those critics still retained a romantic view of NATO's former enemies - despite the evidence of ecological and human tragedy. Others advocated an openly parochial point of view (that nothing beyond our state's borders should concern us). Most were probably moved chiefly by the dream of peace. The fact, as I suppose, that NATO's leaders and loyalists were also moved by just that dream perhaps escaped them.

Ethical Inconsistencies

If we go to war on behalf of the Kosovar Albanians, why did we not go to war on behalf of Serbs, when they were being evicted from what was to become Croatian land?[7] If we insist, with all available force, that the killing in Kosovo must stop, why did we not do the same in Rwanda, East Timor or Chechnya? If Milosević is a target because he is a dictator, why was not the same force used against any number of other dictators who employed even bloodier means to control their people?

The argument seems to have two sides: the psychological and the ethical. On the psychological side, the inference intended is that the *real* cause of going to war is not the explicit 'cause of war': if NATO were moved to war by the occasions that it itemizes it would have gone to war on other occasions and in other theatres. Because it didn't and doesn't its claims are hypocritical. It must have a secret agenda, since the one it claims would have produced very different actions. On the ethical side, the inference is different: if it is right to go to war in Serbia, it must be right to go to war in other, relevantly similar cases. But anyone can see (it is supposed) that in those other cases it would *not* be right to go to war, most often because we cannot go to war in every case. 'We cannot be the world's policeman' - and so should not attempt to police at all.

The psychological claim is not one that I shall consider at any length. There may be many explanations for inaction in putatively 'similar' cases, and a full analysis of those explanations (diplomatic, economic, military, party political, psychological) demands far more knowledge, and experience, than I can muster. It is not necessarily hypocritical to act in one case, and not another, even if the identifiable differences between the cases would not themselves have any general effect. The charge of hypocrisy indeed appears to rest upon too high an opinion of human rationality: it is assumed that everyone has a rationally ordered plan to achieve clear goals, that we can decipher what that plan amounted to by seeing what, in practice, it achieved, and must then disbelieve all statements to the contrary. The chances are, instead of this, that people respond to present stimuli, are rarely very clear-headed about their goals, and routinely make mistakes in seeking to avoid the perils that they see. Actually, this is not necessarily a bad thing. Even where there really *are* no discoverable differences between cases it is not obviously wrong to discriminate at random: the best way of deciding when to drive back from a holiday resort would be for everyone to toss a coin; the best way of deciding when to give coins to a beggar is by random whim.[8] If things work out badly, it need be no-one's design: cock-up rather than conspiracy rules the world.[9]

But there is one more point to make - namely that it is inappropriate to employ such psychological categories at all in considering the actions of a public body. Margaret Thatcher may have earned the scorn of many by her casual denial that there was 'any such thing as society', and it is likely that she herself did not quite know what she meant. But in an important and neglected sense she was entirely right. Neither 'society' nor 'the British electorate' nor 'the British Government' nor 'NATO' names a single personal entity with a stable character and an ongoing purpose. Despite the claims of journalists and politicians, 'the British electorate', for example, does not 'decide' to provide any faction with an overwhelming majority, or a difficult tactical situation as it makes pacts with other factions, nor is 'it' irrational in determining that local councils, regional assemblies, Westminster and the European Parliament have different policies. All these putative entities are changeful alliances in a changing world, and the results of voting patterns need be *no one's* preference. Even personal agents, of course, can be inconsistent without being hypocritical. Organizations and alliances are not bound by 'their own past', nor by a coherent policy. They may be founded for all sorts of reasons which cease to apply even before the ink is dried. Their 'actions', which are only the results of arguments and preemptive actions by the persons who dictate or take immediate responsibility for what is done 'in their name', may make no single sense at all, without our having to denounce any actual, individual persons for that inconsistency.

The ethical argument (or arguments) also depends on our ability to identify the 'relevantly similar case'. Ethical judgements cannot, we are told, be arbitrary. To say that x is right, or A is good, depends upon a prior judgement that *all* cases like x or A are right or good. This theory in turn depends upon identifying 'relevant' descriptions of x or A. Every particular case or entity, after all, must differ from every other in many ways. Nor should the descriptions be merely particular or ostensive: it cannot, we are told, be ethically significant that it is *this* individual, not *that*, with whom we have been previously acquainted, nor that the act has been performed on *one* side of the border, not the *other*. Personal attachments may be individual, and arbitrary. Legal rulings may shift with the territory, or the court conventions. *Ethical* judgements are intended to be binding on *all* moral agents, in *all* significantly similar cases. What matters are the 'real' or 'objective' qualities of the act or agent or subject, not their significance for historically and personally contingent beings. We cannot change the ethical qualities of acts by redescription. How can it be wrong to eat dogs, but not to eat pigs? How can it be right to 'execute' people, but not to 'murder' them, merely because the killer is called a public executioner, or right to bomb them if one is called a 'soldier'? If there is no statable difference between *all* non-human animals, on the one hand, and *all* human animals on the other, must it not be as wrong to enslave, imprison, torment and kill non-human animals as it is to do those things to humans?

One response is simply to insist that the language of moral, ethical, or political judgement expresses contingent attitudes. Freedom fighters and terrorists, kings and tyrants differ only in the names we use, for personal and idiosyncratic reasons. We need not expect those attitudes to be strictly 'rational', any more than love or loathing is. My *love* for Jo does not imply that I even *like* her identical twin sister, even if the only qualities I can identify in Jo as earning my affection are shared not only by her twin but by uncounted others. My loyalty to 'crown and country' depends upon historical circumstance: others may be as laudably loyal to a different crown, and I *might* have been a citizen of many different countries, whether by having a different life, or living in a different history. *The British Isles* need never have been a political unit,[10] and are not now - or ever - socially or ethnically homogenous. The rules, whatever they may be from time to time, that are devized to settle disputes in these islands need never have been considered 'rational', as forming a consistent system deemed binding on all parties. They are only the rules that have, so far, survived. I speak the language that I do by accident, and am similarly, accidentally, bound in loyalty to just these peoples, and legally bound to act or to forebear in ways that need make no *systematic* sense.

Oddly, it may be just this point which has misled some critics of our recent military adventures. Although 'right-wingers' are typically inclined to approve of the use of military means to *defend* or *promote* the interest of the peoples to which they are attached, they are correspondingly disinclined to leap to the defence of *other* peoples, and rather to insist that where there is no 'national advantage' in the victory of one side or the other we should not interfere, whatever calamities ensue. Some of those who rather approve of NATO's intervention in the Balkans, or the UN's efforts to create a peace in East Timor, instead rely upon a sense of human solidarity which must transcend our local, accidental attachments. I share enough of 'right-wing' sensibilities to suspect that *some* claims of 'human solidarity' disguise far more particular and paternalist emotions. There are indeed good reasons to suspect the wit or virtue of any rulers who are too quick to take offence at what is done beyond their ordinary borders. Even if we ourselves do strongly disapprove of what is being done 'elsewhere' we dare not claim the right, and cannot claim the authority, to interfere. Should Kuwaitis be *compelled* to allow women to vote? Should Koreans be *compelled* to stop killing dogs for their dinner by slow strangulation? Should Americans be *compelled* to abandon judicial murder? Should Hindus have been *compelled* to abandon suttee, and should they now be *compelled* to dismantle the caste system? Should peoples around the world be *compelled* to abandon child labour? And - in all these cases - *can* they be?

But the answer to these questions can be in the negative without adopting any universal rule of 'non-interference'. Such a rule, indeed, would be just as contrary to the broadly Burkean attitude that I am here describing, as a universal rule of moralizing interference. There will be occasions when it would be folly to permit our neighbours to conduct themselves exactly as they please. Those who live upstream will not be allowed to foul the waters more than those who live *downstream* can bear. Those who force others into exile, upon pain of death, impose burdens upon neighbouring nations. Those who do vile things to their victims may suddenly and unpredictably discover that even distant nations have been roused against them. Nor are our separate nations really so distinct: shared customs, ancestry and chance acquaintance mean that we may have serious, personal interests in the welfare of neighbouring peoples, and sufficient concern about their treatment to justify our intervention. It is one thing to agree - if so we do - that the wars of distant tribesmen are no concern of ours, and that we have no duty, and maybe no right, to interfere. It is quite another to insist that *European* wars are no concern of Europeans, *African* wars no concern of Africans.

Conversely, even universalists are not required to interfere on every possible occasion. Let us grant that there are universal human rights: it is not just Britons who shall not be slaves, subject to arbitrary arrest, tortured, dispossessed and killed. The same crime is committed against Amerindians, Timorese, Hutu or Kosovar Albanians. Those who commit those crimes deserve our condemnation, and the strongest case for some form of World Government or World Police is just our fervent demand that such crimes should not be left unsolved, unpunished, unresolved. But even though we wish there were a World Police (with whatever caveats about the dangers of such a Power), we must acknowledge that there is no such Power now. We cannot always be obliged to intervene because we are not always *able* to intervene, at least with any reasonable hope of remedying the situation or not making it much worse. We had some reasonable chance of defeating Serbia: our chances of defeating Russia (over Chechnya), or China (over Tibet), are very small indeed. That indeed has been the charge against much military intervention, that it cannot succeed, and must *make things worse*. Once again, this cannot - plausibly - be a universal truth. Some brigands are sometimes arrested and brought to trial. Their victims are sometimes greatly relieved. Even if the price of their release is, in the short term, harsh, they maybe reckon themselves fortunate. After all, if it were widely understood that brigands, bandits, cultists, evil empires, would never be assaulted by a neighbouring power, and their victims *never* rescued or avenged, there would indeed be little hope of freedom. But though we should not give *carte blanche* to bandits by declining any use of forceful intervention, it is still true that we shall not always be able to intervene without ourselves being bandits. The moment of intervention must then be a matter for delicate judgement - and it will, typically, be far too late. We are so anxious not to seem to be oppressors, and also anxious not be too quick to judge, that we shall only ever intervene when evidence of unbearable oppression has itself become unbearable. Even the most interventionist of social workers will only take children from their parents once they have *already* been appallingly abused. Taking them without such concrete evidence is itself an abuse of power, and likely enough to lead to further such abuses.

So even universal moralists will not so easily be 'consistent' in their interventions. Situations differ in an infinite array of ways. We may doubt the evidence of oppression. We may be uncertain of our own capacities. We may be aware of *other* duties. We may be uncertain of our motives, or the chances of corruption once we begin a military escapade. We may not be confident that others will support our case. No doubt it was 'inconsistent' to permit the Reich to attach Czechoslovakia, but find the attachment of Poland an excuse for war. No doubt it was 'inconsistent' to take the Nazis as our enemies, and the Soviets as our allies (since both regimes were already murderous, and both geared up for genocide). But all manner of distinctions could be drawn to defend those differences. No doubt there are many occasions when *all* that we do is wrong, and our only hope is amnesty.

Crimes and the Global Court

Ideally, it is easy to suppose, all crimes against humanity, and indeed all *crimes* that are properly so called, would be acknowledged globally. The Convention against Genocide is one long step towards that goal. We have, perhaps, taken another in judging[11] that a Head of State may properly be called to account for crimes against humanity committed by officials of that State under his or her regime. It is still the case that individual States may offer sanctuary to alleged or proven criminals, and refuse their extradition, whether because their crimes are judged 'political', or because it is thought that they cannot expect fair trials, or because they may be subject to 'cruel or unusual punishments', or because the acts for which they would be tried are not accounted 'crimes', or simply because the relevant State has signed no extradition treaty. If there were sufficient agreement amongst the Powers that certain acts were outlawed, and that no State should ever shelter suspects from the law, a genuinely global Police-force and an authoritative Global Court might be imminent. Even in such a case it might well be that not all crimes, however serious they might be, would earn full global retribution. Local forces and local courts would still be left to deal with almost all such cases, and many suspected criminals would still be able to flee from one local jurisdiction to another without any real fear of being brought before the Global Court, or even being returned to their first jurisdiction. Maybe precise computer records (including universal DNA-identification) would make it easier to track such suspects: the easier it would be to do so, the more likely it might be that the World Police would intervene. But the greatest weight of global disapproval must still be directed at those crimes which directly affect us all. Small-time crooks and cheats are not worth the hassle, or the damage to our privacy - and our respect for law - that would be done by any single-minded pursuit. If everyone must have a number to be judged a proper citizen of the World Community, there will be many otherwise respectable people who decide that this would be the number of the Beast, and foreswear allegiance.[12]

If *all* crimes and all suspected criminals were equally the concern of any powerful Global Court, we would all be citizens, or subjects, of the one World State. Whether such a State could ever be run without creating an Imperial caste to run it, and a totalitarian surveillance system, seems uncertain. Whether it could, in reason, ever allow any cultural or ethical diversity amongst its subjects also seems unclear. If it were founded simply on the interests of some one class or people it might most profitably *ignore* (as the Roman Empire did) most local customs, as long as the tax was paid and any world-class criminals (which is simply, *rebels*) were identified and arrested everywhere. But the State which I am considering here is founded on a universal ethical demand - that *crimes against humanity* or all crimes properly so called are equally the concern of all of us, and that there should be no effective sanctuary for the criminals. There were limits even to the Romans' tolerance. There will certainly be limits to ours - but will *we* be the arbiters? One serious question must be: are we agreed on what thus counts as *crime*? Is infanticide a crime? Clitoridectomy? Serial killing? Pederasty? Sodomy? Indecency? The sale of addictive drugs (including or not including alcohol, nicotine or caffeine)? Attempted genocide? Pollution? Profiteering? Usury? Killing whales? The destruction of whole species? Waste? Idolatry? Apostasy? Secession?

Chesterton had a point: 'The average agnostic of recent times has really had no notion of what he meant by religious liberty and equality. He took his own ethics as self-evident and enforced them; such as decency or the error of the Adamite heresy. Then he was horribly shocked if he heard of anybody else, Moslem or Christian, taking *his* ethics as self-evident and enforcing *them*; such as reverence or the error of the Atheist heresy.'[13] Until we are sure we know what real *crimes* are, we had better not be too enthusiastic about a World Court to enforce obedience, as though it were *obvious* that everyone agreed with *us*.

The authority of such a Global State, after all, cannot rest on any Lockean principle of consent - that its citizens are bound to obey it or else leave. Even now the realistic chance of *leaving* any particular State is small, and our Lockean duties of obedience are suspect. But as long as there are rival regimes there is a residual possibility of abandoning one's birth State for another. For as long as we can prefer to stay, it may be that we have some duty to obey. But no-one can leave the World State: any serious attempt at secession will, inevitably, be treated as rebellion. Maybe there will be no need to send in troops on such an occasion: the offending parties will simply be denied all credit in the Global Market, denied all access to the transport system, communications, necessary drugs or education. Maybe they will be allowed a Reservation, but only for as long as the land is not 'needed' for others. Only those who serve the Beast will prosper - for a while. And what the Beast will require of us, who knows?[14]

So maybe a World State will be illegitimate as well as - possibly - impractical, unless its legitimacy is openly theocratic (that is, founded on a universal, and universally acknowledged, ethical demand). Universal humanism may be as close as we can, at present, get to such a demand: no-one is to be abandoned. Any human being, anywhere, must be remembered and befriended, rather than be left, defenceless and unavenged, to suffer whatever abuse her masters choose. But though such a demand is one whose force I feel (and pray that it is felt by others), it is simply a fact that the sacredness of human life is *not* recognized everywhere. It is a *religious* claim, even if it often lacks the ground, in metaphysical theism, that it once enjoyed. Conversely, I would myself insist that it is not *only* human life that deserves and demands such care. If the abuse of *human* rights may be an argument for military intervention, so may be the abuse of *animal* rights, or the deliberate destruction of whole habitats. There are other religions than the merely humanistic.

Unfortunately, the Imperial caste that will probably run the World State in the name of whatever demand proves powerful is unlikely to believe that it faces any serious challenge, or that it lives under judgement. 'The objection to an aristocracy is that it is a priesthood without a god.'[15] Personally, I prefer not to be governed by any such smug aristocratic class, even one that professed to accept the same demands as I. But in the absence of such a Court, and such agreement, we are thrown back again on what we, locally and tribally, are willing to endure.

The Dream of Europe

But Immanuel Kant - the actual Kant, that is, rather than the Philosophers' Kant[16] - identified a middle ground. Maybe we should not - or would not - welcome a World State, and therefore should be cautious about any attempt to regulate the World in the name of one acknowledged set of values. Any such attempt is far more likely to be an attempt at conquest (by one faction, nation or imperial church), and will necessarily lack authority (whether of the Lockean or theocratic kind). It does not follow that we should reckon everything beyond our accidental borders is beyond our reach, or outside any rational concern of ours. I may have no wish to merge my family within a village commune, and so surrender any special claim on property or on my children's affections. It does not follow that I should seek to rule my family as, so Homer and Aristotle between them tell us, ogres did.[17] Correspondingly, even if I would not willingly surrender 'national sovereignty' to an alien despot, it does not follow that this or any 'nation' can long hold itself aloof from the acts and opinions of its immediate neighbours. As before: even if the wars of *distant* tribesmen are no concern of ours, it is absurd to reckon that *European* wars do not matter to Europeans. We are knit together in a historical association of states, professions, churches, businesses and extended families.

Universal Humanism (the demand that no single human being be abandoned to despair or degradation) may - so far - be a step too far. To insist on such obedience would involve us in another, greater war, and all the usual arguments could be brought against that risk. How can we *compel* people to respect humanity by bombing, starving and eviscerating them? How can we avoid corrupting even such virtue as we now possess? How can we ensure that the world which grows from even a *victorious* crusade is better than the world we lost? Often enough we *have* to abandon people, unrevenged, to despair and degradation since the cost of trying to redeem them is far too high, and our chances of success are far too small. But it does not follow that we should happily or easily abandon children in the house next door to be shamed, abused or killed merely because (we know) there are *other* children in as hideous a plight, and that their would-be or self-styled rescuers are often themselves foolish, wicked or unlucky. Sometimes we should seek to intervene, and if we are virtuous we *must* intervene, even if we *know* that we shall not succeed. Taking a stand may sometimes even be worth defeat, when all we can do is testify.

> 'So we rush them, then?' said Simony. I'm sure of - maybe four hundred on our side. So I give the signal and a few hundred of us attack thousands of them? And he dies anyway and we die too? What difference does that make?'
>
> Urn's face was grey with horror now.
>
> 'You mean you don't know?' he said.[18]

Correspondingly, our frequent failures do not excuse mere indolence when it comes to attempted genocide in a neighbouring nation. When we confess our inability to help the afflicted we judge that they must simply endure their fate, because we cannot justly or practically help them. When we are goaded into mounting a crusade to save them we must similarly judge that there will be other innocents who also suffer for the sake of a half-way decent future, and because we can do no other. Neither course can be required in the abstract, nor yet forbidden. Neither course can be defended on some specious calculation of 'quality-adjusted life-years saved'. And both depend, for their decency, on some version of the principle of double effect: those who reject armed intervention do not *intend* that the oppressed should suffer, though they foresee that they will; those who advocate such intervention likewise do not *intend* the deaths of innocents that they too must foresee.

There might even be situations where the spectacle of one single child, imprisoned and humiliated, would be enough to galvanize one people into military action against another: the spectacle may suddenly be unendurable, whatever nice calculations of political expediency are offered. That, after all, is how wars often start, with a single *cause célèbre* that, in the abstract, may not seem worth the price. But such occasions are most often symbols of some underlying difference of creed and attitude and past behaviour that at last demands a confrontation. Those who deny that we should ever, on any circumstance, be driven to such lengths in effect demand that we abandon the world - and our fellows - to others with fewer scruples. 'Mediaeval men thought that if a social system was founded on a certain idea it must fight for that idea.'[19]

What, at the moment, is the 'certain idea' we have to fight for? As I said, it might be, on occasion, that a single forsaken child could be a cause of war. Universal humanism at least seems to require that all such sufferings demand a response. It would make no difference - except to make it worse - if the victims of oppression were selected randomly, or even (by some notions) 'fairly'. But it seems that we are not all convinced of this: the criticisms of NATO's actions in the former Yugoslavia, remember, sometimes turned on a rejection of the claim of 'genocide'. Only if the Serbs were 'really' intent on 'genocide', it was said, would concerted military action be an appropriate reaction. As it was - so we are to suppose - the victims were merely in the way, and there was no real intention to wipe out a nation. The Serbs just wanted the Kosovar Albanians to leave, or stand aside, or stop requiring independence: maybe their means were violent or oppressive, but they were not 'genocidal'. So NATO had no authority to act because the United Nations - the only available voice of a united humankind - had given it none. If the Serbian intention *had* been genocidal the authority would have been given already.

I have already observed that the definition of 'genocide' or 'genocidal intention' actually does fit the observed events far better than NATO's critics have suggested. I might also reasonably query their sudden faith in another political institution, namely the UN, which seems to have no *greater* hold on anyone's real loyalty than NATO does. Whatever we may hope of it, it is not now, not yet, a genuine World State, speaking for all people - or peoples - of the world according to a single, simple creed. It has neither Lockean nor theocratic authority - nor even an impressive record. But my concluding comments take a different slant. Let us concede that there might be a question whether Serbia was genocidal in intent (or rather, whether Serb leaders, officials, soldiers, partisans were acting genocidally). My point is, emphatically, *not* that NATO's actions could be justified only if the allies were right to suppose that genocide was in progress (though I believe that this was at the least a reasonable belief).[20] As far as I can see, it is unimportant whether, say, Pol Pot's victims were of a single people, distinct from their executioners or from those they spared: if they were, his plan was genocidal; if they were not, it was only murderous. A reasonable humanist, we might be inclined to say, would see no real difference between the cases: either way, tens of thousands died. King Chaka of the Zulus also murdered his many thousands, and should not be excused on the pretext that they too were Zulus. But in practice we may have to admit that only two things would galvanize the neighbours of Pol Pot or Chaka into armed revenge. If a single member of *our* nation, a relative of one of *us*, and especially a child, were to be murdered too, we could be angry enough to intervene. Not humanism, but tribalism would drive us in that case.[21] The other thing is genocide.

Genocide demands an intervention, with all possible speed and careful violence. We will not put up with tribes, states or churches that attempt to eliminate *a people*. That is the bottom line of our religion, and one shared widely enough to be a practicable basis for concerted action. There is an obvious parallel. Some people are moved enough by the suffering or frustration of individual non-human animals to change their ways or urge a change on all of us. So far, that is a minority opinion. But many more are moved by the thought of losing *species*. Sometimes, no doubt, this is a merely (?) prudential calculation: that every species lost is an opportunity lost, and a further strand in the web of life is broken. But we also reckon *species* as forms of beauty, maintained over generations despite the incidental loss of individuals. Nations or peoples or great lineages or languages may evoke - apparently do evoke - a similar emotion.

Often enough, it has been war itself which has cost us nations, peoples, lineages, languages, species. No one remotely sane or sensible *desires* that means of safety. But if we are faced, as we have actually been faced, by genocidal enemies we recognize what we are fighting for, by whatever practical and decent means. Not to oppose such genocide for fear of individual losses, individual pains, is folly. The idea that, by default and perhaps without deliberate intention, we are primed to fight for is just this: that the tapestry of human life, as well as general terrestrial life, be kept intact, and that we not lose the strands that make it up. There are those who would gladly rip that tapestry apart. Let us acknowledge that, in the end, we shall oppose them, the more readily and easily when they are close at hand. Distant nations touch us less, for many not wholly creditable reasons. One reason which fits the rationale I offer here is simply that we do not discriminate so easily between those distant nations: it takes a moment, for Europeans, to distinguish Hutu and Tutsi enough to realize that a genuinely genocidal war is taking place. Africans - and even Britons - would have as great a difficulty in distinguishing Serbs, Croats and Albanians. As our knowledge grows, so also our concern not to lose any distinguishable variant of humanity. Maybe, in the end, we shall progress to a more individual-centred care, and mind as much about the deliberate murder, say, of street-children in Brazil as if they were our neighbours or a distinguishable nation. Till such a religion sweeps the world, we rely on what we have. We will go to war, on occasion, either to save our very own kindred or to save a people. In both cases our aim will often be to insist - with all necessary force - that they are not forgotten. In neither case will we always have been consistent. Consistency in these matters is no virtue.

Notes

1   And by some discussions on philos-1@liverpool.ac.uk, the philosophy email list.
2   The fact that it *was* may turn on a military calculation, that invasion would be too costly or the gain too uncertain. It may also turn upon an ill-defended judgement that state borders should be secure against *all* invasion. It is not obvious to me that Vietnam should have refrained from invading Kampuchea to put a stop to the Khmer Rouge merely because an arbitrary, historical boundary divided the two regions. See Jeff McMahan, 'The Ethics of International Intervention', *Ethics and International Relations*, ed. Anthony Ellis (Manchester University Press: Manchester 1986), pp.24-51. On the occasion of the conference at which McMahan's paper was first presented I agreed that states should not be considered sacrosanct, while also expressing some doubts about the additional powers that licensed intervention gave the intervening state (op.cit., pp.55-56). I retain the doubts - but see no reason to accept the rule of non-intervention as an absolute.

3   78 U.N.T.S. 277, which entered into force on January 12, 1951: see http://www.unesco.com.

4   In its resolution 96 (I) dated 11 December 1946.

5   'For it may happen that the war is declared by the legitimate authority, and for a just cause, and yet be rendered unlawful through a wicked intention. Hence Augustine says (*Contra Faust*. xxii, 74): "The passion for inflicting harm, the cruel thirst for vengeance, an unpacific and relentless spirit, the fever of revolt, the lust of power, and such like things, all these are rightly condemned in war".' (Thomas Aquinas *Summa Theologica* II.2, 40 q.1.)

6   Some recent writers have argued that because the actual occasion of war was the invasion of Poland (and that the subsequent war certainly did Poland very little good), it is somehow a mistake to say that World War 2 was fought to halt a dreadful enemy, the Nazi Reich. This claim is either naïve or offensive.

7   Possibly in response to attempts by agents of the Serbian government to hang on to territory largely inhabited by Croats. The Balkans are, obviously, at least a three-way conflict, in which all sides, at various times, have committed atrocious acts. In the most recent crisis it was the Serbian side that had most fire-power, and apparently least compunction. Suppose that the UK Government, dominated by English politicians, had responded to reports that the English-born were occasionally subject to violence, insult or discriminatory treatment up in Scotland by removing local government and seeking to force the *Scottish* into exile in Ulster, Denmark or North America, at whatever cost to the stability and civil peace within those jurisdictions. Suppose Westminster went on to encourage roving gangs of English thugs to rape, rob and murder any remaining Scots, while blaming any unrest entirely on Scottish Nationalists, demonized as bandits. There is, of course, a certain historical verisimilitude about this allegory.

8   See also Mark Evans, in this volume: 'Selectivity, Imperfect Obligations and the Character of Humanitarian Morality.'

9   Strangely, it seems that critics with a low opinion of our rulers' *morals* have a correspondingly *high* opinion of their cleverness and efficiency. No doubt there are real, and even undiscovered, conspiracies: but only dedicated idealists make good conspirators. Our safety lies in our rulers' inefficiency and idleness!

10 A point constantly neglected by those who would have us abandon our present constitution in favour of their favourite alternative: once the *established* order is in question, why on earth should any of us agree to submit to the judgement of just this group of people in just this territory? And what will be the background of that judgement? Edmund Burke, it seems to me, was entirely right to fear the lucubrations of self-selected constitutional lawyers. 'When antient opinions and rules of life are taken away, the loss cannot possibly be estimated. From that moment we have no compass to govern us; nor can we know distinctly to what port we steer' (Edmund Burke, *Reflections on the Revolution in France*, ed. Conor Cruise O'Brien (Penguin: Harmondsworth 1968), p.172; see also pp.129ff).

11 Or at least the British House of Lords has judged, twice over, that this is so.

12 *Revelation* 13.16: 'And [the miracle-working Beast] causeth all, both small and great,

rich and poor, free and bond, to receive a mark in their right hand, or in the foreheads: and that no man might buy or sell, save he that had the mark, or the name of the beast or the number of his name.' And all those who receive that mark 'shall drink of the wine of the wrath of God' (*Revelation* 14.10). What the prophecy meant originally, who knows? That it will be interpreted as a warning against accepting any such global marker seems quite clear, and that it will therefore be an occasion for - at least - disobedience. Opposition to 'the New World Order' may be premature, or even wrong, but no-one should suppose that it would be easy to appease, nor that it is obviously ridiculous.

13 G.K. Chesterton, *St. Francis of Assisi* (Hodder & Stoughton: London 1923), pp.144ff.

14 See V. Solovyev, *War, Progress and the End of History*, tr. A. Bakshy and T.R. Beyer Jr (Lindisfarne Press: Hudson, NY 1990; first published 1900) pp.159-193, on the Anti-Christ.

15 Chesterton, *St. Francis*, op.cit., p.141: a remark that does not apply only to *military* or *landed* aristocracies. Aristocrats are convinced of their own rectitude, and fear no coming Judgement.

16 Who is routinely depicted as a humourless universalist who cared only that the abstract rules be followed. The actual Kant's picture of international relations is very much more realistic: see 'Perpetual Peace: a Philosophical Sketch' (1796), *Kant's Political Writings*, tr. H.B. Nesbit, ed. H. Reiss (Cambridge University Press: Cambridge 1970), pp.93-130. In the necessary absence of an *international state* (*civitas gentium*) we must hope instead for 'an enduring and gradually expanding federation likely to prevent war' (p.105). I am aware that Kant also advocated the rule of non-interference in the 'internal affairs' of states - a rule which I do not think can be absolute. He was assuming too easily that the federated states would all share some fundamental attitudes and axioms.

17 Aristotle, *Politics* 1.1252b23ff, *Nicomachean Ethics* 10.1180a28, after Homer, *The Odyssey* 9.114.

18 Terry Pratchett, *Small Gods* (Gollancz: London 1992) p.343; see also p.225. It is also possible, of course, to testify by an absolute commitment to non-violence, at whatever cost. But contemporary critics of armed intervention rarely claim to be dedicated pacifists, and reserve the right to use violence in defence of *their own* children or friends. I concede - indeed, I have already stated - that we are entitled to be somewhat parochial in our concerns - but there must come a moment when we can no longer distinguish those who would work evil on *our* children and those who only oppress, as it might be, Jewish or Romany or Slav children. To say that we will *never* defend or testify on behalf of those others is to accept the standards of our enemies.

19 Chesterton, *St. Francis*, op.cit., p.145.

20 The flat assertion that it was a *false* belief, made by some contributors to the discussion on *philos-l* and at the conference seems to me to depend on nothing more than the wish that this was so. That the International Court has begun to find individuals guilty of genocide at least confirms that the belief is reasonable.

21 It may be that the sight of *any* child in terror, of whatever tribe, may come to serve as a

proper cue for violent intervention. Amongst the most moving icons of the age have been pictures of a naked child running down the road in Vietnam, and a Jewish child beginning to believe that people meant him ill. It is pictures like that, along with that of the earth from orbit, that are beginning the long, slow process of civilizing humankind.

Chapter 7

Selectivity, Imperfect Obligations and the Character of Humanitarian Morality

Mark Evans

The Question of Selectivity

One of the most frequently pressed criticisms of 'humanitarian intervention' has been that those with the power and will to intervene invariably appear to be unconscionably selective in their actions. Far from involving themselves with all comparable injustices around the world, these powers devote themselves only to certain ones and not others. Thus they open themselves up to the question: 'why concern yourself with one instance that you think warrants intervention and not a like instance elsewhere?' To take just one recent example, one might ask 'why did Kosovo merit military intervention whilst Chechnya was left to the mercy of the Russians and Rwanda was abandoned to drown in the blood of one of the worst genocides since World War Two?'

This 'selectivity question' can, of course, be asked with respect to any number of other policy acts and omissions, but this observation merely challenges the priorities of the intervening agents still further. One may wonder, for example, why not more is done by the latter - who are usually among the most affluent states in the world - in terms of providing humanitarian *aid*. The terminology of humanitarian policy often operates to isolate the latter from the category of intervention, making this question's pertinence less obvious. 'Intervention' is, or at least claims to be, a type of just war. 'Aid', however, refers to the provision of basic material necessities - food, medicines, clothing, shelter - to the citizens of other states and is not in itself a form of war; at most, the military has a logistical and protective role in its provision. (It is also frequently provided by non-state organizations.) Yet if 'intervention' and 'aid' denote different types of action, one might still ask whether there is any relevant distinctiveness in their moral justifications to legitimize the preference for one over the other.

Where is the difference when the most basic interests of the starving millions in the world are, in effect, as fatally compromised as those of, say, the 'ethnically cleansed' whose plight seems to have commanded so much more political attention in recent times?

There are, of course, some familiar answers to the selectivity question. Sometimes, two instances of humanitarian concern may be very similar in their nature but one presents insuperable logistical obstacles to a successful action or threatens outweighing moral costs should such action ever be attempted. Thus there are sound, morally justified reasons why this instance is not selected for action when the other is. The lack of intervention in support of Tibetan independence, say, can then be accounted for in terms of both the practical difficulties of such an enterprise and the horrors of the conflict with China that would undoubtedly result. Another type of answer is the realist's *realpolitik* (or cynical) response which baldly explains why selections are actually made rather than varnish them with moral justifications. This holds that humanitarian action (and political behaviour generally) is motivated by the typically amoral self-interest of the powers in question and so, regrettably or not, it is only to be expected that they intervene in certain cases and not others. Kosovo, it has been said, merited the concern of the West because of its importance for future access to Caspian Sea oil,[1] whereas strategic interest militated against intervention in Rwanda, or East Timor during the 1970s.

The critics of humanitarian intervention frequently suspect that only *realpolitik* underpins the decisions to intervene - and these suspicions are doubtless often well-founded. Contempt is indeed well warranted for the hypocritical presentation of self-interested policies as supposedly impelled by pristine moral motives. And hypocrisy is not the central fault here: most would agree that amoral self-interest does not generate a *morally* acceptable justification for selectivity even when presented honestly, stripped of moral pretence.[2]

However, politically vital though the criticisms of interventionist policies may be, they do not always pay the attention deserved to those questions about what might be morally justified in a more ideal world, defined as one where genuine humanitarianism would not be subordinated to *realpolitik*. This chapter takes up one of them: could selectivity in a policy of humanitarian action ever be justified? Specifically, is there any morally justifiable opportunity for such discretion aside from that sanctioned by countervailing pragmatic and moral costs? Indeed, given that the latter might perhaps not be sensibly described as a matter of 'selectivity' at all - for a policy which comes with daunting obstacles and unacceptable consequences is unlikely to be considered a realistic choice -

we might reformulate this question thus: 'could there ever be morally justified selectivity in terms of choosing which of a number of *feasible* actions to pursue?'

What makes this question so perplexing is that in general it is profoundly inadequate to describe humanitarian action as a supererogatory affair. Most of us would recognize a deep intuition that humanitarian injustice is the very worst kind of injustice perpetuated by human beings and I shall argue that we cannot explicate this idea if we think that their prevention, rectification or restitution is essentially optional. This should lead us to posit some kind of positive demand that something be done to rectify, prevent and/or punish such injustice which is not grasped by the common (supererogatory) discourse of 'charity'. But even with this claim accepted, I will argue that genuine and substantial discretion in the discharge of such duty may well be unavoidable *in particular under the global institutional circumstances in which we presently find ourselves.* If this conclusion is granted, then although we might still condemn governments for some of the reasons they employ in making their selections we cannot coherently condemn them *simply* for being selective.

The practical purpose of this inquiry is not to excuse the actions or omissions of any particular actor or power; indeed, nothing in what follows should be taken to imply any particular judgement on any specific event in world history.[3] Instead, I suggest that consideration of the selectivity question takes us to the very heart of how best to conceptualize 'humanitarian morality'. It helps us to clarify some profound but often confused intuitions many of us have about the morality of humanitarianism and the argument which follows attempts to present these in their most coherently satisfying form. I shall argue that the inevitability-of-selectivity claim must be understood in a way that, crucially, does not totally exculpate inactivity even when the choice not to act can count as a justified instance of selectivity.

The Concept of Humanitarian Morality

We begin with a clarification of 'humanitarian morality'. It might be thought that this should centre upon the doctrine of human rights, which is the usual currency of humanitarian moralizing. However, the proliferation of 'rights' in such discourse, evident in the sheer size of many of the documents which codify human rights in national and international laws, has made it difficult to ascribe to all proclaimed human rights the kind of normative importance borne by this concept. It would, for example, be bizarre to hold that a human right to life (Article 3 of the Universal Declaration of Human Rights) bears the same significance as a human right to paid holidays (Article 24).[4] So if we wish to defend the idea that violations of some, but only some, human rights may justify humanitarian action, we need to demarcate these particular rights to indicate their possession of this crucial moral feature. 'Humanitarian morality', therefore, seeks to isolate from the full range of internationally ratified human rights the subset of such rights whose neglect or violation is so morally perturbing or reprehensible that no state within whose boundaries they go unrespected could justifiably invoke its claims to sovereignty, should it ever choose to do so, against corrective intervention from without.[5]

Now those who ascribe human rights to human beings tend to assume that such rights should in general hold for evermore, even when they believe the positing of such rights to be a relatively recent and culturally particular event. It is not necessary, though, to view the category of 'humanitarian morality' in quite the same way. As moral and political goals and possibilities shift, so might our conception of which rights engage potentially sovereignty-trumping international concern. Some claim that, as genocide alone has thus far tended to prompt humanitarian intervention, only the violation to a large degree and in certain deliberate ways of the right to life currently counts as humanitarian injustice. In fact this characterization is probably too narrow, overlooking as it does other sovereignty-trumping examples of humanitarian relief, particularly those of non-state organizations such as Médecins sans Frontières. 'Humanitarianism' itself is commonly used in more expansive terms: as Bhikhu Parekh argues, one feature of a humanitarian act is that it is 'intended to address what is regarded as a violation of the minimum that is due to human beings'.[6] We should straightaway recognize the difficulty in arguing for an uncontroversial, culturally neutral definition of this 'minimum', which is one of the reasons why the content of humanitarian morality should be viewed as fluid, contestable, rather than fixed. But we can nevertheless agree that the 'minimum due' to humans must include the basic material necessities which sustain life, as well as the basic security that protects it from other people: the 'limiting conditions of human *being*', we might say. This feature should establish it as the most important element of morality in general, compatible with a wide range of more comprehensively characterized moral theories and political ideologies, but not so vacuous as to be limitlessly permissive.[7]

Another way in which 'humanitarian morality' may lack fixity derives from how the sovereignty-trumping characteristic indicates that it stands at the intersection between state-centric and genuinely cosmopolitan conceptions of the ideal world order. Whilst it embodies principles whose enforceable authority transcends any state's claim to have the authority to act against them, the concept is clearly posited for a world where sovereignty-claims over their citizens by states against other states and organizations are granted *pro tanto* recognition. Many would agree with Parekh that this is a significant fault, undermining its internal cogency by presupposing yet seeking to move beyond the statist paradigm.[8] And one could accept that a move away from statism towards a more substantively cosmopolitan world political order could render the present particular construal of the 'humanitarian' obsolete. However, this potentially transient quality does not make the concepts of humanitarian morality and intervention logically incoherent for the here-and-now. Their time may yet pass but, in the context of a current world order which likewise conjoins extensive but still constrained state-centrism with a small but significant concession to cosmopolitanism, that point has yet to be reached.

Selectivity in the Demands of Humanitarian Morality

Whatever principles we assign to the category of humanitarian morality, I have suggested that their fundamental character places them at the very heart of morality. It is this feature that makes selectivity in engaging with them so troubling.

The disquiet becomes obvious insofar as we possess certain notions about the nature of humanitarian morality that make one well-known strategy to explain and justify moral selectivity so radically unsatisfactory in this case. That strategy is to posit morality's requirements as purely negative, or prohibitive. Leaving aside special obligations, morality is said to have in general a 'thou shalt not' character, stipulating that one should desist from certain actions. Any positive assistance we might render to others is supererogatory - a matter of non-obligatory 'charity' - which, though praiseworthy if performed, is entirely optional and thus not blameworthy if not performed.

Characterized thus, *morality* would not allow selectivity insofar as we would be said to have no choice not to follow its negative strictures (and except in certain tragic situations, it would always be *possible* to act as morality permits or requires). But all that humanitarian morality could then demand of us is that we do not ourselves directly act to compromise the fundamental human rights of others. The question of aiding others who have suffered humanitarian injustice for reasons beyond our control would not be one answerable with reference to the requirements of morality. We would be left free to choose which 'supra-moral', supererogatory acts we wish to perform, and blamelessly free to choose not to perform any.

Common though this view of morality is, reflection upon our heartfelt reactions to acquaintance with humanitarian injustice severely disrupts it. To think that 'positive' responses to humanitarian injustices are purely supererogatory requires one to believe that the moral situation in such predicaments is not worsened when no such assistance is rendered. Yet such is the 'weight' of humanitarian morality on our moral sensibilities that it seems entirely inadequate to treat its concerns as lightly as is entailed by reducing them to matters of charity. When we see images of the victims of genocide, or diseased, starving, dying refugees - those for whom the barest minimum conditions of life are brutally denied - our reaction runs typically along the lines of 'something *must* be done'. *That* is the intuitive obligation-generating import of humanitarian morality, which supererogation cannot express. And such is the urgency of its demands that in principle we are prepared to grant it sovereignty-trumping force.

This argument, however, cannot strip the interventionists' selectivity of all possible moral justification. Even when rejecting the purely negative conception of morality, it is extremely difficult to imagine how any viable moral system might be operationalized without a significant role being granted for selectivity. One of the most potentially anti-selective moral theories is likely to be some form of what Shelly Kagan has labelled 'moral extremism', a doctrine that in principle recognizes no limits to what demands (positive, assistance-rendering) morality makes of us beyond those that would protect our ability to be moral agents.[9] But 'doing what we can to maximize our contribution to the greatest good' may often be little more than a rough rule of thumb to guide action. Imperfect knowledge and the indeterminacy in any calculation of 'amounts of goodness', and the consequent increase in possible actions nominated by this rule, will probably allow even extremist moral agents considerable discretion in their actions. They, too, are likely to select certain moral causes and not others - they will *have* to - which means it is quite possible that some, even serious, demands will go unaddressed. And if we prefer instead to support what Kagan thinks of as 'moral moderation', in which personal non-moral projects permissibly limit morality's demands upon agents, then the general opportunity for selectivity obviously increases significantly.[10]

Furthermore, the unavoidability of selectivity may not be something we should bemoan as an unfortunate limitation in the human condition. We might imagine some kind of arrangement in which the multiple possibilities for action open to moral agents are neatly determined for them according to a comprehensive blueprint which ensures no moral concern goes unmet.

But if we share the predominant Enlightenment view that moral agents are in some fundamental sense free then this can hardly be regarded as an attractive prospect. The rigorous predetermined organization of a life so structured would seem to reduce the agent to a means, a tool, for moral ends whilst having lost sight of morality's very purpose, which I think most (and not just Kantians) would see in some way as about treating people with due respect as ends in themselves. It seems an essential part of what it means to be a human being to have the latitude allowed to determine for oneself how a (positive) moral life should be led: it is, after all, the agent and not the moral theory that should *lead* the life. (Persuasive doubts as to whether social interaction could ever be so neatly structured as to afford such moral predetermination add extra force to this argument.)

Now we ought to be wary of a possible sleight of hand in this pro-selectivity argument: the 'moral agent' thus far appears to have been the individual, yet it is collective bodies - primarily states acting alone and in alliance, but also local, regional, national and international non-governmental organizations - whose humanitarian policies we should primarily scrutinize. Obviously, we should not think that their moral opportunities and constraints are identical to those of individuals.[11] They are almost certainly bound to be configured differently, not least because at least some of these bodies actually exist precisely to overcome the limitations of individuals in spheres of moral concern.

Yet it can nevertheless be argued that some such discretion is also likely to be a permanent feature of their moral behaviour. Their resources are hardly limitless, for example, not least because greater demands than those levied on individuals are invariably made of them, forcing choices - often very difficult ones - to be made between them. A state, for example, may find itself morally overburdened amidst a complex pattern of obligations beginning with its own citizens and stretching outwards to their near neighbours, allies, others to whom they have certain other ties (such as the special responsibilities ex-colonial powers typically presume, and are presumed by some others, to have to their former colonies). It may have treaty obligations as well, which predetermine its moral concerns.

If we accept that these are often just too extensive all to be met, we can see how significant discretion should be admitted in any account of how a state should ideally discharge its moral obligations. And if democratic states are ideally constrained by the demands of their own citizens, then the arguments about individuals' moral discretion come directly back into play here. Ascription of necessary and desirable selectivity in the moral concerns of the democratic state, which we might take as an exemplar of a potential humanitarian-intervening power, actually follows from the arguments concerning selectivity on the part of its citizens, for it is their demands which should ultimately inform the priorities of their governors.

Human Rights and Imperfect Obligations

Thus far, we have concluded that moral agents of whatever type tend inevitably to display selectivity in at least some of the positive moral concerns they may take up (special obligations arising from promises and specific relationships - for example between parent and child - notwithstanding). It follows from this that none of them is necessarily at fault whenever their choices work out such that a particular humanitarian moral demand goes unmet. But can we bring this judgement into equilibrium with the apparently equally strong case developed against treating our responses to humanitarian injustice as merely supererogatory?

I contend that we can do this by conceptualizing humanitarian morality's rights as attended not only by the perfect obligations which attach to them *qua* universal liberty rights (the obligations all moral agents have to refrain from behaviour which illegitimately compromises those rights) but also by *imperfect* obligations of positive assistance whenever the conditions of their enjoyment are not in place. The notion of 'imperfection' here is crucial and we can begin to develop it by considering J.S. Mill's classic definition of imperfect obligations. He says they are 'those in which, though the act is obligatory, the particular occasions of performing it are left to our choice, as in the case of charity or beneficence, which we are indeed bound to practice but not toward any definite person, nor at any prescribed time.'[12] So consider X's right to life, which is at the heart of humanitarian morality: this generates perfect obligations on the part of everyone else not to kill X. Crucially, I propose that it also generates imperfect obligations of assistance if X's life is threatened in certain ways (from genocidal maniacs or famine, say), but *ceteris paribus* their imperfect nature means that they do not fall upon any specific individual or group for their satisfaction.

This association of rights and imperfect obligations is unusual. Mill, for example, writes that 'duties of perfect obligation are those duties in virtue of which a correlative right resides in some person or persons; duties of imperfect obligation are those obligations which do not give birth to any right.'[13] (He goes on to remark that this distinction exactly corresponds to that between 'justice' and the other obligations of morality, which hardly sits well with an attempt to place imperfect obligation at the heart of humanitarian morality.) Onora O'Neill, who has done much in contemporary moral and political theory to revive interest in the concept, says that imperfect obligations 'will belong to identifiable obligation-bearers, but there will be no corresponding rights-holders'.[14]

Clearly, mine is a somewhat unconventional usage of the concept but I contend that it does a better job of encapsulating what is at stake here. Uncoupling 'rights' and 'imperfect obligations' seems to require a particular and contestable understanding of a right as being primarily a claim that can be levied upon *definite* other agents. But our intuitions about the seriousness of humanitarian morality on the one hand and the permissibility of moral selectivity on the other suggest that we should think of such obligations emerging from definite rights - hence addressed to the needs of an identifiable rights-holder - but rendered imperfect (only) due to the inability to locate a corresponding, *designated* obligation bearer. *Qua* obligation, a serious moral deficit is incurred if no one takes it up, which crucially distinguishes such a situation from one of supererogation. Yet still, no one moral agent or group of agents can be held responsible for such a failure (that is what is entailed by the lack of a designated obligation-bearer). Room is thus left for the latitude that moral agents have in responding to the demands of imperfect obligations.

One problem with this approach to selectivity immediately presents itself when we realize that the initial 'something must be done' reaction need not always translate into an '*I* must do something' conviction. For it appears to afford us - by which I mean those who may be in a position to do something about humanitarian injustice - the luxury of 'having our moral cake and eating it too'. We can placate our consciences by calling the demands of the suffering 'obligations' but, by considering them imperfect, effectively absolve ourselves of the responsibility to do anything about them. In failing to meet the requirement of an imperfect obligation, we appear paradoxically to have a moral wrong that wrongs no one, an oddity we would hardly expect in a theory produced through reflective equilibrium.

Another objection seems to bar the integration of this approach into a moral moderate's account of humanitarian morality. There would appear to be a crucial indeterminacy in the notion of discharging limited positive obligations (when one is under a general, limited obligation to do some good but not to maximize one's contribution to the good above all else) if they are deemed to be imperfect. For at what point could one be said to have fulfilled them? Of course, if I do absolutely nothing I am morally culpable in a way that I would not be if there were no such obligations, but what is there to say that I cannot meet the obligation by doing a minuscule amount of good? The contributions of all moral agents could then be so permissibly tiny as to fail lamentably to address the demands caused by humanitarian immorality - and therefore, once again, to fail to do justice to the seriousness with which we think they should be treated.

The moral extremist might here argue that, even though no particular person has a legitimate moral grievance against me if my moral action does not address their demands, it is possible to determine whether I had adequately met the imperfect obligation simply by asking myself 'could I have done more without self-defeatingly crippling my very capacity for moral agency?' Yet if this operationalizes imperfect obligations in a way that moral moderation does not, I suspect we would still demur from saying that extremism grounds an intuitively satisfactory answer to this problem. Even some of its defenders recognize that it may make morality just too demanding in the kind of lives it would be good for us to lead; it is not a moral system we could reasonably be expected to live with.

Now one potential advantage of focusing on the 'humanitarian' subset of morality could be that its requirements - separate from those of morality in general - might be sufficiently satisfiable by a moral moderate to allow an adequate characterization of it to be anyway neutral with respect to the extremism/moderation debate.[15] To be able to leave this particular debate aside here, though, we must answer these objections to moral moderation. We can do so by reconsidering the idea of responsibility entailed by imperfect obligations and by developing further what it means for an obligation to be imperfect.

I suggest that we should think of whatever imperfect obligations are generated when humanitarian morality goes unrespected in terms of a generalized, or universalized, responsibility to be concerned with those members of the human community suffering the worst of plights. We can then say that the responsibility turns into generalized culpability insofar as that community has allowed humanitarian injustice to rise in its midst and, most importantly, go unaddressed.

This proposal can be supported via the strength of the following analogy. Imagine a swimmer in the sea who finds himself in life-threatening difficulties. Ten qualified life-savers are standing on the shore, each of whom is capable of saving the swimmer without endangering their own lives. Only one of them is needed to save the swimmer; indeed, let us imagine that circumstances are such that two or more of them would actually complicate the rescue operation. Yet it so transpires that each of them fails to jump in not only because of some relatively trivial reasons peculiar to each but also because of a tacit assumption that one of the others would do what each would agree ought to be done, and take the plunge. No single one of them has the duty to rescue the swimmer but we can surely say that, despite our inability to blame specific individuals, there is some collective moral failing on their part for their failure to rescue.

Can 'humanity', as analogous by-stander to humanitarian injustice, be nominated as a similar responsibility-bearing moral unit? A compelling affirmative answer is derivable from the idea of 'crimes against *humanity*'. Its meaning is clear: such crimes, deliberate humanitarian injustices, are suffered not only by their direct victims (who, of course, 'suffer' them in the most acute sense) but, in a way, by all of us. The whole human race is wounded, degraded, violated by such acts. In granting this point, it seems natural to insist that it should cut both ways. If 'humanity' is a collective entity against which crimes can be committed, then it can also be a bearer of certain moral responsibilities - not, perhaps, so extensive as to allow us to say that it can commit as well as suffer crimes (although this may be debatable), but enough to deny that it is morally inert and non-responsible. So the proposition is that *some* kind of responsibility falls on *all* our shoulders as a result of humanitarian imperfect obligations and hence *something* has gone wrong in a way that redounds negatively upon us all if they go undischarged. This gives content to the idea of universal moral concern that the oft-cited concept of 'world citizenship' tries to capture.

As individuals, we all share in humanity's responsibilities when humanitarian injustice arises and, if we now agree that the latter in itself does not specify precisely who should respond and how, I think perhaps it should nevertheless prick all our moral consciences in a way that a supererogatory characterization of humanitarianism would not. The response I have in mind may be similar to Karl Jaspers' notion of moral guilt, which he posited in 1947 as one element of the appropriate attitude he believed individual Germans should adopt with respect to the Nazism that arose in their midst. He wrote,

> [E]ach one of us is guilty insofar as he remained inactive ... [p]assivity knows itself morally guilty of every failure, every neglect to act whenever possible, to shield the imperilled, to relieve wrong, to countervail. Impotent submission always left a margin of activity which, though not without risk, could still be cautiously effective ... Blindness for the misfortune of others, lack of imagination of the heart, inner indifference towards the witnessed evil - that is moral guilt.[16]

For whatever reason we might be unable - or we might regard ourselves as unable - to do much when others suffer, but we should still be aware that there are high costs arising from our inactivity, our moral omissions, and that morality does not turn a blind eye and fail to count them against us.

This sensibility is heightened when we confront what Jaspers called metaphysical guilt:

> There exists a solidarity among men as human beings that makes each co-responsible for every wrong and every injustice in the world, especially for crimes committed in his presence or in his knowledge. If I fail to do whatever I can to prevent them, I too am guilty. If I was present at the murder of others without risking my life to prevent it, I feel guilty in a way not adequately conceivable ... That I live after such a thing has happened weighs upon me as indelible guilt.[17]

If some of this might seem a little melodramatic, it nevertheless helps to capture the core thought that humanitarian immorality besmirches the very heart of human being on this earth; if we are to accord its due weight, we must think of it as touching us all in some way that we should not ignore.

But can such attribution of guilt or, perhaps more appropriately, responsibility really be warranted if moral selectivity is unavoidable? Is not the point of the selectivity/imperfect-obligation thesis that none of us could be guilty of all such omissions, as Jaspers proposes, and that therefore no sensible responsibility for them can be attributed to us? Jaspers' emphasis on 'co-responsibility', however, returns us to the 'collective' idea. *Individuals* may not be blameable for not themselves, as individuals, acting to save a life. But together they must take responsibility for living in a world where some urgent moral demand which could have been met was nevertheless allowed to go unmet. *That* is what should trouble them.

At this point, we are now in a position to cash out in full the notion of 'imperfection'. Obligations need institutionalization, just as much as rights do, in order to be operationalized. If this institutionalization is lacking or incomplete, the specific responsibilities for discharging obligations cannot be definitively allocated. Yet we should say not that there are no obligations in such instances but that they have been rendered *imperfect*: the lack of proper institutionalization to identify definite obligation-holders, and not necessarily that of identifiable correlative rights-holders, is the imperfection's source.[18]

So my claim is that humanitarian morality's import is best thought of thus: failures positively to confront violations of humanitarian morality which could be prevented/ameliorated/punished are matters of collective responsibility insofar as the community of human beings has failed to develop the means to convert imperfect obligations into perfect obligations. That is the responsibility in which we all, as human beings, collectively share and which the fact of individual moral selectivity allowable in such a morally sub-optimal world does not wholly excuse. Therefore, a significant difference between the imperfectly obligatory and the supererogatory is that specific moral omissions by any one moral agent may be justifiable as examples of selectivity but still constitute overwhelming reasons to be profoundly critical of, rather than apologetic for or indifferent to, the social and institutional *status quo*.

So selectivity in the midst of humanitarian imperfect obligations signals a case for reconfiguring the world order such that moral responsibilities can be clearly and justly allocated. This exposes a crucial ambiguity in the familiar adage that 'ought implies can'. Some might be tempted to say that, if we cannot reasonably expect all humanitarian demands to be addressed under the present institutions' division of moral labour, the 'ought implies can' principle must challenge the idea that 'we', collectively, ought nevertheless to bear responsibility for such failings. However, no institutional arrangement is the product of anything other than human beings' conscious construction and these *could* be configured differently. We should not allow our estimation of moral possibilities to be illegitimately constrained by the contingencies of the social relationships and understandings through which moral life is conducted. Even to the extent that we cannot now address all of humanitarian morality's demands, there is no reason to reject the idea that we could do so if only we restructured the way in which we lead our moral lives. 'Ought implies *could*' is thus a much better watchword, avoiding any legitimation of moral omissions by the present contingent, changeable institutions.

Making Imperfect Obligations Perfect: Towards a Restructuring of the Global Order

If we are morally obligated not to rest content with the present world institutional order, we must press the questions of what is to be done, and who should do it. These are difficult; the argument of the last section, though it may have something significant to say about what *attitudes* on our part are appropriate, may still look disappointingly thin in terms of practical guidance. We have theorized a general responsibility to try to promote the kind of understandings, practices and structures that would help us convert imperfect into perfect obligations. But in our morally imperfect condition even a responsive moral conscience will find itself somewhat at sea in working out what exactly follows from this recognition, and hence acutely vulnerable to an enervating sense of moral impotence.

Regrettably, we must expect a degree of moral confusion in such circumstances. Where possible (and we may have no determinate way of identifying even where the possibility of positive moral action begins for any agent), perhaps we can say that everyone should do something - *complete* indifference, we can judge, is *ceteris paribus* not morally acceptable.[19] Beyond that: some may devote time and resources directly to the alleviation of humanitarian injustice, others will protest that others are not doing so and/or are acting hypocritically and cynically, and yet others will ruminate on the issues involved in their living rooms, bars and seminars, all in the name of consciousness-raising. And many in particularly difficult personal circumstances may legitimately be excused if they are unable to take up the responsibility thus (it would be ridiculous to think that the poor or the ill to should engage in humanitarian activity to the same degree as the millionaire company director, if at all).

Some might argue that individuals should be absolved of any such attribution of this hazy overall responsibility insofar as truly effective humanitarian moral action clearly requires collective action on an extremely large scale. Yet collective bodies are ultimately comprised of individuals who find they need to be organized together to pursue certain goals, so it would surely be self-defeating to argue that a collectively shouldered responsibility need not impact upon individuals at all.

Individuals can and of course do take the initiative to act upon such responsibility in direct and less-than-direct ways; the recent 'globalize resistance' campaigns amply demonstrate this. If we are tempted to think that engagement with the responsibility is possible only for those 'with the time on their hands' (young, unemployed, no family commitments and so on), then we would do well to reflect upon events such as the UK's fuel tax protests of September 2000, when large majorities of people were happy to support oil blockades that caused serious disruption to their own lives. These show how apposite and actually rather familiar it can be to attribute to individuals significant ability to change their lives for some cause: if they can raise themselves for such purposes to protest against their government, even at the cost of some hardship to themselves, it shows that they *could* do likewise for other, perhaps more altruistic purposes.

To the reply that 'it is impossible to expect people to change their behaviour to fulfil morality's particular demands', it should be stressed that there is in general no question of *physical* impossibility in achieving such a change. The 'impossibility' lies in what is often an incredibly profound reluctance to change thus, and we must admit this is reinforced by the way lives are typically socially structured - but to transform even all this does not require laws of physics to be broken. Overcoming such reluctance is physically and probably psychologically *possible* and that is what makes it valid to criticize people's acts and omissions, and hence to talk of their moral responsibilities to act in different ways should they be failing to live as morality requires.

Still, I think it acceptable to say that the onus of moral responsibility falls on the shoulders of larger bodies; as a rule of thumb in these imperfect conditions, it is reasonable to demand that more be done the more an agency has the resources to do so. In this realm especially, we may not actually be totally rudderless at present. Even where institutionalization has not fully perfected them, we might already identify some pattern of (virtually) perfected obligations in the institutions and relationships we have. Deferring to the state might seem to be an obvious strategy we can adopt to overcome the limitations of individual moral agency, accepting its authority to concretize, codify and organize the discharge of responsibilities. It decides how much we should give, in our taxes, and to whom this wealth should be directed. Clearly, some states are more powerful than others and hence better equipped to bear humanitarian responsibilities and some, such as the US, are clearly capable in many instances of acting alone. But humanitarian concerns may best be addressed when states act in concert, not least to help undermine doubts that individual states are seeking selfish advantage in unilateral action.

For the various non-governmental organizations, often deliberately constituted to respond to humanitarian injustices, there is no good reason to believe that they will not play a significant role in the more ideal world order being envisaged here. But they lack the military force and the overall coordination typically needed for successful humanitarian interventions, which is sometimes also required to support or protect the provision of humanitarian aid. Given the moral division of labour between the NGOs, coordination may also be missing for comprehensive provision of humanitarian aid. NGOs are thus unlikely to be decisive in the process of converting imperfect into perfect obligations.

More generally, states, regional alliances and NGOs alone may not be able to overcome the lack of authoritative institutionalization which threatens to leave some humanitarian injustices unaddressed. Much must surely depend upon legitimated international organizations such as the United Nations which might, with sufficient institutional reform, coordinate global humanitarian action and correct any 'market failings' which arise from the actions of less-than-global moral agencies.

So the logic of this argument certainly suggests that what is needed is something akin to a 'world authority' with the power to require action and enforce compliance. But the responsibilities of any global authority charged with meeting or coordinating humanitarian obligations could fall far short of those much more extensive functions which a nation state ideally discharges with respect to its citizens at present. Whatever reservations may be entertained about the moral adequacy of the 'night-watchman' nation state may not be as pertinent at the global level; its tasks are the most urgent that humanity faces, but they may be relatively few in number. This may be just as well: Kant's worries about a full-blown world state are clearly apposite,[20] and perhaps it would be to indulge our utopianism a little too much to think that we could live in a world where the Westphalian inheritance had been transcended altogether.

Lack of space must curtail further elaboration of these ideas but it is worth concluding by rebutting one fear that might be entertained about the project initiated here, which is that philosophy has all too little to contribute to the quest for a more just world. For appropriate humility in what philosophy can hope to achieve must not become excessive modesty. Philosophy has here been used to refine and balance some profound but often ill-defined and conflicting intuitions about humanitarian morality. Of course it cannot change our world alone, but it can help to shift the mindsets that constitute such barriers to the changes morality requires by showing us how our present thinking might best be expressed and developed. We should neither underestimate the difficulties of overcoming the obstacles to the project nor overestimate the prospects of even a much improved moral order ever being capable of living up comprehensively and continuously to its ideals ('perfected obligations' do not themselves mean a 'perfected reality'). But these cautionary notes should not deter us from ever undertaking the project - and we have already significantly advanced it once we have grasped how we might begin to orient the most fundamental elements of our moral thinking in this, our own distinctly imperfect moral world.[21]

Notes

1   See D. Johnstone, 'Humanitarian War: Making the Crime Fit the Punishment', in T. Ali (ed.) *Masters of the Universe: Nato's Balkan Crusade* (London: Verso, 2000), pp.147-170, esp. pp.155-156.

2   Tariq Ali argues that, precisely because of its inattention to moral considerations, non-morally motivated action is much more likely to generate significant moral costs. These could, of course, outweigh whatever moral case for the action in question may be available. See 'Our Herods' in *New Left Review* 2 no.5 pp.5-14, at p.12.

3   I wish in particular to stress that my argument does not necessarily and is not intended to vindicate the shocking abnegation of responsibility by the United Nations and others in the 1994 Rwandan genocide. For a scrupulously documented indictment of the

international community's behaviour, see Linda Melvern, *A People Betrayed* (London: Zed Books, 2000).

4   The cultural specificity of a 'right to paid holidays' must, of course, challenge its status as a genuinely 'human' right, but the example serves well enough to indicate the general claim that some such rights are clearly much more universally significant than others.

5   What I call 'sovereignty-trumping' is a manifestation of the extreme moral weight definitive of humanitarian morality, though it is not criterial: humanitarian acts can, of course, be invited by the states in question.

6   Bhikhu Parekh, 'Rethinking Humanitarian Intervention', in *International Journal of Political Science* 18 (1), pp.49-69, at p.54.

7   'Humanitarian morality' may well be coextensive with the 'universal minimum morality' theorized by authors such as H.L.A. Hart and Isaiah Berlin. The 'universality' lies first and foremost in its intended domain: those who affirm it believe it applies to all human beings. This belief does not necessarily commit one to believing that all other human beings do or even could agree with and embrace it. However, for those who adopt the heavily influential but highly demanding requirement of 'public justification', this may problematize the belief – but that is an issue left aside here.

8   Parekh, op. cit., esp. pp.63-68.

9   Shelly Kagan, *The Limits of Morality* (Oxford: Clarendon, 1989), esp. pp.1-2.

10 Ibid., pp.2-5.

11 I leave aside here social-scientific considerations concerning the appropriateness or accuracy of conceptualizing these collective bodies as genuinely unified, rather than being typically fragmented in their interests, coordination and so on. All that concerns us here is that they act as if they are unified, in their singular pursuit of (moral) goals.

12 J.S. Mill, 'Utilitarianism', in *Utilitarianism, On Liberty and Considerations on Representative Government* (London: Dent, 1972), pp.1-67, at p.51.

13 Ibid., p.51.

14 Onora O'Neill, *Towards Justice and Virtue* (Cambridge: Cambridge University Press, 1996), p.147.

15 Obviously, this hope rests upon certain assumptions about what would be necessary from us to meet humanitarian morality's demands, an empirical question that might well settle this particular dispute aside from any further philosophical considerations.

16 Karl Jaspers, *The Question of German Guilt* (New York: Dial Press, 1947), pp.69-70.

17 Ibid., p.32.

18 As Bruce Haddock has pointed out to me, the classical idea of 'imperfect' obligation did not imply that they were 'flawed' in this or any other way. I accept this in its earlier usage, but the present argument is intended as a reconfiguration of the concept, one which exploits it rather more fruitfully (and mine is, I think, hardly a forced reading of 'imperfection').

19 The *ceteris paribus* condition is, it must be stressed, much more than notional, for many individuals will surely have good reason to be excused any lack of concern for this generalized responsibility - not least those suffering humanitarian injustice themselves, who are in no position to be expected to reflect upon the issues in the fashion sketched here.

20 See his 'Perpetual Peace: A Philosophical Sketch' in H. Reiss ed., *Kant: Political Writings* (Cambridge: Cambridge University Press, 1991), pp.93-130, at p.113.

21 I would like to thank Bruce Haddock and participants in the Swansea Politics Department's political theory seminars for inspirational criticism of the arguments presented here, Patrick Hayden for detailed commentary on an earlier draft and

enthusiastic support for the larger project of which this is part, and Anne Evans for careful reading of the final draft. I am particularly grateful to the organizers and participants at the Society of Applied Philosophy's 2001 conference, where this chapter received its first public airing and critique.

PART IV
NATIONAL SOVEREIGNTY
AND THE LEGITIMACY OF
INTERVENTION

Chapter 8

Humanitarian Intervention and International Political Theory

Chris Brown

Humanitarian intervention is an important topic, too important to be left to political scientists and diplomats; the kind of questions it raises about the obligations we have to a wider humanity are precisely questions of applied philosophy, and it is good that applied philosophers are increasingly interested in them. It is, however, important that this interest should be based on an understanding of the international political theory of intervention under both the so-called 'Westphalia' system and the currently-emerging post-Westphalia system.[1] The usual account of intervention and the Westphalia order identifies strict rules of non-intervention and respect for the rights of sovereigns: these rules de-legitimate humanitarian actions. Since 1945, it is held, Westphalian norms have been in conflict with an alternative set of rules, the modern international human rights regime, which purport to oversee the way in which states exercise their domestic jurisdiction, and which make possible legitimate external intervention on humanitarian grounds. The argument presented here will be that while some parts of this story are accurate enough the overall picture is misleading. The Westphalia order was actually characterized by interventions of all shapes and kinds, and 1945 was significant for two reasons not one; it certainly instituted a set of new human rights but it also, *for the first time* introduced a strict norm of non-intervention - in other words both human rights and non-intervention are substantially new ideas, and it is a mistake to regard one as representing an old order displaced by the other. After presenting this argument, the putatively-humanitarian interventions of the 1990s will be discussed.

Part of the argument here posits that there is no clear-cut divide between 'humanitarian' and other kinds of intervention. The general idea behind the category of humanitarian intervention is that it represents intervention in the affairs of another state in the interests of its inhabitants, and this is seen as in sharp contrast with other kinds of intervention which are more selfishly motivated. This is misleading for two reasons - it rests on a tendentious account of foreign policy behaviour and is too much oriented towards questions of motive. Humanitarian intervention is generally seen as a non-realist, even anti-realist, notion, but the idea that there is, or might be, a separate category of state behaviour that can be characterized as 'humanitarian' owes its existence to the very *dominance* of realist assumptions about international behaviour.[2] According to realists, states are rational egoists who act in pursuit of their material interests; it follows that when they do something that, on the face of it, seems *not* to be egoistic and *not* to relate to a material interest, some kind of special explanation is required. Realists believe that this only rarely happens, and that behaviour that seems not to be self-seeking usually will turn out to be so once closely inspected, but, on the rare occasions when this turns out not to be the case, a term such as 'humanitarian' is required to mark the fact that something unusual and extraordinary is going on.

The problem with this position is clear; even those who wish to argue for a predominantly materialist understanding of the taproots of state behaviour can hardly deny that material interests need to be conceptualized before they can influence policy, and, in any event, a more ideational account of interests seems inherently more plausible than a purely materialist notion. This is the burden of the constructivist turn in international relations theory, but is also reflected in mainstream thinking.[3] If, however, we assume that foreign policy behaviour is at least in part ideas-driven - that is to say, using older language, if we assume that through their foreign policy states desire to project their sense of themselves on to the world stage - then the necessity for a separate category of specifically humanitarian action becomes much less clear.

Further, the emphasis realists place on motivation is a little puzzling; it is, apparently, a widely-held assumption that for an action to count as humanitarian it must be motivated unambiguously by altruism. But, although we might be unwilling to describe as humanitarian an intervention that was wholly motivated by non-humanitarian motives and whose humanitarian results were solely a by-product of less noble impulses, it seems unnecessary to demand that action be entirely motivated by humanitarianism in order for it to count as humanitarian, especially since in this, as in other areas of human endeavour, motives are almost always mixed. The word 'count' here is important - one of the reasons for an emphasis on motive is a desire to assign praise and blame, and underlying this is the medieval notion of 'right intention' which was important in determining what effect the use of force by particular actors would have on their immortal souls. This is all very well, but the beneficiaries of putatively humanitarian action are less likely to be impressed by such a exclusive concern for the moral well-being of the actor. It would seem, on the face of it, that a concern for effects is at least as justified as a concern with motive, although it is clearly important that the motives of state behaviour should not actually undermine humanitarian efforts.[4] This is not an abstract point because in the history of the Westphalia system it has frequently been the case that more or less unambiguously humanitarian effects have followed from action motivated by very un-humanitarian concerns. Moreover, when humanitarian motives have actually been present they have frequently been accompanied by ethnocentric, racist assumptions.

Humanitarian Intervention and the Westphalia System

Martin Wight, one of the leading theorists of international society, argues that the norm of non-intervention is basic to the Westphalian order, but that consistent with 'Western Values in International Relations' this norm may be breached in response to 'gross violations of human dignity'.[5] Sovereignty is the norm but there are some (extreme) circumstances in which this norm may, legitimately, be broken. The historical record supports this proposition but only with two important qualifications - first, Wight does not distinguish sufficiently between relations among the core members of the system and their relations with others, while, second, it is by no means clear that notions of 'human dignity' have remained constant throughout the last four hundred years.

In an influential essay, Martha Finnemore has described the ways in which a norm of humanitarian intervention has been constructed over the last two centuries.[6] Her argument is that this period has seen a change in terms of who is considered to be 'human'; in the nineteenth century humanitarian interventions were carried out by the Western powers in order primarily to rescue Christian communities under threat from non-Christian rulers - for example, Greece in the 1820s, the Maronite Christians of Lebanon in 1862/3. The, often more outrageous, oppression of non-European, non-Christian communities attracted much less attention, especially, of course, when actually conducted by Europeans. She argues that this situation has changed in the late twentieth century - the category of 'human' is now genuinely universal, and the interventions of this period have been less overtly ethnocentric, although it should be noted that those states with the power to intervene are still disproportionately of European origin and still inclined to regard the oppression of fellow Europeans more seriously than that of non-Europeans. Finnemore's work represents a genuine advance on that of Wight, but does not quite capture the ambiguities in the way in which ideas of race and empire worked for the expansionist powers of the Westphalia system, in particular, the way in which ideas of racial inferiority and superiority actually proved compatible with some kinds of humanitarian concern for the welfare of the so-called 'lesser' races. Moreover, stress on the notion of human dignity understates the extent to which interventions explicitly designed to serve the selfish interests of the imperial powers could have beneficial results. Two examples will serve to illustrate these points.

In the first half of the nineteenth century, the British Government led a determined effort, spearheaded by the Royal Navy, to end the slave trade. This campaign is usually characterized as either unqualifiedly humanitarian, or as an attempt to undermine Britain's competitors who were still reliant on slave labour. Recent work by Chaim Kaufman and Robert Pape undermines both of these stereotypes.[7] They demonstrate that this was genuinely costly action, a yearly average net cost of 1.78% of the national product; even as a ballpark figure this is far higher, for example, than current aid budgets. Perhaps more interestingly, they argue that the campaign was adopted as a response to developments in British internal politics, and in particular the need on the part of the governing elite to generate support for the political order from increasingly important low-church and non-conformist sections of the community. The latter took the issue of slavery very seriously, not because of any great affection for the slaves, much less because of beliefs in racial equality, but rather because they held that to own and trade in another human being - even an 'inferior' - was inherently wrong, and would lead to divine punishment. To be against the slave-trade was quite compatible with racist and imperialist allegiances and a selfish concern for British interests, although the latter were not defined in the materialist way favoured by realists. At the same time, it would be difficult to argue that the suppression of the slave trade - and the later campaign against slavery more generally - was *not* a humanitarian action. It is only an excessive concern for motivation that could lead to this conclusion.

The second case is the issue of the so-called standards of 'civilization' whereby the European powers imposed restrictions upon the sovereignty of 'uncivilized' non-European powers whose legal codes and general conduct of affairs did not meet European standards; in such case a 'regime of capitulations' was established and countries such as China and Japan were coerced into surrendering their jurisdiction over Europeans in their territory.[8] The idea here is clear - full members of international society are entitled to exercise general jurisdiction because they have 'proper' legal systems; foreigners are entitled to call upon consular assistance to ensure fair play, but that is all they are entitled to specifically as foreigners. However, European traders, missionaries and travellers in countries which do not have proper legal systems cannot be expected to put up with being treated the same way as the natives; European (including American) power was employed to ensure that this was not the case by establishing special courts and extra-territorial jurisdiction for cases involving foreigners (either as plaintiffs or defendants).

These arrangements were unambiguously racist, and deeply offensive to peoples every bit as entitled to be considered as civilized as the Europeans who plundered their wealth, sold them opium and wantonly destroyed their cultural artefacts. On the other hand, by obliging the Chinese and the Japanese to adopt legal codes in which the arbitrary power of the ruling elites - including sometimes the right to dispense summary capital punishment at will - were curbed, it could well be argued that the results of this policy were highly beneficial for the ordinary people of the countries concerned. Such was certainly not the primary motivation for the establishment of the policy, but, whatever the motivation, the effect was largely humanitarian. It is sometimes suggested that the international human rights regime of the twenty-first century involves the re-creation of the 'standards of civilization' under new clothing. If so, this need only be considered wholly undesirable if motivation is taken to be the most important defining characteristic of humanitarian action.

Similar considerations apply to imperialism more generally. For the most part imperialism was certainly motivated by the desire to exploit colonies economically, and where this was not the case the search for prestige was central; it was equally true that racial theories provided a context for European imperialism. Moreover, these propositions remained true even when the Europeans themselves came to employ language which suggested that they were ruling on behalf of the 'natives'. Nonetheless, even taking these points on board, it is still possible to argue that in some, perhaps many, cases imperialism had humanitarian *effects* - although the importance of the mental scars left by imperialism and racism should not be underestimated.

Pulling these points together, throughout the Westphalian period at least two sets of norms concerning intervention were in place. Amongst the full members of international society, the norm was non-intervention and although interventions often took place they were rarely humanitarian in either motive or effect. On the other hand, in their relations with peoples not deemed members of international society, that is - prior to the admission of the Ottoman Empire to this status in 1856 - non-European peoples, no such norm of non-intervention was held to apply.   States considered themselves free to intervene in the affairs of the non-European world whenever it was in their interests to do so, and whenever the local balance of forces allowed them the option.   Such interventions were only rarely motivated by explicitly humanitarian concerns, but, quite frequently, they may well have had humanitarian effects.   Such was the situation in the closing years of the nineteenth century.   The story of the first half of the twentieth century is that of these two sets of norms gradually converging.

The Emergence of a Strong Norm of Non-Intervention

In the late nineteenth and early twentieth century, the rhetoric of European imperialism underwent a change, with increasing emphasis on the idea that imperial rule was undertaken in the interests of the inhabitants of the colonies.   The very high-profile campaign against the savage rule of King Leopold of the Belgians in the so-called Congo Free State was a symptom of this shift.[9] The legitimacy of imperialism as such was not challenged by this campaign - indeed the campaigners often explicitly referred to the allegedly enlightened nature of British rule in Africa in order to make a contrast with the slavery and mutilation associated with Leopold's greed - but the traditional justifications of imperialism were.   The idea that colonies were held in trust for their inhabitants was given a boost by the adoption in 1919 of a system of Mandates held under the League of Nations as a way of disposing of former German colonies.

The Mandate system was not extended to existing colonies - and in a more explicit endorsement of the double standard, the Versailles Conference rejected a Japanese proposal to condemn racial discrimination - but even so the new system had unforeseen long term consequences.   All Mandates were expected *eventually* to qualify for self-government, quite quickly in the case of Class 'A' and 'B' Mandates, in the longest of long runs in the case of the, predominantly African, Class 'C' Mandates.   This almost certainly had some effect in terms of changing the prevailing sentiments about colonies and it is interesting that, more or less simultaneously, the British declared, in a radical change of tack, that the ultimate intention was that India should become an independent member of the British Commonwealth, with a similar status to Canada and Australia (which after the Westminster Conference of 1931 equated in effect to full independence).   As Robert Jackson has emphasized in a classic study, it was not anticipated that any colony would achieve independence before it reached a level of economic development and administrative competence that would allow it to exercise effective self-rule and qualify it for membership of international society, and, in many cases, the date at which such an achievement would be realistic was assumed to be many years in the future.[10] This latter assumption was made by figures on the left as well as by apologists for imperialism. After the independence of India in 1947, the post-war Labour Government in Britain set up a commission on the future of the colonies which recommended that her African colonies be also prepared for self-government; it assumed that the more advanced of them would be ready for self-rule by the end of the twentieth century.

By then, of course, the general situation had changed quite radically. The terms under which the Second World War was fought did much to undermine racial ideologies, and to promote a strong norm of self-determination; such a norm was built into the UN system, and the Trusteeship Council that took over the Mandates of the League pushed much more enthusiastically for the independence of colonies. The outcome of the war was to weaken the traditional European Empires - British, French and Dutch - while strengthening the position in world affairs of the Soviet Union and the United States, both of whom claimed to be anti-imperialist. The Dutch were not in a position to retain control of the East Indies, French efforts to remain in Indochina failed, and once Britain's Indian Empire disappeared, the economic rationale of her African colonies more or less disappeared with it. Within less than a generation, the only remains of the colonial empires - apart from a scattering of small islands - were those colonies where a large European population had settled and was unwilling to give up its privileges without a fight (as in Algeria, Rhodesia, and South Africa) along with those colonies maintained as status symbols by the authoritarian regimes of Spain and Portugal until the 1970s.

The result of these shifts was the establishment for the first time in four hundred years of an international system with a single norm concerning non-intervention - the old rules that applied only to fellow members of the European states-system now applied universally. The human rights norms contained in the UN Charter and the *Universal Declaration on Human Rights* in 1948 were always qualified as not interfering with the legitimate exercise of state sovereignty, and the norm of self-determination was now applied more or less irrespective of the capacity for self-government of the collectivity in question. The Cold War saw a great many interventions driven by the desire to maintain the boundaries of the two camps but these interventions were almost always described as counter-interventions to exclude the opposing ideology/superpower. Neither side in the Cold War claimed a right to intervene on humanitarian grounds; each explicitly endorsed the notion of non-intervention as a concomitant of self-determination, however much they might both break such a norm in practice.

Non-intervention became the norm of a single international society - but with a high price tag attached. The first of the major crises in former colonies came with the descent of the former Belgian Congo into anarchy in 1960, immediately after the independence for which it was manifestly unprepared. A UN army was despatched with no clear mandate, and became involved in the military politics of the Congo, eventually being used to end a secession in Katanga; the UN Secretary-General died in a plane crash while visiting the operation - probably as a murder victim - and, generally, the experience of trying to be helpful in this difficult case was so awful that UN forces were not used in such a role for a generation thereafter.[11] The Nigerian Civil War of 1967-70 also provided pointers for the future. There was no question here of direct foreign intervention; the international aid agencies (governmental and non-governmental) provided assistance to both sides until the Spring of 1968, when the Federal authorities forbad assistance to the rebels. The official agencies, including the International Committee of the Red Cross (ICRC) withdrew, but the unofficial agencies led by Oxfam continued with an airlift to Biafra, the result of which was to prolong the war by perhaps a year, with an additional 200,000 deaths - the fear had been that defeat of the Biafrans would result in genocide, which proved, in fact, not to be the case.

The experience of the Nigerian Civil War was instructive in a number of ways. This was a humanitarian intervention but by non-state actors. The British aid agencies came away from Biafra in penitent mood, their own investigations having confirmed that their intervention had actually prolonged the war to no good purpose. They resolved that in future they would adhere strictly to the non-intervention norm, acting in future humanitarian disasters with the official agencies and with the approval of the state in question. Others took a different view; a group of French doctors left the ICRC over its decision to suspend aid to Biafra and formed *Médecins sans Frontières* (MsF) under the leadership of the charismatic and controversial Bernard Kouchner, who was later to break away from MsF to form yet another group, and, later still, to be a minister in various French Socialist Governments and, in 1999-2000, the head of the civilian administration in Kosovo. Kouchner articulated the doctrine, taken up more widely in France, of '*le droit d'ingérence*' - a phrase that could be translated as a 'right to interfere' or a 'law of intervention' - which asserts that in cases where there are violations of human rights, the international community has the right to act, the terminology used implying, albeit ambiguously, that this is a *legal* right.[12] This doctrine, little known in the English-speaking world, has had considerable impact in France, especially when Kouchner's star has been in the ascendant, and also where French is spoken; this latter point became of some significance when the Francophone Egyptian Foreign Minister Boutros Boutros-Ghali became UN Secretary General in the late 1980s.

For most of the 1970s and 1980s the doctrine of non-intervention reigned supreme. Nicholas Wheeler has shown in detail that on three occasions in the 1970s - India's war with Pakistan as a result of the West Bengal crisis of 1971, Vietnam's overthrow of the Pol Pot regime in Cambodia in 1979, and Tanzania's overthrow of Idi Amin in Uganda, also in 1979 - when states might plausibly have claimed justification on humanitarian grounds they did not do so, preferring to cite as prime justification for their action a threat to 'international peace and security'.[13] To these examples one might add the US intervention in Grenada against the murderers of the elected Prime Minister of that country, which was justified in terms of counter-intervention (against Cuban engineers) and the rescue of US citizens, but, judging by the positive reactions of the Grenadines, could equally well have been seen as a humanitarian act. Still, by the end of the 1980s some movement was visible in international law; the use of force to protect aid workers gradually came to be seen as legitimate, and in 1988 UN General Assembly Resolution 43/131 summarized the new understanding by simultaneously restating the doctrine of non-intervention, but legitimating humanitarian action in rebel held areas, which had been a key issue in the Nigerian Civil War, twenty years earlier.

Thus, the stage was set for the dramatic developments of the 1990s, and the re-emergence, under radically different conditions, of the occasional willingness of the international community to intervene on humanitarian grounds. This is a re-emergence because the idea of a strict norm of non-intervention *applied on equal terms to all members of international society* was itself of comparatively recent origin. This re-emergence was partly a function of contingent factors, but the ending of the Cold War was a necessary, if not a sufficient, condition for its occurrence. Given the reluctance that, in any event, many states have shown to acknowledge that there has been any change in this area, it is clear that without the ending of East-West conflict no such development would have been possible. For the first time in decades, in the 1990s the major powers were faced with situations where it was actually possible to respond positively to calls for humanitarian action. These cases provide ample material for an examination of developments in the international political theory of humanitarian intervention in the 1990s.[14]

Reflections on Humanitarian Intervention in the 1990s

The decade began and ended with interventions that were justified on humanitarian grounds. UN Security Council Resolutions 688 (1991), concerning 'safe areas' in Northern Iraq, and 794 (1992), explicitly authorizing the use of force on humanitarian grounds in Somalia, were genuinely innovatory. However, the lack of success of the interventions of 1991-93 in Iraq and Somalia led directly to an unwillingness to act in response to genocide in Rwanda in 1994, while the response to atrocities in former Yugoslavia in the early 1990s was almost equally tepid.[15] Partly in response to a sense of guilt over the consequences of inaction, the end of the decade saw a return to a more active stance in Kosovo and East Timor in 1999, although, in the former case, NATO acted without the sanction of a UN Security Council Resolution.[16] The ambiguous results of these latter interventions suggest that this action-reaction cycle may continue into the 2000s.

What can be said in general terms about this experience? There are a number of propositions that can be asserted dogmatically; all interventions involve *the exercise of power*; all involve, in one way or another, *taking sides in local political conflicts*, and the *motives for all interventions are mixed*. On a number of occasions in the 1990s, the UN or other groups of states have attempted to disprove these propositions, but in the event, merely demonstrated their force. Other issues are more complex; what kind of *international authorization* is required for a legitimate humanitarian intervention? Do humanitarian interventions usually, or perhaps ever, actually make a positive contribution to the relief of suffering?

Interventions involve the exercise of power, but in both Somalia and Bosnia the attempt was made to avoid the implications of this proposition by intervening with forces mainly, or at least significantly, drawn from countries without a tradition of exercising extensive political power and employing troops who were in no sense elite fighting forces - this was very much in the tradition of UN peacekeeping over past decades. In Somalia the initial commitment in 1992 ('UNOSOM I') involved Pakistani peacekeepers, and again in 1993 ('UNOSOM II') Pakistani, Bengali, Malaysian and other Muslim troops were placed in key roles, as an explicit decision to replace the US troops who made up the bulk of the 'tactical force' ('UNITAF') sent in in December 1992. It was thought that the

Somalis would find it easier to relate to fellow Muslims, a rather orientalist assumption that proved inaccurate. 'Peacemaking' is different from 'peacekeeping'. These troops were largely outgunned by the forces of the Somali clan leaders and, without the superior fire-power of the US, control on the ground could not be established. The situation was very unlike that of, say, UN forces in Cyprus, where the capacity of the UN to police the 'Green Line' between the two communities rests on the consent of the communities, and the moral force of the UN uniform. In Somalia the communities had not given their consent to be policed, and showed no respect for the blue helmets of the UN, as the Pakistanis found out to their cost in June 1993. Thereafter the superior fire-power of US Rangers and Delta-Force commandos was brought to bear, but the relatively small size of the US contingent ensured that they became simply one more participant in a local power struggle; this was as opposed to the overwhelming American strength earlier in the year, during the UNITAF period, which created a window of opportunity when intervention could have been successful and the clan armies largely disarmed.

In Bosnia, the use of troops from a large number of countries, many of whom had very little experience of the conditions they would face, was also the product of a deliberate desire for the intervention not to be seen as the exercise of brute force. The intention was that these forces would be involved in humanitarian activities and therefore would not need to overwhelm the forces with which they would have to deal - they would act neutrally and therefore would be treated as neutrals, and in such circumstances reliance on combat-hardened soldiers would be unnecessary, indeed quite possibly counter-productive. In the event, what transpired demonstrated both that the idea of a neutral intervention is a chimera, and that, when neutrality is not respected, there is no substitute for fighting spirit. If privation of civilians is being used as a weapon of war, as was the case here, to provide humanitarian aid will be seen as a political intervention whether the interveners want it to be seen in this way or not. And, even when the policy appears neutral, a degree of strength on the part of the interveners may be necessary.

The fate of the 'safe areas' for government-supporting Bosnians is exemplary; the troops that were supposed to be protecting the safe areas had neither the numbers nor the will either to prevent those inside from using them as bases to attack the Serbs, or to prevent the latter from overwhelming them and committing atrocities. The Dutch battalion at Srebrenica were badly let down by their superiors, but their own lack of willingness to assert themselves as soldiers certainly contributed to the atrocity that took place in this unsafest of safe areas. It is not too fanciful to suggest that a battalion of French Legionnaires or British Paratroopers might have been rather more willing to find out whether the Serbs were actually prepared to fight OSCE/UN troops; at the very least they might have been less willing to hand over their equipment undamaged to the Serbs - the use by the latter of UN uniforms and vehicles to lure their victims from hiding was particularly humiliating for the peacekeepers. It is also difficult to imagine a Legion commander allowing himself to be filmed by Serb TV accepting a bottle of wine and flowers for his wife from a Serb commander who has just murdered between 5 and 10,000 unarmed prisoners, a fate that befell the hapless Dutch commander.

In short, effective humanitarian intervention is an act of power; it involves taking sides, choosing which of the various parties to support and enforcing one's choice by superior strength. This may not be a pleasant sight - to be blunt, the aim must be to bully the bully; the behaviour of the successful intervener may not be particularly attractive, and may indeed involve temporarily contributing to humanitarian distress. This will appear particularly unpleasant because the motives for intervention are unlikely to be purely altruistic. Critics such as the journalist John Pilger have made a point of stressing this absence of purity, to the point of denying that there are any occasions when action has taken place for unselfish non-materialistic reasons, a good example of this approach being his condemnation of the intervention in East Timor as designed to preserve the territory for global capitalism.[17] Apparently the local inhabitants would disagree and this is a particularly absurd exaggeration, but the general point has some force. Even if the war in Kosovo was not part of some implausible master plan for the US to control the Eurasian continent, it certainly was fought partly in order to preserve NATO's credibility, and while no material interest lay behind the US intervention in Somalia, the desire on the part of the defeated Bush administration to 'go out' with a foreign policy success should not be ignored. Equally, the decision in 1999 to attack Serbia's infrastructure undoubtedly imposed costs on innocent civilians - in addition, of course, to those who became victims of the inevitable mistakes that accompany a military campaign.

One answer to this point is to put emphasis on effects not motives, in which case most of the interventions of the 1990s can still be seen as broadly unsuccessful, but for the rather more sensible and prosaic reason that they generally did not produce the results intended. It could be that this is a general characteristic of armed humanitarian action and that a more subtle approach will almost always bring better results. The Somali experience is instructive; the UN's representative in Somalia in 1992 was Mohamed Sahnoun, an experienced Algerian diplomat; his approach was to work with clan elders and persuade them to use their authority to undermine the more warlike clan leaders - this was the traditional way in which conflicts between the clans were restrained in Somalia and it may have been successful on this occasion, especially if backed by financial aid. Sahnoun was fired by Boutros Boutros-Ghali, and we will never know whether such a strategy would have worked, but the alternative certainly did not, and the unintentional killing of many clan elders by the US in July 1993 was the single biggest disaster of the affair.

The work of critics such as Pilger and, in a different key, realists such as Michael Mandelbaum and Colin Gray manages at times to convey the impression that armed 'humanitarian' action was a common event in the 1990s.[18] In fact, of course, the most striking feature of the period was the relatively small number of occasions on which action replaced inaction. The biggest single disaster - the Rwanda genocide - produced no helpful intervention, and in general the civil wars and massacres of Africa, especially in Angola and Zaire/Congo, were ignored by those who had the power to act. That the interveners were so selective in their interventions is often held against them, although it is not clear whether the critics actually want more interventions or fewer. Selectivity in itself is more or less inevitable and it is equally inevitable that the criteria for selection will not simply be humanitarian; to take a fairly obvious example, armed intervention to stop the Russians doing to Chechnya what the Serbs wanted to do to Kosovo would be equivalent to a declaration of war on a power which is still in possession of large scale armed forces and a nuclear capacity - unsurprisingly no one has seriously suggested such a course of action, but it is not clear why this reluctance should be taken to de-legitimize intervention in Kosovo where similar considerations do not apply. The search for a law-like moral rule that will determine when intervention should take place is unlikely to be successful.

The relative infrequency of humanitarian interventions provides a context for Nicholas Wheeler's study of the emergence of a norm of humanitarian intervention.[19] He approaches the subject as a theorist of international society with constructivist leanings; his underlying premise is that the way in which states describe what they are doing when they act influences the actions they take, perhaps even determining what action they can take. He examined the public utterances of states, in particular in the context of their votes on key resolutions in the UN Security Council, in order to find out whether they claim that a right of humanitarian intervention actually exists, or whether they actually invoke more conventional positions, such as the right to self-defence, or right to respond to a threat to international peace and security. He found that during the

1990s there were genuine innovations in international law and that the language states employed did change significantly during the decade. By the time of the Kosovo War a highly qualified right of humanitarian intervention was being asserted by some states, although important members of the international community such as China, Russia and India remain opposed to this development. This is a fascinating study, the best yet on the experiences of the 1990s, but, while it might be the case that there has been a shift in the normative foundations of IR over the decade, and that the firm bar on intervention has been partially lifted, whether this will actually affect in any substantial way the future behaviour of states is another matter.

The fate of the Kosovo intervention is instructive here; the official justifications employed to support the intervention certainly claimed or implied a right to intervene, even in the absence of explicit UN authorization.[20] Moreover, one very influential voice, that of Jürgen Habermas, went so far as to see the action as just possibly serving as a precursor to the emergence of a more Kantian international system, a Pacific Union of liberal-democratic states.[21] On the other hand, the post-Kosovo War experience of the NATO/UN protectorate in Kosovo has been sufficiently depressing to make it highly unlikely that any state is likely to enter into such an action again in the near future. Further, the effect on the UN of the Kosovo war could well be quite serious. In the past it had been understood that a resolution with the formula 'all necessary means' would be needed before UN-authorized violent action could follow; on this occasion it was argued by NATO that earlier UN resolutions condemning human rights violations and calling on the Federal Yugoslav authorities to end them could provide legitimation for action. If such an argument came to be accepted, the probable result would be that, in future, resolutions with this latter wording would be vetoed by states that did not want to see this slippage occur. The difficulty here is clear; norm-creation requires a broader base in the international community than has been present over the last few years. The claim of the powerful, affluent Western states of Europe and North America to be able to create such norms without the consent of the rest of the world is bound to be resisted, and rightly so. It may well be better to accept a firm norm of non-intervention which is broken occasionally and in exceptional circumstances, than to try to create a norm of humanitarian intervention in the absence of wide consent to such a move.

Would the general interest actually be compromised if no norm of humanitarian intervention were to be established? This is an interesting point because the usual assumption is that it is good to intervene to stop a violent conflict. Is this always so? Edward Luttwak has recently argued that in some cases the general welfare would be served better if military force were to be allowed to settle matters - this would, at least, prevent conflicts from dragging on unresolved, which, given the absence of authoritative conflict resolution mechanisms in the current system is likely usually to be their fate.[22] This is a counsel of despair, but, in any event, there is a wider point raised here, which is the issue of counterfactuals - the difficulty of assessing the consequences of actions that did *not* take place.

Consider, for example, the situation in Rwanda in early 1994. The commander of the small UN Force in Rwanda ('UNAMIR'), General Dallaire, requested the authority and resources to allow him to confiscate weapons stockpiled by Hutu extremists. This request was denied, but suppose that authority to act had been granted. This might well have led to violence, and the UN could have found itself engaging with, and outgunned by, Hutu militias and even part of the Rwandan Army; the Rwandan Government might well have been replaced by more extreme elements, and the Tutsi-dominated Rwanda Patriotic Front might have gone on the offensive, effectively acting with UNAMIR. There is very little doubt that had this quite plausible chain of events come about, we would now be analysing what went wrong in Rwanda, seeing this as a case similar to that of Somalia, where an overactive UN stepped into a conflict it did not understand, and made things worse. What we would *not* be doing is comparing this chain of events with what actually happened, because the genocide, on this account, was prevented - in our world we know that, but in the new world created by relatively effective but very messy UN action, this would be a matter for speculation only. Equally, events in Kosovo need to be seen in this light - we simply do not know what would have happened had NATO not intervened as it did, but there is at least some reason to think that things would have been worse than they actually are for the people most closely affected.

One final point should be made. Humanitarian intervention, as conventionally understood, is something that states do, or not, as the case more usually is. But non-state aid organizations are also involved heavily in actions that look very like interventions while bodies such as Amnesty International are more widely involved in promoting human rights. If what we are actually interested in is a growth in international *humanitarianism* then these activities are highly relevant and it would be a mistake to judge the current situation simply in the context of the kind of headline events discussed above. On the other hand, the major sources of human misery in the world today are poverty, malnutrition and stunted life-chances. The international community may respond to actual famines, but the misery of constant but non-dramatic malnutrition attracts much less attention. In the case of actual or possible humanitarian interventions there is usually an identifiable enemy who can be held to account - but the global inequalities that generate such extremes of poverty are less easy to personalize. It is often asked whether it is right that soldiers be asked to risk their lives on behalf of foreigners, but a similar question arises just as forcefully, although rather less dramatically, when the relief of poverty is at stake. What obligations do the rich owe to the poor, when the latter are not their fellow citizens? This is, perhaps, the most important current question in international political theory - and one rather less embedded in existing Westphalian discourses than the issue of humanitarian intervention; because the latter is actually graspable in Westphalian terms without a great deal of conceptual innovation, it may, unfortunately, draw attention away from the more serious issue of global inequality.[23] It is important that those who would wish to promote a just world order should not be distracted from the consideration of the deeper obstacles to its achievement by the more immediate dramas of armed humanitarian action.

Notes

1   The 'Westphalia' system is a convenient way of referring to the system of states established in Europe in the sixteenth/seventeenth centuries, although Stephen Krasner points out that the Peace of Westphalia that ended the thirty-years war in 1648 was not, actually, very 'Westphalian' in content; *Sovereignty: Organised Hypocrisy*, Princeton NJ: Princeton University Press, 1999.

2   For realism in international relations theory see Chris Brown, *Understanding International Relations* 2nd ed. Basingstoke: Palgrave, 2001, Chapters 2 and 3.

3   For 'constructivism' see, e.g. Alexander Wendt, *Social Theory of International Politics*, Cambridge: Cambridge University Press, 1999; for the mainstream, Judith Goldstein and Robert Keohane, eds., *Ideas and Foreign Policy*, Ithaca, NY: Cornell University Press.

4   This last point is stressed by N.J. Wheeler in *Saving Strangers*, Oxford: Oxford University Press, 2000; Oliver Ramsbotham and Tom Woodhouse, *Humanitarian Intervention in Contemporary Conflict*, Cambridge: Polity Press, argue convincingly for a shift of attention from motive to effect.

5   See Wight, 'Western values in international relations', in Herbert Butterfield and Martin Wight, eds., *Diplomatic Investigations*, London: George Allen and Unwin, 1966.

6   Martha Finnemore, 'Constructing Norms of Humanitarian Intervention' in Peter Katzenstein ed., *The Culture of National Security*, New York: Columbia University Press, 1966.

7   'Explaining Costly International Moral Action: Britain's Sixty Year Campaign against the Slave Trade', *International Organisation* (53) 1999, 361-368.

8   See Gerritt Gong, *The Standard of 'Civilisation' in International Society*, Oxford: Oxford University Press, 1984.

9   See Adam Hochschild, *King Leopold's Ghost*, New York: Houghton Mifflin, Co., 1998.

10 Robert Jackson, *Quasi-states: Sovereignty, Independence and the Third World*, Cambridge: Cambridge University Press, 1990.

11 Conor Cruse O'Brien, a UN official in the Congo, produced the best book on the Congo; *To Katanga and Back: A UN Case History*, London: Hutchinson, 1962.

12 See Tim Allen and David Styan, 'A Right to Interfere? Bernard Kouchner and the New Humanitarianism', *Journal of International Development* (12) 825-842.

13 Wheeler, *Saving Strangers*, op. cit.

14 The following discussion is based on a number of general studies and collections, including Wheeler, *Saving Strangers*, op. cit., the best overview, with William Shawcross, *Deliver us From Evil*, London: Bloomsbury, 2000 as an alternative, journalistic account; the best collections are John Moore ed., *Hard Choices: Moral Dilemmas in Humanitarian Intervention*, Lanham MD: Rowman and Littlefield, 1998 and James Mayall ed., *The New Interventionism*, Cambridge: Cambridge University Press, 1996.

15 Linda Melvern, *A People Betrayed: The Role of The West in Rwanda's Genocide*, London: Zed Books, 2000; James Gow, *Triumph of the Lack of Will: International Diplomacy and the Yugoslav War*, London: C. Hurst & Co. 1997.

16 The Independent International Commission on Kosovo has produced a reasonably balanced account of the intervention: *The Kosovo Report*, Oxford: Oxford University Press, 2000. For East Timor, see Tim Dunne and Nicholas Wheeler, 'The Australian-led Intervention in East Timor', *International Affairs* (77) 4, October 2001.

17 'Under the influence: the real reason for the United Nations' intervention is to maintain Indonesian control', *The Guardian*, 21 September 1999.

18 Michael Mandelbaum, 'A Perfect Failure', *Foreign Affairs* (98), 1999, 2-8; Colin Gray, 'No Good Deed Shall Go Unpunished', in Ken Booth ed. *The Kosovo Tragedy: The Human Rights Dimension*, London: Frank Cass, 2001.

19 Wheeler, *Saving Strangers*, op. cit.

20 See Tony Blair, 'Doctrine of the International Community', Speech in Chicago, 22 April 1999.

21 'Bestialität und Humanität', *Die Zeit* (18), 29 April 1999.

22 'Give War a Chance', *Foreign Affairs*, (78), 1999, 36-45.

23 International social justice is discussed in Chris Brown, *Sovereignty, Rights and Justice*, Cambridge: Polity Press, forthcoming 2002, which also contains a discussion of humanitarian intervention upon which this chapter draws.

Chapter 9

On the Justifiability of Military Intervention: The Kosovan Case

Brendan Howe

Introduction

The NATO action in Yugoslavia appears to have rested on shaky legal foundations. It was not an action of individual or collective self-defence, had not been sanctioned by the UN Security Council, and, however distasteful the actions of the Belgrade regime, Serbian forces were not technically waging a war of aggression. President Clinton claimed that '[w]e act to prevent a wider war; to diffuse a powder keg at the heart of Europe that has exploded twice before this century with catastrophic results'[1] yet this was an exaggeration of the threat posed to international security by the situation in Kosovo, besides which, Article 39 of the UN Charter states that it is up to the Security Council to decide upon such definitions. Had Kosovo been an independent state, Yugoslavia's act of aggression in violation of international law would have justified NATO collectively defending the Kosovars in anticipation of a Security Council ruling. However, Kosovo is more accurately viewed as an integral part of a sovereign state, against whose territorial integrity and political independence NATO acted. Importantly, from an international legal standpoint, the Belgrade authorities had exercised *de facto* and *de jure* control over the province for an extended period of time.

International law *does* provide for intervention in civil conflicts, but again the indicators are not good for NATO claims. In the Nicaragua Case, the International Court of Justice upheld the neutral non-intervention rule, whereby states are prohibited from aiding either side in a civil war, stating that in the absence of any justification unequivocally provided for by the UN Charter 'the use of force could not be the appropriate method to monitor or ensure...respect [for human rights]'. Nevertheless, here we may have the beginning of a case for defending NATO intervention. Codified international law does recognize the right of self-determination of peoples, and some authorities have advocated a right to intervene on the side of people struggling to establish their own political identity in the face of oppressive and coercive actions from the dominant community to which they currently belong. This view is also widely reflected in *state practice* (the Reagan and Brezhnev doctrines); and the Paquete Habana Case established that international law *can* be created through such means. This is reflected in Article 38 of the Statute of the International Court of Justice. Also cited by the Statute are 'the teachings of the most highly qualified publicists of the various nations, as subsidiary means for the determination of rules of law'. The 1974 Definition of Aggression (a General Assembly resolution) specifically recognized not only the right to self-determination, but also the right to seek and receive support against alien domination, and it might be claimed that ethnic differences between the invading Orthodox Serbs and majority indigenous Muslim Albanians in Kosovo are such as to fulfil this last criterion.

Furthermore, while we might have a duty not to intervene in the affairs of other states, the doctrine of non-intervention does not explain why this is a moral duty, or tell us what to do when it comes into conflict with other acknowledged duties, moral or otherwise.[2] International law has increasingly become concerned with another such acknowledged duty - that owed to the individual, *especially* where it comes into conflict with state prerogatives, thus human rights are often seen as rights against states. Such developments led the former Secretary General of the UN, Boutros Boutros-Ghali, to make it clear in his *Agenda for Peace* that he considered the age of the sovereign state to be at an end. If sovereignty can be challenged, and there are certain things that states may not do to or with their citizens, then the normative value attached to non-intervention must be weighed against that attached to other commonly held values that are being violated in order to judge the legitimacy of intervention. This implies a crucial theoretical shift from a purely positive interpretation of international legal obligations, but whether we have reached a natural law style universalist position is still open to debate. Are the rights of individuals determined by their membership of political communities, or do these rights pre-exist such communities, belonging to all individuals by virtue of their common humanity?

Walzer, Community and the Legalist Paradigm

For Michael Walzer the most appropriate unit for normative analysis is the political community that underlies the state.[3] For him, aggression is a singular and undifferentiated crime because, in all its forms, it challenges rights that are worth dying for. In the context of international law these rights may be summed up as territorial integrity and political sovereignty. 'The two belong to states, but they derive ultimately from the rights of individuals, and from them they take their force.'[4] Thus the political community itself is based on shared experiences and co-operative activity, a 'common life' which has a right to be protected, and the legitimacy of a state depends on the closeness of its match to the community of shared values.[5] 'If no common life exists, its own defence may have no moral justification. But most states do stand guard over the community of their citizens, at least to some degree: that is why we assume the justice of defensive wars.'[6] In particular, it is this 'presumption of legitimacy' that precludes external intervention.[7]

Walzer rejects attempts to come up with neutral, value free or universal theories of justice as at best impossible and at worst counterproductive. There are human rights, but due to the problem of the particularism of history, culture, and membership, the political community to which individuals belong, rather than uninformed external interference, is the best agency for their defence.[8] For Walzer, the political community (*qua* state) is the closest we can come to a world of common meanings as it is where language, history, and culture come most closely together to produce a collective consciousness.[9] Thus community itself becomes a good. Membership cannot be handed out by some external agency, as, in the absence of a global community, values are constructed through internal decision, and the state represents the largest unit for legitimation.[10] So NATO was not in the moral position to criticize the actions of Belgrade towards members of its own community, still less to launch a criminal act of aggression. Only the people of Yugoslavia as a community could declare their regime to be illegitimate, and there was insufficient evidence of such a sentiment.

Liberals, however, are distrustful of the state, often seeking to minimize it, and always to differentiate state from society.[11] Walzer acknowledges that in reality 'countries are likely to take shape as closed territories dominated, perhaps, by particular nations (clubs of families), but always including aliens of one sort or another', yet considers that the only right such minorities have is not to be expelled. If they are large enough to constitute a separate political community, and irredeemably alienated from the political whole, he accepts the desirability of setting up separate states for each community when boundaries are drawn.[12] However, within an established community, Walzer advocates coercion in the pursuit of conformity.[13] Thus Belgrade's actions may be seen as legitimate and those of the KLA as illegitimate.

Community and Intervention

From such principles Walzer has drawn together his justification of the international norm of non-intervention, and the community rights of territorial integrity and national sovereignty. 'All the groups that achieve statehood and all the practices that they permit... are tolerated by the society of states. Toleration is an essential feature of sovereignty and an important reason for its desirability.'[14] It is not for us to judge other societies, but rather, if by their own values they are unjust, it is up to the members of those societies to reform themselves. Statesmen do deal with 'intolerable' states, and recognize them as sovereign members of international society.[15] Aggression, or forcibly intervening in another state's affairs, is the only crime in international relations.[16] Thus international norms required NATO to refrain from intervening. Only if the Yugoslav government was unacceptable to the community it claimed to represent (i.e. the whole country) would insurrection be justified, and even then salvation would have to be attained internally. From this central hypothesis Walzer postulates six principles:

1. There exists an international society of independent states....
2. This international society has a law that establishes the rights of its members - above all, the rights of territorial integrity and political sovereignty....
3. Any use of force or imminent threat of force by one state against the political sovereignty or territorial integrity of another constitutes aggression and is a criminal act....
4. Aggression justifies two kinds of violent response: a war of self-defence by the victim and a war of law enforcement by the victim and any other member of international society....
5. Nothing but aggression can justify war....
6. Once the aggressor state has been militarily repulsed, it can also be punished.[17]

The communitarian basis of Walzer's work means that he is unable to accept intervention for any reason other than to counter aggression (i.e. to reverse an earlier intervention). From a starting-point of justice, morality and rights being culturally specific and embodied in historically distinct political communities, Walzer claims that the citizens of these communities are the only ones with the right to change the regime under which they live, and may insist upon conformity within their geographical borders. In international relations terms, this translates as a norm of non-intervention, and the protection of political sovereignty and territorial integrity.

The Liberal/Universalist Critique of Communitarianism

Kymlicka reacts against the communitarian notion that we cannot and/or must not stand back and judge social arrangements. He rejects Taylor's accusation that 'complete freedom would be a void in which nothing would be worth doing, nothing would deserve to count for anything', pointing out that '[f]reedom of choice is not pursued for its own sake, but as a precondition for pursuing those projects that are valued for their own sake'.[18] By treating freedom of choice as just another culturally specific value which may be weighed against other community-embedded values and then justly rejected if considered less important, communitarians miss the point that it is a necessary pre-requisite for protecting the community values of all groups within the larger political society. Furthermore, in contrast to the communitarian claim that someone who is nothing but a free rational being would have no reason to choose one way of life over another as they would have no evaluative criteria with which to make the choice, liberals counter that such individuals could actually insert such criteria, yet still remain free to change them if they do not produce pleasing results. This is a freedom conspicuously denied by Walzer's historical, epistemological approach.

Communitarians claim that it is impossible to retreat to a neutral, value-free standpoint, but liberals believe that it must be possible to see oneself encumbered with alternative motivations, in order to have some reason to choose one over others. The self is, in this sense, perceived prior to its ends, that is, one can always envisage oneself without one's present ends.[19] In an attempt to refute the charge that liberalism ignores the way we are embedded in our social roles (what Taylor refers to as 'atomism'), Kymlicka claims that liberals do not deny interaction in search of perfection, just Walzer's premise that the coercive state is the appropriate forum for such a search.[20] The search is further facilitated by liberal values of freedom of speech, assembly and association. Perhaps the best conclusion to this particular debate is a compromise position. The communitarians are correct to make reference to the 'inescapable frameworks of the self' - that if we really were able to escape our values and preferences, we would no longer be agents capable of decision - but although we cannot in practical terms escape the framework that defines our identity, it has long been acknowledged that we can do so in theoretical terms. It is possible to imagine possessing a different set of frameworks. Hyland has termed this process epistemological self-transcendence.[21]

A more severe and complex criticism of Walzer concerns his notions of justice, spheres of justice, and the boundaries of community. Walzer talks of pluralistic principles of justice and distribution based on historically and culturally generated divergent understandings of social goods. What he fails to acknowledge is that these understandings of social goods may historically and culturally have been generated in the interests of only a small and distinct section of the community - in the case of Yugoslavia, the Orthodox Serbian ascendancy. Kymlicka identifies this as a general failing of communitarian theory.[22]

Walzer claims society and its structures are always subject to revision should the existing distribution of social goods not find favour with the majority of citizens. However, this opens him to a number of other criticisms. Firstly, he explicitly assumes that the disadvantaged have the means to conduct social revision. Secondly, he implicitly assumes that what the majority want is correct for that community, and that the rights of minorities may be sacrificed on the altar of conformity through the instrument of state coercion. His third assumption is that a majority will be able to form a revisionist ideology and movement if the distributions of social goods are contrary to their interest. Yet a person or group may lack the physical and/or political resources to overthrow the unjustified monopolies to which Walzer refers. Even if there is access to political resources, some groups may be so handicapped in their ability to utilize those resources that not only are they ultimately ineffective, but also they never even get to the stage of making their demands heard. Finally, Cohen has attacked the notion of community values. Although for Walzer the *subjects* of values are in the first instance *political communities*, and not the individual members of those communities, consent to a political order can result from combinations of fear, disinterest, narrow self-interest, a restricted sense of alternatives, or a strategic judgement about how to advance values not now embodied in the political community, rather than a commitment to preserving and advancing a way of life of that order.[23] Furthermore, what are the 'shared understandings' upon which communitarian justice is based? If they are seen as existing social practices, the process is inherently conservative and resistant to revision. If they are distinct from practices, what evidence will there be that we have the values right? If a consensus is sought by asking everyone's views, then there exist no shared understandings, and we still have to weigh justly one view against another.[24]

Liberal/Universalist Critiques of the Legalist Paradigm

Walzer assumes homogeneity and a normative consensus within political communities. Although he acknowledges there might be more than one community sharing the geographical boundaries of a nation state, he assumes that there must either be conformity, or separation of the distinct socio-ethnic components. In other words, he claims that if there is irresolvable conflict concerning substantial conceptions of the good, questions of justice and distribution, then we have more than one community masquerading as a single political entity. Thus, he would contend, his premise remains true, and the anomaly can be removed by the simple expedient of geographical separation. This is a false assumption on two levels. Firstly, internal plurality is the norm for modern societies. Secondly, it is often impossible to separate conflictual groups within a community. It may be that minorities who want out (or whom the majority want expelled) do not live in a geographically distinct region, do not exist in large enough numbers to survive as an independent political community, or do not have sufficient resources to strive for independence against the wishes of the dominant group. It would seem that the Albanian ethnic group in Kosovo would meet at least two of these criteria.

These points lead us on to a critique of the final manifestation of Walzer's communitarian outlook, the legalist paradigm. The central question is 'when is it justifiable to wage war?' Leaving aside the extreme realist answer (always) and the extreme pacifist (never), there remains a broad spectrum of debate. One response has been that war may only be resorted to once all other avenues have been attempted and have failed. However, as Walzer points out, this is simply to revert to pacifism, for we can never reach 'lastness', or we can never know that we have reached it.[25] In addition, if we assume that our objective is to minimize human suffering through our actions, then it may be that war achieves our aims in a less harmful way than say blockade, sanctions or sabotage. Walzer's solution is to lay down rules for when it is just or even when it is our moral duty to go to war, and also to stipulate when it is illegal, unjust or morally repugnant to do so. In doing so he draws heavily upon his communitarian background, and his six principles extensively reflect his defence of the rights of political communities *qua* states.

The morality of Walzer's argument has been extensively criticized concerning whether it goes far enough in sanctioning war. There is something of a consensus against Walzer's fifth principle, that nothing but aggression can justify war. For David Luban, 'if the rights of states are derived from the rights of humans, and are thus in a sense one kind of human rights, it will be important to consider their possible conflict with other human rights'.[26] He agrees with Doppelt that an illegitimate and tyrannical state cannot derive sovereign rights against aggression from the rights of its own oppressed citizens, when it is itself denying them those same rights,[27] and is concerned that in the communitarian justification 'somehow oppression of domestic vintage carries a prima facie claim to legitimacy which is not there in the case of foreign conquest'.[28] In his opinion, the majority of states have forfeited their rights which in truth are only *privileges* granted them in trust. Thus although not every infringement is a casus belli (the doctrine of proportionality still applies), he implies that every state has a duty to intervene in those with inferior human rights records. Unless we say that morality is conditional upon the nationality of the aggressor, we have a duty to defend the victims of internal as well of those of external aggression. Thus a just war is (i) a war in defence of socially basic human rights (subject to proportionality); or (ii) a war of self-defence against an unjust war. An unjust war is (i) a war subversive of human rights, whether socially basic or not, which is also (ii) not a war in defence of socially basic human rights.[29]

This leaves us in a position where 'the legitimacy of the state is conferred in two forms: externally by other members of the society of states, and internally by its own citizens'.[30] For Walzer, we must always act internationally 'as if' the states we are dealing with are legitimate. Or as Robert Jackson has put it, '[j]ustice between states as between individuals involves mutual respect and forbearance'.[31] If a state does not embody the interests of its citizens, it is up to them to rebel. This is essentially a Millian position that people cannot be set free by external force but must rely on 'self-help'.[32] Thus to a certain extent societies get the governments they deserve, as they reflect something within the society that threw them up. Luban's response is that governments can 'fit the people the way the sole of a boot fits a human face: after a while the patterns of indentation match with uncanny precision. In this way the politics of "as if", in which we acknowledge rights but turn our backs on their enforcement, fails to take our values seriously. It raises politics above moral theory.'[33]

The Value of Rules

Luban's position raises serious questions of its own - namely, if we are to give the right of intervention to those states who are morally superior, who decides which states qualify and on what criteria? Furthermore, what constitutes a human right, and when do we decide that it is being infringed? Or, as Walzer himself responds to his critics,

> to whom is this far-reaching license granted? Who is to make the crucial calculations? In principle, I suppose, the license is extended to any and all foreigners; in practice, today, the officials of foreign states; tomorrow, perhaps, to some set of global bureaucrats acting by themselves or as advisors to and agents of a Universal Assembly.[34]

A common concern is that those values purporting to be universal are in fact merely an extension of the world dominance of western culture.[35] Thus perhaps a truly just international society would in fact follow George Bernard Shaw's maxim: 'Do not unto others as you would that they should do unto you. Their tastes may not be the same.' Furthermore, we may ultimately side with Walzer's firm stance on non-intervention because international society is unlike domestic society 'in that every conflict threatens the structure as a whole with collapse. Aggression challenges it directly and is much more dangerous than domestic crime, because there are no policemen.'[36] Without states there would be no international society, merely permanent war or universal tyranny.

However, this is where we uncover a major contradiction in Walzer's work. He champions 'shared values' for a community of a certain size, but not for smaller (sub-state) communities, or the larger international community. In *Spheres of Justice* Walzer states that there are no shared global values.[37] The question is, does anyone have a taste for such things as genocide? If so, then the plurality of cultures is probably not worth preserving if some of these cultures are so inhumane. In fact, it could be argued that there is something approaching a global normative consensus with regard to some of the more extreme abuses of human rights. This argument is somewhat similar to that put forward by Roger Spegele in placing pluralism somewhere between relativism and absolutism (or communitarianism and universalism).[38] There may be no absolute, universal conception of the good, but this does not necessarily preclude us from recognizing a universal conception of the 'bad'. 'Pluralism does not commit one, as subjectivism does, to "anything goes" in morality.'[39]

We may not be in a position to judge the values of Serbian society, but this does not preclude us from saying that their actions in Kosovo were an affront to all notions of human dignity and worthy of international reaction in the form of intervention in order to put a stop to them. For Donnelly there is a 'remarkable international normative consensus on the list of rights' found in the Universal Declaration of Human Rights, and according to Dunne and Wheeler, '[w]hat further strengthens Donnelly's claim that there is a normative consensus underlying the human rights regime is the fact that in the daily round of diplomacy, state leaders justify their human rights policies in terms of these standards'.[40] Even Walzer concedes something along these lines, stating that 'sovereignty also has its limits, which are fixed most clearly by the legal doctrine of humanitarian intervention. Acts or practices that "shock the conscience of humankind" are, in principle, not tolerated.'[41] Is not the 'conscience of humankind' a case of shared global values?

Walzer still attempts to differentiate between domestic and international regimes in terms of permissive and prescriptive morality.[42] However, this further weakens his argument. Distinguishing between two forms of political community purely on the basis of voluntary or compulsory defence of norms is dubious in itself, and begs the question of the grounds on which he makes this distinction. His critics would also claim that this is precisely what is wrong with Walzer's argument - he does not acknowledge a moral imperative to defend human rights in all their forms. By acknowledging that in certain cases intervention to stop abuses is justified if they are bad enough, he is hoist by his own petard - who decides what is 'bad enough'? What degree of force is appropriate? He ends up in the same position as his critics, but without the support of a value neutral set of criteria for just intervention.

Theoretical Fusion

There is considerable consensus (which ironically includes Walzer himself) that in its unrevised form Walzer's legalist paradigm is not morally defensible. However, with limited revision along the lines suggested by Luban (that is, consider the conflict between state and other human rights and weigh both in the balance) the reverse is true. We must, in general, recognize a rule of non-intervention in international relations, as there is considerable utility in avoiding conflict. However, in extreme circumstances, the utility involved in preventing abhorrent practices may outweigh that of following the rule. Although Luban and Walzer reach their final positions from opposing theoretical starting points, in the end their practical differences are little more than a matter of degree. We cannot escape Luban's insight that 'no description of just war is likely to address all of the difficult cases adequately - and there is no realm of human affairs in which difficult cases are more common. Seat-of-the-pants practical judgement is a necessary supplement to one's principles in such matters.'[43]

Thus we have reached a point where we accept that there are individual human rights, shared values within communities that constitute state rights, and a certain degree of global consensus or shared norms. What is needed is a way to reflect these three competing demands upon our evaluation of justice. Rawls has come closest to providing an answer. Starting with a value neutral liberal approach to the rights of individuals, he accepts that we are historically situated, but contends we have become historically situated in liberal individualism. Thus most contemporary societies (those not rejected by international society as pariah regimes) give a high priority to the freedom to choose. His theory of 'overlapping consensus' is as applicable to the international community of nation states as it is to multi-cultural pluralistic domestic communities. This approach places less emphasis on the supposed value-free universalism that Walzer found so objectionable. However, it remains resistant to the notion of values embedded in the political community, precisely because *no* political community reflects an absolute consensus view of its citizens regarding conceptions of the good, and any attempt to create such conformity will rely on coercion. For Rawls, justice as fairness abandons the idea of political community if by that is meant a political society united on one (partially or fully) comprehensive religious, philosophical or moral doctrine. 'That conception of social unity is excluded by the fact of pluralism; it is no longer a political possibility for those who accept the constraints of liberty and toleration embodied in democratic institutions.'[44]

Although democracy itself could be challenged as a culturally specific norm, such a discussion would constitute a paper in itself, and Walzer implicitly accepts many of the concepts that underline majoritarian democracy. Indeed, like aversion to genocide and condemnation of aggression, the idea of 'democracy' comes close to being viewed as a global norm.[45] Rawls does not rule out community embedded values in spheres other than the political.[46] However, with regard to the political, he identifies his overlapping consensus as the only community shared value likely to endure without coercion - an institutionalized guarantee of tolerance of diversity *within* communities as opposed to mere toleration of diversity between communities.[47] He is also concerned with majoritarian popular support for regimes, but unlike Walzer is convinced that in order to get a substantial majority of citizens to give their support freely, a political doctrine is needed 'that a diversity of comprehensive religions, philosophical, and moral doctrines can endorse, each from its own point of view'.[48]

Any state which does not practise this degree of toleration of diversity leaves itself open to condemnation from the international community. Any state which does not practise this degree of toleration *and* conducts itself in a manner towards its own citizens that any rational being would find abhorrent *is* guilty under international law according to the shared norms of international society, the works of eminent publicists, the practice of states and the intents and purposes of the United Nations. As such, should the abuses be sufficient (according to the doctrine of proportionality) to outweigh the possible harm that would be done by external intervention, then every state of superior moral standing not only has the right, but also the duty to intervene.

Conclusion

It would certainly have been preferable for NATO to have obtained UN endorsement, as this would (presumably) have satisfied even the positivists. This not being the case, we need to consider whether the human rights abuses were severe enough to warrant intervention. NATO justified their actions under the 1948 Genocide Convention and other general humanitarian principles on the grounds that if they did not intervene, ethnic cleansing on a genocidal scale would have occurred. As little could have been achieved through the usual UN channels due to the inevitable veto by Russia and China, and NATO felt that action was demanded, the strict written rule of international law had to be overridden by demands of human compassion. This amounted to a claim that today human rights are no longer of exclusive concern to the particular state where they may be infringed, but rather their abuse may be used to justify interventions into otherwise internal disputes. Increasing intervention by the international community, through international bodies, in internal conflicts where human rights are in serious jeopardy was used as evidence.[49] NATO argued that in the light of reports by international organizations testifying to the magnitude of human rights violations, in turn acknowledged by the UN,[50] and as Yugoslavia consistently defied resolutions and decisions of the Security Council, itself crippled by indecision,[51] it was entitled similarly to intervene.

As is often the case in international affairs, the controversy may ultimately be reduced to whether or not we desire a world of 'positive peace' and the realization, sometimes imposition, of justice, or 'negative peace' which is simply the absence of armed interstate conflict. As pointed out by Dunne and Wheeler, the Universal Declaration of Human Rights established a standard of civilized conduct which applies to all governments in the treatment of their citizens, and a regime that from the outset recognized a concern for both sets of rights.[52] Their answer to the question 'why are there all these human rights standards but the bodies keep piling up?' is that either states fail to live up to the universal standard or political communities interpret universal human rights very differently.[53] This is not the whole story, and these are not the only two possible answers. Matters are further complicated by inadequate definitions of the rules concerning human rights and what may be done should they be compromised, and lack of 'back-up' rules that would then make these provisions fully legal, binding and enforceable. The key questions are 'who decides?' and 'who implements?' Will newly energized but self-interested post-Cold War regional entities be allowed to impose peace? Or will the post-world war UN, more representative but grindingly slow, continue to determine the global defence of international peace and security? Even if there has been a shift in the practice and interpretation of international law, this has not yet been adequately enshrined in the constitutive documents of international organizations or reflected in codified treaty law. This situation needs to be rectified, lest the anachronisms of codified law serve to discredit the international legal system as a whole.

> Formality strengthens a rule by making its normative character clearer, in the process separating it from rules that are normatively more ambiguous (conventions for example)... Agents are inclined to make rules legal and to follow them if they are legal because they know what the rules are, how much they matter to other agents, and what consequences they can expect from not following them.[54]

As codified international law still overwhelmingly reflects the desires and interests of the political units we call states, this means that in the interest of authority and clarity states must agree to a significant slate of legislation that will actually serve to undermine their central position in the international legal system - a difficult proposition, but maybe the only one that will serve to bring together the various strands of existing international legal norms.

Notes

1   Statement by the President to the Nation, March 24, 1999.
2   Luban, David, 'Just War and Human Rights' in Beitz, Charles R. et al. (eds.), *International Ethics* (Princeton, Princeton University Press, 1985) p.199.
3   Walzer, Michael, 'The Moral Standing of States: A Response to Four Critics' in Beitz et al., op. cit., p.218.
4   Walzer, Michael, 'The Rights of Political Communities' [extracted from *Just and Unjust Wars*] in Beitz et al., op. cit., p.167.
5   Ibid., p.168.
6   Ibid., p.168.
7   Walzer, 'The Moral Standing of States', p.220.
8   Walzer, M. *Spheres of Justice: A Defence of Pluralism and Equality* (Harvard, Martin Robertson, 1983), p.5.
9   Ibid., p.28.
10 Ibid., p.29.
11 Kymlicka, Will, *Contemporary Political Philosophy: an Introduction* (Oxford, Clarendon Press, 1990), pp.222-223.
12 Walzer, *Spheres of Justice*, p.62.
13 Ibid., p.68.
14 Walzer, M., *On Toleration* (Yale, Yale University Press, 1997), p.19.
15 Ibid., p.20.
16 Walzer, M., *Just and Unjust Wars: A Moral Argument with Historical Illustrations*, 2nd edition (Cambridge Ma., Basic Books, 1992), p.51.
17 Ibid., pp.61-62.
18 Kymlicka, op. cit., pp.208-209.
19 Ibid., p.212.
20 'It is of course true that participation in shared linguistic and cultural practices is what enables individuals to make intelligent decisions about the good life. But why should such participation be organized through the state, rather than through the free association of individuals?' Ibid., p.221.
21 James L. Hyland, *Democratic Theory: The Philosophical Foundations* (Manchester University Press, 1995).
22 Kymlicka, op. cit., p.227.
23 Cohen, Joshua, abstract of 'Review of Spheres of Justice' in Will Kymlicka, *Justice in Political Philosophy Volume II: Critiques and Alternatives* (Edward Elgar, 1992), pp.325-328.
24 Ibid., pp.329-333.
25 Walzer, *Just and Unjust Wars*, op. cit., p.xiv.
26 Luban, 'Just War and Human Rights', p.201.
27 Ibid., p.204.
28 Ibid., p.214.
29 Ibid., p.210.
30 Hoffman, Mark, 'States, Cosmopolitanism and Normative International Theory', *Paradigms* 2, No.1 (1988), pp.60-75.
31 Jackson, Robert H., 'Dialectical Justice in the Gulf War', *Review of International Studies* 18, No.4 (1992), p.337.
32 Walzer, *Just and Unjust Wars*, p.90.
33 Luban, 'The Romance of the Nation-State' in Beitz et al. (eds.), *International Ethics*, p.242.

34   Michael Walzer, 'The Moral Standing of States', p.232.
35   'Shue may put security and subsistence above all other rights... But what of those who would put the right to worship God in their own way above either? Or the right to honour their ancestors?' Chris Brown, 'Cosmopolitan Confusions: A Reply to Hoffman', *Paradigms*, Winter 1988-89, Vol.2, No.2, p.106.
36   Walzer, *Just and Unjust Wars*, p.59.
37   Walzer, *Spheres of Justice*, p.30.
38   Segele, R.D., 'Political Realism and the Remembrance of Relativism', *Review of International Studies* 21 (1995), pp.224-225.
39   Ibid., pp.224-225.
40   Dunne, T. and Wheeler, N.J. (eds.), *Human Rights in Global Politics* (Cambridge University Press, Cambridge, 1999), p.7.
41   Walzer, M., *On Toleration* (New Haven, Yale University Press, 1997), p.21.
42   'Given the weak regime of international society, all that this means in practice is that any member state is entitled to use force to stop what is going on if what is going on is awful enough... But no one is obligated to use force; the regime has no agents whose function it is to repress intolerable practices. Even in the face of obvious and extensive brutality, humanitarian intervention is entirely voluntary.' Ibid., p.21.
43   Luban, 'Just War and Human Rights', p.216.
44   Stephen Mulhall and Adam Swift, *Liberals and Communitarians* (Blackwell, Oxford, 1992), p.198.
45   'We agree that there are tables, chairs and other people. Similarly, we agree that democracy is a good thing and that the political system inside which we currently operate is a democratic system. Democracy surrounds us like tables and chairs and the air we breathe, normally totally taken for granted. Right across the world, in obviously different political systems, the form of government is taken to be democratic and democracy is unquestionably taken to be a good thing.' Ross Harrison, *Democracy* (Routledge, London, 1993), p.1.
46   'Note that what is impractical is not all values of community... but only political community and its values.' In Mulhall and Swift, op. cit., pp.199-200.
47   Ibid., p.198.
48   Rawls, J. 'The domain of the political and overlapping consensus' in Copp, David et al. (eds.), *The Idea of Democracy* (Cambridge, Cambridge University Press, 1993), p.250.
49   As early as 1990, the Organization of African Unity attempted to mitigate the Liberian civil war, and continues to try and find a solution to the problems besetting the former African state of Zaire. Somalia in Eastern Africa has seen international intervention, while in Central Africa a rather belated attempt was made in Rwanda to stop the genocide of Tutsis in the mid 1990s.
50   Security Council Resolution, 1199 (1998).
51   See the draft resolution sponsored in the Security Council by Belarus, India and the Russian Federation (UN Doc. S/1999/328).
52   Dunne and Wheeler, op. cit., p.1.
53   Ibid., p.2.
54   Onuf, N.G., 'Constructivism: A User's Manual' in Kubalkova, V., Onuf, N.G., Kowert, P., *International Relations in a Constructed World* (New York, Armonk, 1998), p.69.

Chapter 10

Intervention and Collective Justice in the Post-Westphalian System

Jamie Munn

To what extent is intervention, and particularly military intervention, ruled out by a requirement of respect for self-determination? In this piece I will challenge the common assumption that respect for self-determination requires an almost exceptionless doctrine of non-intervention. Let me start by explaining how I understand the notions of 'intervention' and 'self-determination'.

In the post-Cold War world, states have increasingly come under pressure to intervene in conflicts that have begun to follow an identifiable pattern whereby such 'interference' takes place. A wave of violent inter-ethnic warfare has carried with it a parallel crisis that is in many ways more difficult to control. Severe humanitarian emergencies have been on the rise as the flood of refugees from a war-ravaged country pose security and economic strains on those countries to which they flee. Typically such crises occur in regions that are lagging behind 'first world' status, and therefore such disasters come to rest on the shoulders of powers such as the United Nations.

International practice has been that the context and circumstances surrounding each of these disasters must be taken into account. And the context of the Somali crisis describes what amounted to the richest nations on the earth intervening in one of the poorest (widely known as 'the most ambitious humanitarian mission in modern history'). The massive humanitarian intervention that was undertaken by many UN member nations saw UN soldiers deployed in an effort to assist in and protect the efforts of aid workers in the region. The UN Security Council commanded these peacekeepers to patrol all ports and airfields where food and supplies were to be delivered in order that aid reached its rightful destinations. The peacekeepers were also given the specific task of helping to re-establish a stable government in Somalia. As the then President, George Bush, implored American citizens to support a cause to alleviate the famine and starvation that was destroying the lives of a little known people half-way around the world, there were many adherents to the philosophy that until 'the hungry were fed...might would make right'.

The primary reason the UN went to Somalia was to halt a humanitarian crisis in the region that was largely the result of anarchy. The mentality of the 'survival of the fittest' arising from this state of anarchy saw a perpetuation of tribal conflicts as competing attempts were made to gain control of the nation state. The lack of government in Somalia from which approval for humanitarian operations could be gained was instrumental in the UN Security Council's decision that the Somali case deserved precedence over other countries in need of urgent humanitarian aid.

Intervention has proven to be most controversial in situations analogous to that of Somalia where operations are carried out within the border of a state where no effective government is in place, such as the Congo and in Cyprus, and where civil warfare is not bound by Security Council decisions or other regional agreements, as in Lebanon and Bosnia-Herzegovina. Yet traditional methods of intervention that demand a ban on the use of force, except in cases of self-defence, has proven to be inadequate in other cases, such as in the former Yugoslavia and in Somalia. In conjunction with peacekeeping standards, both these situations saw cease-fire agreements signed and pledges of cooperation made between the relevant warring parties. Yet these measures proved ineffectual, and in each case further action had to be taken by the Security Council in an attempt to break down the velocity of these destructive cycles.

In Somalia, in accordance with UN law, the UN soldiers acted justly in self-defence. The battle that ensued in Mogadishu on 5 June 1993, between Aidid's faction and Pakistani soldiers, that saw the Pakistanis - who had been flying the UN flag over Aidid's weapons depot - shot down and their bodies later mutilated by a crowd of belligerent faction members, was clearly a resort to the use of force in self-defence on behalf of the UN. This particular crisis tipped off a string of increasingly hostile confrontations over the following couple of months. Instead of recalling the UN forces however, the decision was made under resolution 814 to 'use all means necessary' to apprehend Aidid and bring him to justice for the crimes he had apparently ordered. These actions were taken and justified within the context of self-defence as stipulated in just cause.

Post-Westphalia and Authority against the Principle of Non-Intervention

The end of the Cold War has seen a breach in the norm established in the Westphalia revolution: non-intervention. It encompasses several cases in which the UN or NATO has sanctioned military force to remedy an injustice within the boundaries of a state, or has taken on the administration of typically domestic matters. In using military force, the UN often has acted often without the consent of the target state's government or the cooperation of the parties in a civil war. Thus it has departed from the tone of pre-Cold War peacekeeping operations. The purpose of these interventions has included the delivery of humanitarian supplies, the ending of civil war, the enforcement of democratic elections, the rebuilding of failed state institutions, and the arrest of war criminals. The venues have included Iraq, the former Yugoslavia, Somalia, Rwanda, Haiti, Cambodia, Liberia, the Sudan, and elsewhere. Some have been failures; some have had mixed successes.[1] Paul Taylor argues that they represent new conditions whereby the UN system places collective self-determination above internal sovereignty, such that 'they [states] are now accountable to a higher authority for upholding certain standards of civilised behaviour'.[2]

Under certain conditions, when states fail to uphold minimal standards of justice - usually peace, order, basic human rights - some will be subject to the intervention of outside states acting in cooperation with an international authority. The target states are no longer absolute in their sovereignty. In the history of Westphalia this trend is significant, for it departs from non-intervention, which is perhaps the most enduring and prominent tenet of the Westphalia settlement. Non-intervention's most recent historical articulation occurs in the UN Charter, which states the principle more than once, and in subsequent UN resolutions and declarations. Throughout the Cold War, the principle remained robust as the UN consistently refrained from endorsing actual interventions, including unilateral humanitarian interventions in Uganda, Cambodia, and Bangladesh.[3]

But this conceptual significance must be balanced by a recognition of the limits of the practice. First, the intervention has been limited and selective. Depending on exactly how one interprets intervention since the end of the Cold War, it has been practised upon somewhere between five and fifteen states out of a total number of 190 plus, yet at the same time it has failed to occur in many states with injustices similar to those warranting intervention. Second, intervention is legitimate only when authorized by the UN Security Council, whose right to authorize force is prescribed by Chapter VII of its Charter. Intervention is far from a unilateral right. Third, the legitimacy of the intervention is not universal. Countries like China often dissent, although notably China has refrained from vetoing any of the above interventions in the Security Council. Fourth, in most cases of intervention, the Security Council has claimed a 'threat to international peace and security', signalling its refusal to openly label its actions intervention or depart radically from its traditional interpretation of the Charter. Although the construal is implausible, for the conflicts and injustices eliciting intervention were all primarily internal, it does reveal the UN's reluctance to endorse a general doctrine of intervention.[4] Finally, it is not clear how robustly the post-Cold War precedent of intervention will continue. The interventions thus far have enjoyed mixed success; the practice is far from a durable fixture in a new world order. Despite these caveats, however, intervention - widely endorsed and significantly practised - now seems well within the Security Council's legitimate authority.

Popular discourse *for* intervention has been highlighted by a sense of moral disgust at gross violations of human rights, whether in mass starvation in Somalia, Bosnian Serb concentration camps, or genocide in Rwanda. Although all of these cases are very different, their power to evoke emotions has come from the individual identifying with *rights* perceived to be universal to all humanity. This moral assumption is often manifest in the practical policy of institutions such as the UN, a fact which contributed to difficulties in formulating a unified doctrine of intervention.[5]

Intervention by one state in the affairs of another is normally objectionable for a variety of reasons, many of them moral. Most actual instances of military intervention, for example, are motivated entirely by the interests of the intervening state and tend to be unjust and exploitative. Even where there is a moral reason - or just cause - for intervention, the intervening state is almost certain to exploit its advantage in ways that are harmful to the target. Even in pursuit of a just cause, a military intervention typically will fail to satisfy the requirements of the traditional theory of the just war. It will fail to satisfy the 'requirement of necessity' if there is an alternative means of achieving the just cause that is less destructive but has a comparable probability of success. And it will fail to satisfy the 'requirement of proportionality' if the probable harm it would cause exceeds the probable good involved in achieving the just cause, taking due account of such considerations as the innocence or non-innocence of those benefited or harmed.[6] Because of the threat of counter-intervention and wider war military intervention often involves disproportionate risks or costs.

Intervention may be objectionable for non-moral reasons as well. Even if there is a just cause that can be achieved only by military intervention, and even if the expected costs of intervention would be proportionate, those costs may be prohibitive for any single state. Realists, indeed, hold that *any* costs to the intervening state are prohibitive unless they are outweighed by greater benefits to that same state.

Despite the consensus that these considerations establish a formidable presumption against the permissibility of intervention, there has been an increasing willingness in recent years to recognize that humanitarian intervention can in principle be legitimate. The various objections just cited have thus increasingly come into conflict with the perceived imperative to protect innocent individuals in other countries. The salience of this conflict has led some observers to suppose that the traditional prohibition of intervention has always been grounded in considerations of international stability and prudence. J. Bryan Hehir, for example, claims that 'the ethical calculus supporting the rule [of non-intervention] involves a clear consequentialist choice to give priority to order over justice in international relations'.[7]

This ignores the role of one historically important objection to intervention, namely that it violates the right to self-determination of the citizens of the state that is the target of the intervention. Intervention - whether military or non-military - has been thought to involve an imposition of an external will on those subject to it, a usurping of the people's right to shape and direct their own collective life. And because this is unjust, the conflict between the requirement of non-intervention and the requirement to protect the right to self-determination may be understood not just as a conflict between order and justice but also as a conflict between competing demands of justice.

This is to describe the conflict in terms of justice. Those more concerned with the political and legal dimensions of intervention may wish to phrase the problem in terms of the notion of sovereignty.[8] They will say that the further objection to intervention is that it is inconsistent with respect to state sovereignty, which is one of the essential foundations of the current international order. However, as the concern of this chapter is principally with the justice of intervention, it will not focus on considerations of sovereignty. But some of the claims will have implications for political and legal concerns.

Intervention

Intervention is the use of coercion, compulsion, or manipulation by some external agent or agents in an effort to effect or to prevent changes in the policies or practices of a state.[9] This understanding is more restrictive than one that sometimes appears in political discourse, according to which *external assistance* to a state that is intended to help the state defeat its internal opponents also counts as intervention. This broader notion is perfectly acceptable.[10] But since this chapter explores the conflict between intervention and self-determination, where the latter is commonly supposed to be expressed through and protected by the states, it will sharpen the focus of the inquiry to use the more restrictive definition.

Two further points should be highlighted. One is that intervention appears to require certain intentions. An act does not constitute intervention simply by virtue of causing or preventing changes in the policies of another state. To count as intervention, the act must be intended to cause or prevent the changes.

The other qualification of intervention is that action that is intended to thwart aggression by one state against another appears not to count as intervention, at least in ordinary language, even if it is intended to compel, coerce, or manipulate the target state. Suppose that Britain unjustly attacks the United States. Suppose further that the United States then resorts to compulsion, coercion, or manipulation in order to end or repel the UK's aggression or that a third party, Canada, does so. Neither response to Britain's aggression seems to count as intervention. Thus military self-defence and other-defence fall outside the category of intervention. The question of whether or not there are forms of military intervention that are morally justifiable is therefore equivalent to the question of whether or not there are just causes for war other than self-defence and other-defence.

Self-determination

The notion of collective self-determination is as elusive as the notion of intervention and is variously understood in the literature.[11] It is sometimes assumed that for a collection of people to be self-determining it is imperative for them to have their own state. On this view, the right of collective self-determination is the right to independent statehood.[12] This does not exhaust the understanding of self-determination. A collection of people may have its own state and yet be under foreign domination.

During the Cold War, for example, the Poles had their own state, yet they were not self-determining in any sense of the term since they were effectively controlled and dominated by the Soviet Union.

A more plausible view that avoids this objection is that a group of people is self-determining if it has a state that is effectively sovereign and politically independent. According to this view, that right of a people to self-determination may be violated by any action that denies them a state or that compromises the *de facto* sovereignty or political independence of their existing state. There is an obvious way of reading this proposed understanding that is highly misleading. For it suggests that all the citizens of any effectively sovereign and independent state are *ipso facto* self-determining. In one important sense they have a sovereign and independent state: they are citizens of one. But mere citizenship of an independent state is not sufficient to guarantee that one is a member of a self-determining collective. For the state may operate effectively on behalf of, or as the agent of, some subgroup of its citizens rather than of the citizenry as a whole. When this is the case and some other subgroup rightly feels that the state systematically subordinates its interests and claims to those of the other, who control the organs of the states, they will not be self-determining.[13]

These considerations suggest a third proposal. A group of people is self-determining if it has an effectively sovereign and independent nation-state that is the state of the group as a whole.[14] What makes a state *the* state 'of the Xs' is a complicated matter. There is a weak sense in which a state is the state of the Xs if it is controlled by - that is, if the government consists largely of - individuals who are identifiable as Xs. The 'rule by one's own kind' is, however, compatible with the possibility that the rulers are entirely corrupt and act with complete disregard for the interests and concerns of others of their kind. Thus one might insist on a stronger criterion whereby a state is the state of the Xs only if it represents or acts on behalf of the Xs as a whole. Alternatively, and even more strongly, a state might count as the state of the Xs only if all of the Xs living within its territory are able to participate in the formulation and administration of its laws and policies.[15]

These three variants of the last proposal all constitute acceptable notions of collective self-determination. They do not, however, capture all of the ways in which the notion of collective self-determination is legitimately used, for they all presuppose that there is an analytical link between self-determination and independent statehood; but there are common understandings of self-determination in which this is not the case.

There were self-determining political bodies that preceded states. And even today, when the world's peoples and territories are divided into sovereign states, it is not incoherent to suppose that a political community could be self-determining even if its political character were not embodied in or expressed through the medium of a state. In short, it is not a contradiction to suppose that there could be a politically organized community that was self-determining and yet was either stateless or incorporated within a state that was essentially the state of another group. Federal arrangements or schemes for regional autonomy seem capable of providing robust forms of self-determination.[16]

From the foregoing discussion, one can find three broad notions of collective self-determination. To be self-determining, a group must (1) have its own state (that is, the state must be the state of that group), (2) have effective political control over those areas of its collective life, or (3) be such that all of its members are able to participate in the governance of its political affairs.

One can refer to these three dimensions as 'statehood', 'internal control', and 'democracy', respectively. Statehood alone is neither necessary nor sufficient for either internal control or democracy. A group can have statehood and yet be subject to external domination. And, though some have denied this, a group can exercise effective control over its own essential affairs without having a state of its own.[17] Furthermore, a state of some particular group can have any one of a number of non-democratic forms of government, while a group that lacks its own state can nevertheless adopt democratic decision-making procedures for those areas of its life over which it exercises effective internal control.

This suggests that the core notion of self-determination is the second - internal control. The importance of statehood is derivative: the achievement of independent statehood is, in the preponderance of cases, the most effective means by which a group can ensure internal control. Of course, the importance of internal control is nominal if the indigenous regime is tyrannical. Nevertheless in modern times despotic internal control has generally been thought to be preferable to even the most liberal and benign forms of foreign control.[18]

Because self-determination is multidimensional, it is a matter of degree. A group that has a state of its own is at least minimally self-determining even if the state is effectively under foreign domination. That group would be self-determining to a higher degree if its state were effectively sovereign and independent (or perhaps, if it enjoyed autonomous status within the independent state of another group). And, among those groups that have their own effectively sovereign states, those with democratic political systems are more self-determining than those governed by non-democratic regimes. In short, full self-determination may require a combination of statehood, internal control, and democracy.

While it may be desirable for a group to be maximally self-determining, what the group has a right to may be something less. The right to self-determination is primarily the right to internal control.[19] If conditions are such that independent statehood is indispensable for the requisite degree of internal control, then perhaps the right to internal control implies a right to independent statehood. If it does, the latter right will be defeasible - that is, it may be overridden by countervailing considerations. Moreover, the right to internal control does not obviously imply a right to democracy, except to the extent that it implies an obligation among external agents not to impose a different form of government if internal control in fact results in democracy.[20]

Not only is there not always a right to those forms of self-determination that would be most desirable, but self-determination itself is not always desirable. There are some groups for whom self-determination is in no way desirable: for example, the group of all left-handed people, a group of Scientologists, or a group of vegetarians. Self-determination is an ideal that applies only to groups that are unified in certain *meaningful* ways. In order to fall within the spectrum of the ideal of self-determination, a group of people must together constitute a unit. And the degree to which self-determination is desirable for a group varies with the importance of the bonds that unify the group.

What sorts of unifying relations make self-determination, understood here as internal control, highly desirable? And why is it desirable for groups to be unified in these ways? It will be helpful to distinguish two types of unifying properties that are widely recognized as making self-determination desirable.

The first consists of shared characteristics, including commonalties of language, religion, ethnicity, territorial boundaries, tradition, and culture and custom generally. Groups whose members are unified by various sorts of commonalties constitute *cultural communities*. Nations are the obvious example of cultural community. Because the members of a cultural community share certain values, interests, and something called 'a way of life', it is important to them, as individuals, to live together, collectively pursuing their conception of the good life. The relevant commonalties also project a collective identity that assumes relative importance in the lives of the individual members, who identify with the community. The actions of the community and those within it become a source of pride and shame. Thus others accord the community recognition and respect. This acts as a well-being and self-esteem indicator of its individual members.[21]

The second type of unifying bond is essentially political. A collection of individuals can be firmly united by a common commitment to certain political, social, and economic ideals and institutions even if the bond that unites members of cultural communities does not unite them.[22] People may, for example, be unified by a commitment to liberal democratic principles even if they are 'multicultural'. Canada and (to some extent) the United States are examples of pluralistic, multinational states whose internal unity is more political than cultural or ethnic in character. Thus, for groups united by common political commitments, internal control is necessary if the individual members are to realize their shared political values and ideals.

Both in the case of cultural commonalties and in the case of shared political commitments, the relevant unifying features have a subjective dimension that is essential to the justification for self-determination. In order for a group to count as a cultural community there must be some recognition among its members that they constitute a group with a unique identity, a group that will or should have a common fate or future. Membership is in part a matter of mutual recognition.[23] But the members of the community must have a stable desire to live together in order to have a firm claim to self-determination. Of course, this flows naturally from the various commonalties that define their collective identity. Similarly, the fact that people share a commitment to certain political principles does nothing to make self-determination desirable unless they want a common life together governed by those principles. Although Canadians and Americans share a commitment to democratic political institutions, it does not follow that they desire to share their future through common self-determination. In short, it is a precondition that the individuals involved should, in Walzer's words, have 'some special commitment to one another and some special sense of their common life'.[24]

The important points are as follows. In order for it to be morally important that a group be self-determining - in the sense that its essential affairs are governed by members of the group rather than by non-members - the group must be unified in certain special ways. The desirability of self-determination depends both on the objective character of the unifying features within the group and on the presence of certain subjective factors, such as a shared desire to build a life together and, perhaps, a shared sense of collective identity. And the degree to which it is desirable for a group to be self-determining in this sense is one important consideration in determining whether or not, all things considered, the group should have an independent state of its own.

Walzer's Doctrine of Non-intervention

According to Walzer, 'the survival and independence of ...separate political communities', in which 'men and women freely shape their separate destinies', are 'the dominant values' of international society.[25] Walzer argues that intervention undermines these values by wresting from people in the target state control of their lives. However, he identifies three cases in which the otherwise rigid rule against intervention is relaxed. In order to evaluate and discuss the relationship between intervention and collective self-determination I want to critique Walzer's theory of non-intervention, in particular the three exceptions to the principle of non-intervention.

The three exceptions to the principle of non-intervention are summarized by Walzer as follows:

1   *Secession*: 'when a particular set of boundaries clearly contains two or more political communities, one of which is already engaged in a large-scale military struggle for independence; that is, when what is at issue is succession or national liberation.'
2   *Counter-intervention*: 'when the boundaries have already been crossed by the armies of a foreign power, even if the crossing has been called for by one of the parties in a civil war, that is, when what is at issue is counter-intervention.'
3   *Humanitarian intervention*: 'when the violation of human rights within a set of boundaries is so terrible that it makes talk of community or self-determination...seem cynical and irrelevant, that is, in cases of enslavement or massacre.' (Later he adds mass expulsion to the list of grievous abuses that may justify humanitarian intervention.)[26]

The first two of these three exceptions are corollaries of the idea that non-intervention is required by respect for self-determination. The first exception - secession - implicitly recognizes that the ideal of self-determination applies only in the case of groups that are unified in certain ways. This exception in effect defines the condition in which the borders of the state do not encompass a single political community. In these conditions, the presumption against intervention based on respect for self-determination fails to apply in the usual way since the ideal of self-determination itself does not apply to the population of the state as a whole. For the population of the state does not constitute a unit of the requisite sort but is divided into separate and distinct political communities.

However, there is a second reason why intervention on behalf of a secessionist movement is compatible with respect for self-determination. For not only does the population as a whole possess no right of self-determination that would be violated by intervention but, Walzer suggests, intervention would also support the secessionist community's own self-determination because it represents a different political community. Walzer states that the rule against interference is nullified as 'a foreign power, morally if not legally alien' is already intervening in the affairs of the political community.[27]

The second exception is also a corollary of the principle of non-intervention. The rationale behind this principle is that the only way to resolve conflicts within a state that is compatible with self-determination is to allow the outcome to be determined by the internal balance of power. When this balance is disrupted by external intervention, counter-intervention is justified in order to restore the initial balance, cancelling the effect of the previous intervention. 'The outcome of civil wars should reflect not the relative strength of the intervening states, but the local alignment of forces.'[28]

Only in the case of the third exception is the ideal of self-determination overridden. Walzer appears to assume that these are cases in which intervention involving a violation of self-determination is justified because the violation of human rights within the target state is so egregious that it outweighs the importance of respect for self-determination. The exception for humanitarian intervention is so weak precisely because the requirement of respect for self-determination is so strong.

I now want to work toward a fuller understanding of intervention by means of a critical examination of Walzer's account. Walzer correctly notes that not just any secessionist movement qualifies for assistance in the form of intervention. But the restrictions he imposes do not seem to me to be the right ones. In the passage quoted earlier, he insists that there should already be a 'large-scale military struggle' in progress, though he later suggests a weaker requirement of 'political or military struggle sustained over time'.[29] These conditions are, it seems, held to be necessary evidence that a large community supports the movement committed to independence. But insofar as the conditions reflect an insistence that members of the secessionist community be numerous, they seem to me to be a mistake. For a group with the right sort of unity for self-determination could in principle be quite small - too small, in many instances, to mount a credible military struggle, or even an effective political struggle, against the vastly greater power of the government of the state in which it finds itself. If Walzer's theory is confined only to military intervention, then of course the size of the secessionist community may be relevant, since it would obviously be wrong to go to war when the stakes are comparatively small, especially if there is not already a war in progress. But the objection to intervention in this case would be based entirely on considerations of proportionality. Respect for self-determination would favour intervention, but this consideration would be overridden by the disproportionate cost of war.

While the size of the secessionist community seems irrelevant except where considerations of proportionality are concerned, there are various other reasons why intervention on behalf of the secessionist movement may be wrong - some of which derive directly from reasons why the attempt at secession may itself be wrong. I believe Walzer readily accepts the assumption that if certain people within a state constitute a distinct political community to which the ideal of self-determination applies then they must have a right to secede or otherwise free themselves from control by the state.[30]

In the case of the second exception, McMahan objected to Walzer's doctrine of counter-intervention on the grounds that it is incompatible with the exceptions made for intervention on behalf of secession and in response to egregious violations of human rights.[31] The assumption behind this objection is that the doctrine of counter-intervention applies in these cases - that is, Walzer holds both that intervention on behalf of secession (or in defence of human rights) is permissible and that counter-intervention intended to cancel the effect of the initial intervention is also permissible. And this seems absurd. If the initial intervention is just, how can it be permissible to counter-intervene to restore the presumably unjust status quo? The mistake, however, seems not to be Walzer's.[32] His intended point is that counter-intervention is permissible only to cancel the effects of previous interventions that have violated the principle of non-intervention. Since certain interventions on behalf of secession or in defence of human rights both violate this principle, the doctrine of counter-intervention does not apply in these cases.

198 Human Rights and Military Intervention

In fact, Walzer's doctrine of counter-intervention is presented and developed with one specific type of case in mind, one in which 'a single community is disrupted by civil war'.[33] Civil war is distinguishable from secessionist conflict in two ways. First, the conflict occurs within a single community rather than between communities; and second, both parties to the conflict seek to establish control of the whole territory they occupy, that is, each seeks to assert control over the other. In a secessionist conflict one of the parties does not seek to control the other but to withdraw from its control. It seems clear that the principle of non-intervention has maximum plausibility when applied to civil war. When a single community is struggling to resolve an issue and all parties to the conflict will have to live with the outcome, it is plausible to suppose that the outcome should be determined only by those whose future is directly at stake - by the members of the community. It is, therefore, in these cases that the doctrine of counter-intervention also has maximum plausibility. Again, it is evident that this combined doctrine of non-intervention and counter-intervention follows from a commitment to respect for collective self-determination. When the members of a state have a collective identity of the requisite sort and what is at issue is their collective future, then it is their right to shape their future as they see fit.

This doctrine of non-intervention is overly restrictive, partly because it is based on too broad a conception of collective self-determination.[34] I will advance several objections, beginning with two that may already be familiar and work from these to others that are more fundamental and which bear directly on the relation between intervention and collective self-determination.

One problem with Walzer's account is that it contains a pernicious bias toward governments. This is clearest in the case of civil war. According to Walzer, in a civil war it is at no point permissible for an external power to intervene on behalf of the opponents of the government (provided, of course, that the government does not commit atrocities that make humanitarian intervention permissible). But Walzer appears to accept, as compatible with his account of the morality of intervention, the view of international law that it is permissible to assist 'the established government - [for] it is after all, the official representative of communal autonomy in international society - so long as it faces nothing more than internal dissension, rebellion, and insurgency'. Only if the opponents of the government demonstrate their capacity for 'self-help' by establishing 'control over some substantial portion of the territory and population of the states' does it become impermissible to provide military assistance to the government.[35]

But it is the nature of governments that they have numerous advantages over their domestic opposition: they can collect taxes, receive non-military aid from abroad, control the dissemination of information, and so on. If they are in addition permitted to call on military assistance from other states to suppress incipient dissent or rebellion, this may make it impossible for the minority groups ever to free themselves from repressive control by the state. It may make it impossible, for example, for a minority nation ever to meet the conditions that Walzer insists it must meet in order to establish itself as a distinct community that may legitimately be aided in its struggle for self-determination. In short, allowing intervention on behalf of governments in the early stages of domestic conflicts adds enormously to the inherent advantages of these governments and permits legitimate struggles for self-determination to be stopped before they start.

A related objection arises from the assumption that non-intervention allows for self-determination because it permits the outcome of conflicts within a state to be determined by the internal balance of forces. The problem is that the internal balance of forces may not reflect or even closely approximate the real strengths of the contending parties. One reason for this is that the government enjoys the entrenched advantages just noted. But there are many other ways in which the distribution of power may be skewed, so that the power of some groups is altogether disproportionate to their numbers. Bosnia is a case in point. In the Bosnian State, the Serbs were a minority that did not control the government. Yet they had access to weapons left in place by the Yugoslavian Territorial Army, which was dominated by Serbs. This, together with certain forms of support from their co-nationals in Serbia, gave them a degree of power far greater than their numerical strength. If one can think of the combined populations of Bosnia as constituting a unit to which the ideal of self-determination applies (an assumption that seemed plausible several years ago but is increasingly implausible now), then there is a clear sense in which their self-determination is not furthered by such non-interventionist practices as prohibiting external agents from supplying weapons to the Bosnian government. If counter-intervention can be justified as a means of restoring the distribution of power within a state that has been disturbed by a previous intervention, then it seems that intervention could also be justified in other instances when it would have the same desired effect. The effect would be that of eliminating advantages that one party to a conflict may have and that give it power disproportionate to its numbers, when these advantages result from factors no less arbitrary and irrelevant to self-determination than external intervention.[36]

A third objection seeks to expand the scope of Walzer's third exception to the rule of non-intervention: humanitarian intervention. As I said earlier, Walzer thinks that this exception is extremely restricted, allowing intervention only in the most extreme circumstances, since the abuses have to be grave enough to justify overriding the value of collective self-determination, which for him constitutes the supreme value in international ethics. But this conception of the right of collective self-determination is in tension with the understanding of the right of self-determination at the individual level. In short, the scope of the right of individual self-determination is constrained by the rights and even the interests of others. Admittedly, it is true that an agent's right to self-determination may protect certain acts that are both wrongful and injurious to others, so that others may not forcibly intervene to stop them. For example, a parent may be acting within her rights if she inflicts an excessive punishment on her child. Yet, if the harshness of the punishment exceeds certain limits, others may intervene. The fact that the point at which intervention becomes permissible is beyond the point at which the punishment becomes excessive does not mean that, even within the intimate setting of family life, the right of self-determination is unconstrained.

It is reasonable to assume that the right of collective self-determination is similarly restricted. It does not give a political community a licence to do whatever it pleases. The right is limited by other elements of morality, including the rights of individuals. Most people acknowledge this in cases in which the victims of a state's wrongful action are the citizens of another state. Walzer, however, seems to assume that matters are different when the victims are members of the same political community as the wrongdoers. But why should this matter if the action is seriously wrong? Why should the right of collective self-determination protect such action?

It might be argued that, in this case, the right of collective self-determination belongs to the victims as well. How can their right to collective self-determination be limited by their other rights (that is, rights that forbid their being victimized in the relevant way)? Some, indeed, have supposed that the right of self-determination covers all purely internal action by a state because all such action is relevantly self-regarding. This, however, is to take the fiction of a collective self too literally. When the government wrongly harms certain citizens of the state it controls, it is absurd to suppose that this can be described as a single self-determining unit harming itself. It is obviously possible for members of a subgroup within a single political community seriously to wrong or harm the members of another subgroup, and there is no reason to suppose that such action is protected by a right to self-determination possessed collectively by the members of both groups. For, at least beyond a certain point, any right at all does not cover this action. There may be good reasons why others outside the community ought not to intervene, but the claim that intervention would violate a single right of self-determination possessed by the agents and their victims alike is not among them.

Walzer's theory may draw plausibility from the fact that it is, primarily, a theory about military intervention. For it is not unreasonable to suppose that military intervention is warranted only when violations of human rights begin to reach the level of atrocity. Even if a government is acting outside the scope of its right to self-determination, military intervention may be a disproportionate response in that the harm it would cause would outweigh the harm it would prevent. If true, this would be a decisive objection.[37] But it derives from the military character of intervention, not from considerations of self-determination.

The Limits of the Ideal of Self-determination

So far it has been assumed here that certain categories distinguished by Walzer coincide. There are, first, cases in which a state encompasses two or more distinct political communities whose interests and perhaps efforts at self-determination are in conflict. The only explicit discussion of these cases in *Just and Unjust Wars* occurs in the subsection entitled 'Secession', in which Walzer defends the first exception to the principle of non-intervention. Interestingly, while the subsection in which the third exception is discussed is called 'Humanitarian Intervention', the subsection in which the second exception is defended is called not 'Counter Intervention' but 'Civil War'. In a summary of this section in a subsequent article, Walzer observes that it deals with cases in which a 'single community is disrupted by civil war'. This suggests an assumption that conflicts between distinct political communities within a single state take the form of struggles for secession or national liberation. When there are problems, struggles, or conflicts within a state that do not take this form, Walzer believes that we are to assume that they involve a single political community.

But this leaves out what is arguably the most common form of conflict within a single state: namely, that in which two or more distinct political communities are engaged in a struggle for control of the entire state. These conflicts do not fit either of the categories distinguished above. They are not instances of secession or national liberation, since neither community seeks independence; rather, each seeks effective control of the other. Nor are they civil wars as understood by Walzer in his discussion of the counter-intervention. It would be a mistake to assume that Walzer defines civil war so that the category excludes conflicts between distinct communities, none of which seeks separation or independence. Nevertheless these conflicts are ones that he does not explicitly consider.[38] Yet I suspect that they may be more common than civil wars that occur within a single political community. For when the conflict between two groups has reached the point of war, with each side strong enough to control substantial amounts of territory, it becomes difficult to see the groups as constituting one community, much less a political community with a common political unity. If the groups had sufficient political unity to constitute a political community, they would not be at war.

Cases in which two or more indigenous and apparently distinct communities are struggling for control of a jointly occupied territory are covered by Walzer's theory of non-intervention. Since such cases do not fall within any of Walzer's three exceptions to the principle of non-intervention (unless they involve massacre, enslavement, or mass expulsion or there has been prior unjust intervention), Walzer's theory implies that they are off-limits to intervention. Why is this? Recall that the three exceptions to the principle of non-intervention are intended to state the conditions in which the principle either does not apply or is overridden. In the absence of one or another of these conditions, intervention is ruled out because it would violate the right of collective self-determination of the community within the target state.

Yet in cases of civil war between distinct political communities, each vying for control of the whole, it is highly doubtful that the two communities share a single right of self-determination that might be violated by intervention. For, as was noted earlier, a group must be unified in certain ways in order for it to be reasonably ascribed a single right of self-determination. But if it is appropriate to describe the groups involved in a civil war as distinct political communities, then that suggests that they are together not unified in one of the ways that are sufficient for the possession of a single right to self-determination.

This point can be expressed in another way. Self-determination is a matter of domestic or internal control. As Walzer acknowledges, it has less to do with self-rule in the sense of rule through democratic institutions than with the absence of external control or domination. But the distinction between domestic and foreign assumes that there is a unit in the relevant sense: a community with a shared sense of identity, a set of common political goals, and so on. The less unity there is within the group, the less clear and important the distinction between domestic and foreign, or internal and external becomes.[39] Thus, in conflicts between two distinct political communities within the same state, the two may in effect be foreigners to each other. Each may have more in common with some nominally external group than with other groups within their state. This is the case, for example, with the Serbs, Croats, and Muslims in Bosnia. In cases of this sort, the population of a state as a whole may not form a unit with respect to which the distinction between domestic and foreign has its normal significance. And, if that is the case, the notion of domestic control or communal self-determination may, when applied to the population as a whole, be largely empty.

The main challenge to Walzer's theory of non-intervention is that if a state contains two or more communities that are sufficiently divided to be at war with one another, then the population of the state may not possess a single right of self-determination that would be violated by intervention.[40] In these circumstances, the case for intervention would parallel Walzer's own argument for the permissibility of intervention in secessionist conflicts. If intervention is permissible on behalf of a representative secessionist movement because the state as a whole no longer constitutes a single community with a single right to self-determination, then it should also be permissible (other things being equal) in other cases in which this is true but in which the conflict between communities is not over secession or national liberation. Just as in the case of secession the concern for self-determination must focus on the claim to self-determination of the seceding group rather than on that of the population as a whole, so in the case of civil war the belligerent groups may all be striving to define their own conflicting claims to self-determination. There is no longer only one unit whose self-determination is at issue. It may be radically unclear what respect for self-determination requires. But it no longer unambiguously requires non-intervention.

To this it might be replied that there remains an important difference between secession and civil war. In the case of secession, the secessionists seek self-determination for themselves but do not seek to impose their own rule on the other citizens of the state from which they seek to withdraw. But the group that controls the state and opposes the secession does seek to continue to impose its rule on the secessionists, as for example in the recent conflict between East Timor and Indonesia. There is an asymmetry between the claims of the secessionists and the anti-secessionists - one that makes intervention on behalf of the secessionists prima facie compatible with respect for the self-determination of both parties. For the goal of the secessionists is compatible with self-determination for both groups while the goal of the anti-secessionists is not. In the case of civil war, by contrast, there is no such asymmetry between the goals of the contending parties. Each seeks to impose its rule on the other. Thus intervention on behalf of one is necessarily incompatible with respect for the self-determination of the other (or others, if more than two groups are involved as in Bosnia). This, it might be argued, is why the case for intervention on behalf of the secessionist movement does not automatically transfer to intervention in a civil war.

Thus, it suggests that, other things being equal, the presumption against intervention in a civil war is stronger than that against intervention on behalf of the efforts at secession. But it leaves the earlier conclusion standing – namely, that intervention in a civil war between two distinct political communities is not ruled out simply by a requirement of respect for the self-determination of the population as a whole. As noted, what is required by respect for self-determination may be radically unclear, since the efforts at self-determination of different groups are in conflict. Yet there will be cases in which intervention may on balance promote the value of self-determination.[41]

The Hard Cases for Collective Self-determination in a Post-Westphalian System

My argument is that interaction between political communities, in which the principles of collective self-determination and non-intervention are embodied, needs a protective component in the form of an internal control structure, and the Westphalian order (nation state plus international anarchy) is the historical form that this structure has taken over the last couple of hundred years. The crisis of this Westphalian order and the emergence of what Richard Falk has called 'pathological anarchies' also implies a crisis for the nation state, and consequently, the principle of non-intervention, as we know it, is being undermined as the protective component constituted by the nation state, in other words, the modern form of state, is being eroded.[42]

As the recent crisis in Chechnya shows, the major threat for a substantial part of a population in a state can come from the state, or rather the regime in power. In the case of one group holding the power and authority over the entire state, which includes the obligation of the state to protect 'its' people, the victims of 'failed states' can do nothing but appeal to the compassion of 'foreigners', that is, other states, and trust that they will conceive a need for intervention.

Humanity as such is not yet an international political actor. Humanitarian action is carried out in the name of humanity, by states (normally in the formal UN context) that have reached a consensus that enough is enough, or by international NGOs. However, in order that they may help victims of war or victims of political oppression in undemocratic and conflict-ridden states, internationally active NGOs are ultimately dependent on protection from 'decent, democratic states'. Instead of wide-reaching human security the year 2000 retains the reality of what might be called 'selective humanitarianism'.

All this underlines the need for better understanding of the world order emerging beyond the 350-year-old Westphalian system. Certainly, there is more than one scenario for such a new world order. Thus the maintenance of human security and welfare, or peace and development, in this new world will become no easier than the tried and traditional.

Post-Westphalian rationality implies that the state has lost its historical usefulness, and certain new solutions to problems of security must increasingly be found in the form of multinational collective decision-making and action. It may be correct to insist that the state has not disappeared (very few institutions do), but at the same time both the capacity of the state as actor and the principle of collective self-determination have changed so as to make the role of state and citizen in post-Westphalia qualitatively different from the Westphalian era.

Conclusion

We are finally moving from the security of the sovereign state to the security of humanity. The constraints of the Cold War meant that the UN could only tackle human rights at the level of enunciating principles (as in the two 1966 human rights covenants) and passing resolutions. In most cases it could not intervene in countries to enforce its principles, nor could it give forces a mandate to defend human rights and protect vulnerable populations.

Now, in the post-Cold War era, some of the constraints which prevented the UN from authorizing action within states have gone. In many debates of the 1990s human security had been presented as a key approach to security issues. As the Commission on Global Governance said, 'Although it is necessary to continue to uphold the right of states to security, so that they may be protected against external threats, the international community needs to make the protection of people and their security an aim of global security policy.'[43]

As so often in life, the principle is fine. The devil is in the detail. It is extremely difficult to work out a coherent UN-based system of 'human security'. In the 1990s the UN did in fact intervene in an unprecedented number of conflicts. UN Security Council resolutions in respect of northern Iraq, the former Yugoslavia, Somalia and Rwanda have all put great emphasis on humanitarian issues as justification for the use of outside forces. In July 1994 it went so far as to authorize military action against Haiti to change its government - an intervention which eventually took place in September 1994.

As the experience of the 1990s has shown, enforcing humanitarian and human rights norms in distant conflicts is a very uncertain business. International forces seem less willing to accept sacrifices in such causes than would be the case if their own interest was directly involved; also they may fail to understand important aspects of the culture in which they are intervening (returning in thought to the Somali crisis first mentioned in the introduction). Further, there are strong arguments about the selectivity of UN actions. Why restore democracy in Haiti, but not in Burma or China? The answer, of course, is that traditional great power calculations, and traditional considerations of prudence, still play a key role in contemporary international intervention as Walzer forcefully, yet for this author unconvincingly, argues.[44]

Notes

1 Ramsbotham, O. and Woodhouse, T., *Humanitarian Intervention in International Conflict* (Cambridge: Cambridge University Press, 1996); Whittaker, D., *Conflict and Reconciliation in the Contemporary World* (London: Routledge, 1999).
2 Taylor, P., 'The United Nations in the 1990s: proactive cosmopolitanism and the issue of sovereignty', *Political Studies*, Vol.47, 1999, pp.548-550.

3   Article 2(4) prohibits unilateral intervention in the form of 'the threat or use of force against territorial integrity or political independence of any state, or in any other manner consistent with the Purposes of the United Nations', whereas Article 2 (7) is directed against the intervention of the United Nations in matters which are in states' domestic jurisdictions.   Subsequent UN Documents even more directly condemn intervention, especially unilateral intervention.   For arguments that UN law forbids intervention, see Damrosch, L., 'Commentary on Collective Military Intervention to Enforce Human Rights', in L. Damrosch and D. Scheffer (eds), *Law and Force in the New International Order*, (Boulder: Westview Press, 1991), pp.215-223; Pease K. and Forsythe, D., 'Human rights, humanitarian intervention and world politics', *Human Rights Quarterly*, Vol.15, 1993, pp.290-314.

4   Scheffer, D., 'Toward a broader doctrine of humanitarian intervention', *University of Toledo Law Review*, Vol.23, 1992, pp.253-294; Copra J. and Weiss, T., 'Sovereignty is no longer sacrosanct: Codifying humanitarian intervention', *Ethics and International Affairs*, Vol.6, 1992, 95.

5   Donaldson, T. (1995) 'International Deontology Defended: A Response to Hardin, R., "International Deontology"', *Ethics and International Affairs*, Vol.9, 1995, pp.133-139.

6   McMahan, J., and McKim, R., 'The Just War and the Gulf War', *Canadian Journal of Philosophy*, Vol.23, 1993, pp.506-518 and 523-30.

7   Hehir, J.B., 'Intervention: From Theories to Cases', *Ethics and International Affairs*, Vol.9, 1995.

8   Lauterpacht, E., 'Sovereignty - Myth or reality', *International Affairs*, Vol.73 (1), 1997, pp.137-150.

9   Walzer, M., *Just and Unjust Wars* (New York: Basic Books, 1977), pp.61 and 72; Walzer, M., 'The Moral Standing of States: a Response to Four Critics', in C. Beitz, M. Cohen, T. Scanlon, and A.J. Simmons (eds), *International Ethics* (Princeton: Princeton University Press, 1985), pp.217-37; Beitz, C., 'Justice and International Relations', in Beitz et al., ibid., 1985, pp.282-311; Roberts, A., 'The Road to Hell...A Critique of Humanitarian Intervention', *Harvard International Review*, Vol.16 (1), 1993, p.10.

10   Hoffman, S., *Duties beyond Borders: On the Limits and Possibilities of Ethical Politics* (Syracuse: Syracuse University Press, 1981).

11   By employing the adjective 'collective' it is hoped the chapter will show the distinction between this notion and individual self-determination or autonomy. I avoid the more common term 'national self-determination', which might be thought to imply that the ideal of collective self-determination properly applies only to nations. See Rawls, J., *A Theory of Justice* (Oxford, Oxford University Press, 1980), pp.378-379. Rawls puts forward the principle that justice (internationally) requires the right to self-determination and therefore the right to self-defence. Also see Beitz, C., *Political Theory and International Relations* (Princeton: Princeton University Press, 1999), pp.104-105, 110-112, 115 and 134.

12   Also it is important to note that some communitarians argue in rejection of the claim of Particularism: Sandel, M., *Liberalism and the Limits of Justice*, (Cambridge: Cambridge University Press, 1982), pp.55-59 and 152-154; Walzer, M., *Spheres of Justice* (Oxford, Blackwell, 1983); French, S. and Gutman, A., 'The Principle of National Self-determination' in V. Held, S. Morgenbesser and T. Nagel (eds)

Philosophy, Morality and International Affairs (Oxford: Oxford University Press, 1974), pp.138-153.

13 Taylor, C., *The Malaise of Modernity* (Concord, Ontario: Anansi Press, 1991), pp.25-30; Miller, D., *On Nationality* (Oxford, Clarendon Press, 1995), p.80.

14 This is to say there exists a belief in the idea of the common good, or as Rousseau called it the General Will. Kymlicka argues that in liberal societies there is a notion of the common good, 'but it is adjusted to the preferences and the conceptions of the good of the people who live in them'. Kymlicka, W., *Contemporary Political Philosophy* (Oxford: Oxford University Press, 1990), p.206.

15 McMahan, J., 'The Ethics of International Intervention' in K. Kipnis and D. Meyers (eds), *Political Realism and International Morality: Ethics in the Nuclear Age* (Boulder: Westview Press, 1988), pp.75-101, on p.83.

16 Daniel Philpott defines self-determination as 'a legal arrangement which givers [a group] independent statehood or greater autonomy within a federal state'. Philpott, D., 'In Defense of Self-Determination', *Ethics* 105 (1995), p.44; Buchanan, A., *Secession: the Morality of Political Divorce, from Fort Sumter to Lithuania and Quebec* (Boulder: Westview Press, 1991) p.50.

17 Michael Walzer writes that 'to give up the state is to give up any effective self-determination'. What Walzer seems to mean here, however, is not that a community cannot be self-determining without a state of its own, but that other means of achieving self-determination require as a background condition that there be sovereign states. Walzer, *Spheres of Justice*, op. cit., 1983, p.44.

18 This is difficult in cases where the political subgroup constitutes a great majority of the population. The case of 'failed' states appears to be less problematic than those in which the state or political subgroup has become the predator such as in Rwanda where the Hutu majority massacred the Tutsi minority. See Clarke, J.N., 'Ethics and Humanitarian Intervention', *Global Society* 13 (4) (1999), pp.498-500. Also, McMahan cites this as a possible outcome in similar circumstances. He cites Christopher Morris: 'until this century the norm for most peoples, European included, was rule by foreigners. Just and efficient rule by foreigners seemed preferable to most people to unjust or inefficient rule by one's own.' See Morris, C., *An Essay on the Modern State* (Cambridge: Cambridge University Press, 1997), ch.8.

19 Raz, J. and Margalit, A., 'National Self-determination', *Journal of Philosophy*, Vol.87 (9), 1990, pp.439-461, on pp.443-447; Taylor, C., *Philosophy of the Human Sciences* (Cambridge: Cambridge University Press, 1985); Walzer, *Spheres of Justice*, op. cit., 1983.

20 Rawls, J., 'The Idea of an Overlapping Consensus', *Oxford Journal of Legal Studies*, 1987, pp.20-25; Halliday, F., 'States, Discourses, and Classes', *Millennium*, Vol.17 (1), 1988, pp.72-80.

21 These are claims elaborated in McMahan, J., 'The Limits of National Partiality' in McKim, R. and J. McMahan (eds), *The Morality of Nationalism* (Oxford: Oxford University Press, 1998); Tamir, Y., *Liberal Nationalism* (Princeton: Princeton University Press, 1993); Taylor, C., *Philosophy of the Human Sciences* (Cambridge: Cambridge University Press, 1985); Walzer, 'The Moral Standing of States', op. cit., 1985; and to a certain extent Raz and Margalit, 'National Self-determination', op. cit., 1990.

22   An example of this is a constitutional patriotism such as that seen in Habermas, Ingram or one that Margaret Canovan argues against. I tend to agree with Canovan in that Habermasian constitutional patriotism is disappointing with respect to reconciling universal humanitarian principles and particularistic political commitments. See especially Habermas, 'Citizenship and National Identity', p.514 in Appendix II of Habermas, J., *Between Facts and Norms: Contributions to a Discourse Theory of Law and Democracy* (Cambridge, MA: MIT Press, 1996); and Ingram, A., 'Constitutional Patriotism', *Philosophy and Social Criticism*, Vol.22 (6), 1996, pp.1-18.

23   There are various sources of support for this in the literature: see White, S., 'Freedom of Association and the Right to Exclude', *Journal of Political Philosophy* Vol.5 (4), 1997, pp.373-391; Iveson, D., 'Modus Vivendi Citizenship', *Rusel Working Papers* 31, Department of Politics, University of Exeter, 1997; Connolly, W., *The Ethos of Pluralization* (Minnesota: Minnesota University Press, 1995) for a general discussion; and Connolly, W., *Identity/Difference: Democratic Negotiations of Political Paradox*, (London: Cornell University Press, 1991), pp.64-68; McCormack, N., 'Is Nationalism Philosophically Credible?', in W. Twining (ed), *Issues of Self-Determination* (Aberdeen: Aberdeen University Press, 1991).

24   Walzer, *Spheres of Justice*, op. cit., 1983, p.62.

25   Walzer, *Just and Unjust Wars*, op. cit., 1977, pp.61 and 72.

26   Walzer, *Just and Unjust Wars*, op.cit., p.90; Walzer, 'The Mortal Standing of States', op. cit., 1985, pp.225-226.

27   Walzer, *Just and Unjust Wars*, op. cit., p.93.

28   Walzer, 'The Moral Standing of States', op. cit., p.101.

29   Walzer, *Just and Unjust Wars*, op.cit., pp.93-94.

30   I cannot argue against this assumption here although many have provided very good arguements elsewhere. See Buchanan, A., *Secession: The Morality of Political Divorce from Fort Sumter to Lithuania and Quebec* (Boulder: Westview Press, 1991), ch.3. For a recent defence of a position between those of Walzer and Buchanan, see Philpott, D., 'In Defense of Self-Determination', *Ethics*, 1995; Galston, W., 'Pluralism and Social Unity', *Ethics*, 1999, pp.711-726; and Pogge, T., *Realizing Rawls* (Ithaca: Cornell University Press, 1989).

31   McMahan, 'The Limits of National Partiality', op. cit., 1988, p.96.

32   Though his occasional presentations of a seemingly unqualified permission to intervene to balance previous interventions may be misleading.

33   Walzer, 'The Moral Standing of States', in C. Beitz et al., op. cit., 1985.

34   J. Bryan Hehir has a strong position on this point. He argues: 'the ethical calculus supporting the rule of non-intervention involves a clear consequentialist choice to give priority to order over justice in international relations'. Hehir, 'Intervention: from Theories to Cases', op. cit., 1995, p.4.

35   Walzer, *Just and Unjust Wars*, op. cit., 1977, p.96.

36   Raz, J., *The Morality of Freedom* (Oxford: Clarendon Press, 1986), ch.9.

37   McMahan and McKim, 'The Just War and the Gulf War', op. cit., 1993.

38   There is a footnote spanning pp.54-55 of *Just and Unjust Wars* in which Walzer refers to 'the problem of national minorities - groups of people who do not fully join (or do not join at all) in the contract that constitutes the nation'. There he claims that, unless they are subject to 'radical mistreatment' (in which case their situation would fall under his third exception), they do not affect his argument.

39   Parfit, D., *Reasons and Persons* (Oxford: Clarendon Press, 1984), p.339.
40   This point is explored in great detail by Linklater, A., *The Transformation of Political Community* (Cambridge: Polity Press, 1998), esp. p.103n; Linklater, A., 'Citizenship and Sovereignty in the Post-Westphalian State', *European Journal of International Relations*, Vol.2 (2), 1996, pp.77-103; Hoffman, M., 'Agency, Identity and Intervention', in Forbes, I., and Hoffman, M. (eds.), *Political Theory, International Relations and the Ethics of Intervention* (Basingstoke: Macmillan, 1993), pp.194-211; and McMahan, J., 'Intervention and Collective Self-Determination', *Ethics and International Affairs*, Vol.11, 1997, pp.1-24.
41   Clarke, J.N., 'Ethics and Humanitarian Intervention', *Global Society*, Vol.13 (4), 1999, pp.489-509; Hardin, 1995, pp.133-139.
42   Falk, R., *Predatory Globalization: a Critique* (Cambridge: Polity Press, 1999).
43   Commission on Global Governance, *Our Global Neighbourhood*, 1995, p.82.
44   I would like to thank David Armstrong, Richard Newman, Oliver Richmond, Nigel Pleasants, Nicola Pratt, Bice Maiguashca, and all the participants at the 2001 conference of the Society of Applied Philosophy for their helpful contributions in completing this chapter.

Chapter 11

Repression, Secession and Intervention

Paul Gilbert

1.

Here is an all too common scenario. First, nationalists launch an armed rebellion in some portion of an established state. Second, the state employs repressive measures against members of the population that the nationalists represent.[1] Third, external powers mount, or at least consider mounting, some form of military intervention in the established state on humanitarian grounds. How are we to assess the ethics of such an intervention, remembering that, in the absence of authorization from the United Nations Security Council, which is unlikely to be forthcoming, such intervention seems contrary to international law since it involves the use of force 'against the territorial integrity and political independence of a state'?[2] Should we adopt the increasingly influential view that, despite such prohibitions, the existence of borders is not relevant to the moral justification of military intervention to prevent gross human rights violations?

This paper is concerned, in a very limited way, to examine this cosmopolitan defence, as I shall call it, of humanitarian intervention in the sort of scenario sketched out above. I shall be comparing the cosmopolitan view with a position that draws on the resources of just war theory, which, I shall argue, cosmopolitans cannot as plausibly do. I shall suggest that this older way of thinking about such intervention may both more accurately capture its character than contemporary cosmopolitanism and provide a better account of what sort of action can be justified.

First, though, I need to indicate more precisely what I intend here by 'cosmopolitanism', while acknowledging that there are many ways of filling out this position. Central to the position described here is, first, the idea that there are certain universal human rights, graspable independently of their particular institutional forms. While their scope is debatable, they at least include rights to life, liberty and the sort of settled existence that

212 Human Rights and Military Intervention

rights of residence and property have traditionally guaranteed. Second, that such rights should be safeguarded imposes a general duty upon others. Thus, while for pragmatic reasons the duty may best be allocated to the authorities of the right-holder's own state, it follows, third, that 'national boundaries do not, with this approach, have any ultimate moral significance'.[3] From this we can infer that where the state fails in this duty it falls upon others to carry it out. The right of humanitarian intervention within such a state may be defended by cosmopolitans as needed so that others can act on behalf of all of us in safeguarding the human rights that are being violated. It is worth noting that on this cosmopolitan view, in contrast to some others, international agreement of the sort embodied in UN Security Council decisions is not needed to confer a right of intervention. While it would be desirable to institutionalize the transnational duty to safeguard human rights, this is a moral duty whose performance can require no such sanction. Nevertheless, the cosmopolitan defence of intervention does imply that current legal prohibitions have no moral basis and, other things being equal, should be amended to allow the transnational safeguarding of human rights where necessary.

International law depends as much upon what behaviour by states comes to be accepted as upon international declarations and the like. But such behaviour requires a rationale and contemporary cosmopolitanism increasingly provides one for the armed interventions which have been launched in recent years without any clear legal mandate, as, for example, in Yugoslavia. Such widely accepted interventions give rise to emerging norms of international behaviour which contrast with earlier practices, and one of the aims of this paper will be to pose against cosmopolitanism what I shall term the statist objection to acceptance of these new norms. The objection is that the principle of non-intervention which proscribes even humanitarian action should not be qualified to permit it and that, in its unqualified form, it reflects a *moral* right of states and thus a respect in which boundaries that are in some sense national do have a significance which is not merely administrative.

2.

In considering the statist objection I want to sidestep an abstract discussion of sovereignty or territorial integrity in order to concentrate on how it arises naturally from the kind of objection a state actually or potentially intervened in on putatively humanitarian grounds might make in the sort of scenario we are considering. As I am presenting it, the statist objection to relaxing the principle of non-intervention hinges on the idea that without authority to take military action within the borders of a state, which they would possess if invited in by its government, interveners are, whatever their good intentions, acting unjustly.[4] They are engaged in an act of aggression against the state. The cosmopolitan response is, of course, to assert that where humanitarian intervention is justified the interveners do have authority to use force to protect human rights, just as it is the state that normally has it. Thus, just as the state does not think of its military actions in quelling low level rebellion as war, but rather as the prevention and punishment of crime, so intervention is often similarly viewed not as war against the state[5] but as a kind of policing operation. Indeed, there is often a kind of Lockean argument that it is the government of the repressive state that are now the rebels committing crimes which need to be prevented or punished.[6] So one way of presenting the contrast is as a dispute over whether intervention constitutes war, as statists claim, or something different in principle if not in practice, as cosmopolitans do. And this issue turns precisely on whether there is a right to cross borders to protect rights when the state fails, as cosmopolitans claim, or there is not.

One way an objection to intervention might be developed is this. The established state will allege, in the scenario we envisage, that the rebels lack any authority in their resort to force, for authority to use force within its borders rests solely with the established state. Intervention, however benevolent in intention, will constitute support for the rebels and interveners will possess no more authority than rebels do. The notion of authority involved here requires some clarification. It depends, in the first step of the argument, on an appeal to the just war principle that not just any armed group may justly wage war, but only one that operates under 'proper authority'.[7] There are two aspects to this. One is that those who fight should be under effective control so that the rules of war which determine *jus in bello* are observed. Anti-state rebels may well not be under such control and may not respect these requirements. In particular, nationalist rebels may show little concern for the welfare of civilians who are not of their own nation. The other aspect of proper authority is that of being in a position to decide to go to war for the right sort of reasons, to ensure, at least in one's own eyes, *jus ad bellum*. The established state denies that rebels are in this position since it claims sole responsibility for the defence of its own citizens. In denying the political claims of the nationalist minority it *ipso facto* denies rebel forces the authority to defend their people. The overall conclusion drawn is that rebels lack proper authority to fight and so should not be assisted by external intervention. Such intervention lacks authority.

This second step of the argument which denies interveners authority in virtue of their effective support for rebels who back it may at first sight seem to depend upon a serious equivocation. What the rebels allegedly lack is authority to fight a war. But that is something that intervening powers will possess simply in virtue of being states themselves. What they allegedly lack is authority to enforce the protection of human rights within another state's borders. Yet in drawing upon just war ideas the objection to intervention relies upon the close connection made by that theory between the authority to wage war and the authority to govern. In the classical theory the proper authority in war is a ruler, or, in modern terms, a state. The implied reason is that only a ruler can represent the vital interests of those they embroil in war, since the only good reason for going to war is to protect a territory within which these interests can be preserved through the rule of law. The objection, then, is that interveners would have the authority they claim to enforce respect for rights in a territory only if the rebels there did. But, lacking the powers of government, the rebels do not, so interveners can only be regarded as waging war upon the established state.

There are, I believe, two conflicting conceptions of a state's authority involved in the cosmopolitan and statist positions. The cosmopolitan regards the authority of the state as dependent principally upon its role in safeguarding human rights. The principle of non-intervention is there simply to enable it to fulfil this role, so that it is entitled to defend itself when attacked just because such an attack threatens its people's human rights. If, however, the state fails in its role then there is no reason not to intervene and no entitlement of self-defence against intervention which upholds rather than threatens rights.

The statist conception of authority is less straightforward and can, doubtless, take several forms. The contrast I wish to draw here is between the cosmopolitan's purely administrative view of the state, which loses authority through maladministration, and a view of it as a moral entity responsible for jurisdiction over a people. As such it is the source of law for the people within a given territory, so that different jurisdictions may quite properly be expected to be quite different, reflecting the different circumstances to which people have had to adapt. That the fundamental human rights of life, liberty and settled existence mentioned earlier are to be found in states generally may be taken simply to reflect the fact that they are necessary to anything that we would want to call a state, that is to say, an organization which maintains order by enforcing law,[8] rather than a tyranny, which reduces people to subjection. That such rights are ostensibly universal in states does not, then, need to reflect the existence of some source of law which lies beyond the state and by which its actions are to be judged. The authority of the state depends, rather, upon its fulfilling its jurisdictional role and is, indeed, lost if that is lost. But its right of self-defence is necessary for it to preserve its jurisdiction within a territory; for there could be no system of specific jurisdictions without a general principle of non-intervention across borders. It is along such lines, I believe, that the statist conceives of authority.

There are, if I am making the distinction aright, different consequences of embracing these contrasting conceptions which explain the different attitudes of cosmopolitans and statists to intervention, but before developing them I want to head off an objection that the statist position, as I have sketched it, is either unmotivated or depends for its plausibility upon cosmopolitan assumptions which should lead all the way to the cosmopolitan conception. The objection is that the statist conception presents jurisdictional rule as preferable to tyranny only because the former safeguards human rights while the latter violates them, so a full blooded cosmopolitanism is the natural conclusion to draw. But this objection simply begs the question: Why should we not say instead that human rights are valued, not as independently identifiable goods, but as aspects of living under jurisdictional government? And why do we value that? Well, the statists can assert, generalizing from Aristotle's observations on the Greeks,[9] people just do, as is evident from the kinds of society they are tolerably happy in.[10]

3.

Let us turn, then, to the sorts of way an external power might respond to a state's denial of their authority to intervene, and see whether these are best made sense of on a cosmopolitan or a statist conception. As will now be obvious, what such a power must do is claim that the state intervened in has lost its authority in the relevant respect. The authority of external powers cannot, therefore, be attacked as trespassing upon the state's authority but rather derives from alternative sources in the absence of it. This response admits of a number of different versions depending both upon its theoretical grounding and on the particular circumstances prevailing. Analytically it is important to distinguish several cases even though in practice they may be composited or confused.

The first is that in which authority is lost because the established state can no longer control a part of its territory so that there is a breakdown of law and order within it. In this case another state may justify intervening as required to maintain order and thereby prevent the violation of human rights which may result from disorder. Assuming that the intervening power does have some authority in such a case,[11] it is important to see that the scope of this sort of justification is quite restricted. Few cases of intervention have this structure. In most, disorder is only a temporary effect of civil strife, not a chronic condition requiring this sort of action. Indeed, we should be careful not to exaggerate the extent of cases of breakdown of authority by assimilating to them situations in which a state is acting to put down insurgency. Since the state needs such powers to maintain its jurisdiction it cannot lose its authority just because it must use coercive measures to restore jurisdictional ones.[12]

I want to contrast cases of a breakdown of authority with those that are more typically exemplified in our scenario, namely where the established state supposedly *forfeits* its own authority because of its repressive behaviour. Two different claims could be involved here and they need to be distinguished. The first is that the state forfeits authority globally, that is, across the whole of its territory. This could be argued for on the grounds that it behaves so badly throughout, and not just in a part of, its territory that its claim to exercise authority no longer holds good anywhere. This is not the situation in our scenario where only a portion of the population is badly treated. But here too an argument for global forfeiture of authority can be made, rather than for merely local forfeiture in that part of the territory where the badly treated portion lives.

The case is made by claiming that a state which grossly violates its subjects' human rights loses its title to political authority because this depends precisely upon its upholding their rights. For a state's upholding their rights gives citizens some reason to accept its commands as in their general interest and thereby to recognize the state as having authority and not just power. If it acts otherwise then people *qua* citizens, rather than *qua* members of the dominant group which is not mistreated, have no reason to obey its injunctions just because it is the state which issues them. Intervention in such a state, it may be suggested, cannot trespass upon an authority the state has lost by its own bad behaviour. The intervener's own authority derives from its acting to protect citizens just as a properly functioning state should do and which, indeed, gains its authority precisely by so doing.

Now this, it seems to me, is the position which a cosmopolitan is likely to espouse, for *qua* administrative unit the state has failed in its duty to protect human rights and has, in fact, violated them. That this has been of only local effect does not alter the fact that the state forfeits its office in this regard so that others may perform it. That it continues to protect rights over the rest of its territory does not affect the issue. Indeed, it only reveals its partiality and consequent failure to grasp the moral purpose, and hence universal application, of human rights. The natural corollary of this global forfeiture of authority is that a change of regime is needed,[13] and that is just what numerous contemporary interventions set out to achieve, so that their work is done when a more enlightened regime which does protect human rights is in place. Such a view resembles older ideas of the right to depose tyrants. But, I shall argue, those ideas do not consort well with the cosmopolitan picture of what humanitarian intervention should be like, in our scenario.

A state that acts as we are hypothesizing in going beyond what is needed to put down unrest is, in the terminology of classical just war theory, tyrannical. The only exception that the theory allows to its requirement that the proper authority for waging war be a ruler is that rebels or tyrannicides can have that authority when they act on behalf of a tyrannized political community simply to restore the *status quo ante* of jurisdictional rule.[14] A more modern version of the doctrine would hold that the state has lost authority under its present repressive regime, so that its authority passes to the rebels. However, the classical theory assumes that within any particular realm there is but one single political community, even if only some troublesome section of it is tyrannized. Yet in the scenario we envisage the dominant majority may well collude with the regime to repress the minority. Indeed, it will normally be impossible for a regime to act as it does without such collusion. In these circumstances it is doubtful whether a mere change of regime will be adequate to protect the minority. It is also unclear whether, in these circumstances, we should grant that those who seek to depose the regime exercise authority on behalf of the whole population of the state, rather than merely the minority. This applies as much to interveners as to internal forces. In these circumstances, then, it is not obvious that the anti-tyranny model can be applied to justify action on behalf of an assumed single political community.

We need to remember that in our scenario there is a civil war or something close to it. In these conditions coercion is the order of the day and its permissible limits are unclear. They cannot include, though, outrages against the civil population which would be contrary to the rules of war in international conflicts. Suppose such outrages were to occur there. Then there might be an analogous case for humanitarian action in such an international conflict as in a domestic one. But here, it would seem, we would have no special kind of action, detached from the main conflict. Rather, we would witness an entry into it on the side of those who principally suffer. Such alliances are, of course, not what the cosmopolitan envisages. For she thinks of her sort of intervention as essentially unmediated by such a relation to a warring party, but rather as the introduction of a third party with the distinct and limited agenda of safeguarding human rights, and as such not really war at all. Yet it is unclear why a domestic differs from an international conflict in this regard, and if the cosmopolitan picture is implausible for the latter then it is implausible for the former too. The upshot of these considerations is, I suggest, that humanitarian intervention in our scenario cannot credibly be viewed as action on behalf of the whole population of the state intervened in, with a change of regime the solution to their problems. It is inevitably slanted towards aiding the repressed part of the population. Its authority is, on a statist account, to be sought in its relation to that part, as we shall now go on to see.

4.

It should not be thought that statists cannot contemplate the possibility that some rebellions are justified. After all, many states, perhaps most, are the products of rebellion. What may justify rebellion is the forfeiture of the established state's authority locally rather than globally, namely in respect of that part of its population whose human rights it is violating. For suppose the state is repressing a national or other minority in its territory. Then it seems natural to say that it forfeits authority over them specifically, since the fact that it does not treat them like other citizens as benefiting from the protection of the law releases them from the normal obligations they have to it. The state retains its authority over those who enjoy jurisdictional governance, and loses it over those who do not. And on this kind of account authority over the latter will pass to an opposition body willing and able, in principle, to exercise jurisdiction in their part of the territory.

It is because authority over a part of the established state's original territory passes to another political organization in that part that external military assistance to secure this transition need not be thought to breach the principle of non-intervention which statists wish to uphold. For the external power will typically recognize a new state in that part so that, in its eyes, intervention in the established state's territory has not occurred. While we may continue to think loosely of external assistance in this situation as intervention, as doubtless it will be so thought of by the established state and perhaps even in international law,[15] it is important to see that on statist principles it does not have to be so regarded and, if its true character is properly grasped, is better not. What sort of situation, though, would justify external assistance for a rebellion?

In the circumstances of our scenario a regime change may not be an adequate remedy for the minority's wrongs. For here what is being suggested is that it is the state itself, not just the regime, which has forfeited authority because its very structures of domination and subordination are what permit the minority to be repressed. Constitutional change is what is needed, and the constitutional changes required to prevent repression may involve redrawing boundaries so that the minority gains a separate state. This is the case I shall concentrate on here because it is theoretically the simplest one. But I want to distinguish two easily confused ways in which the case for secession may be made, one of which, I shall argue, may justify external assistance to achieve it, while the other probably does not.

The first kind of case is this. Authority is lost, as we said, because the minority no longer has obligations to a state which represses it. They lack obligations because acceptance of the state's commands cannot reasonably be expected when these are tyrannical rather than jurisdictional. Indeed, far from being under any obligations the repressed minority has a right to defend itself against the consequences of disobeying tyrannical commands. Insofar as a right of secession is being claimed here, under which authority rightfully passes from one state to another, it depends upon the rights of people to defend themselves when unjustly attacked. In the circumstances they are in they may need to secede to exercise these rights, if only a separate state can protect them. Their right of secession is, therefore, what I shall call a *circumstantial* right.[16] This is very different analytically from allowing what I shall call, by contrast, a *systemic* right of secession, that is to say a right which derives not from the circumstances the group finds itself in but from the kind of group it is, for example a national group. Their right of secession, if they have one, would derive from a group of this kind having a right of self-determination.[17]

However, external assistance to secure secession should not be thought of as necessarily aimed at advancing self-determination. It may promote such political separation simply as a defence against human rights violations.[18] It is easy to overlook this when the group whose rights are violated is, by some criterion, a national group and especially when it is a group claiming a systemic right of secession. Indeed, the grounds one may have for thinking that the repressive state's authority over the group is permanently forfeit may be that the state represses them *qua* members of a separate national group, rather than just as any group of rebellious subjects. For if this is the case then their prospects for obtaining just treatment within the existing state may well be remote. The state itself has, by its own behaviour towards them, acknowledged their distinctiveness and implied that it is unprepared to treat them on all fours with other citizens within a common polity. In these circumstances it is *as* the supposedly national group that a separate political organization is sought for them. But it is sought *because* members of that national group are mistreated, not because the group is a national one.

5.

The distinction I have just drawn between external assistance in support of secession for a national group because it is repressed and support for its exercise of self-determination enables those engaged in humanitarian action to answer, I believe, the charge that they lack authority because they are interfering in the self-determinative process whose outcome establishes where authority lies. This sort of charge is associated with Michael Walzer, although Walzer himself does not specifically consider the *authority* under which interveners act, perhaps because, as has been noted,[19] his defence of just war theory curiously omits mention of proper authority altogether. However, filling out Walzer's qualified opposition to intervention in an appropriate way we may take the objection to depend on the assumption that where there is no clear locus of internal authority there can be no authority for external intervention, which must, *ceteris paribus*, be derivative from it, and on the view that such loci are established by self-determinative struggles. That Walzer assumes something of the kind seems to be implied by the fact that he is prepared to countenance intervention on behalf of secessionists when 'a community actually exists whose members are committed to independence and ready and able to determine the conditions of their own existence',[20] and do so by armed struggle. For then they show themselves to constitute a separate political community acting by popular consent which, in Walzer's view, bestows legitimacy upon them. Similarly counter-intervention against other external interveners is permissible only 'on behalf of a legitimate regime, one that possesses the required "fit" of contractual consent between the governed and their governors, and which has passed the self-help test'.[21]

Walzer does countenance humanitarian intervention in those most extreme cases of massacre and enslavement 'that shock the moral conscience of mankind'.[22] But here we may take him to assume that questions of the authority of interveners fall away from consideration, since they cannot be linked to internal authority when 'we must doubt the very existence of a political community to which the idea of self-determination might apply'.[23] In any other than these extreme cases humanitarian intervention would interfere with the self-determination processes which require people to help themselves and not rely on external military assistance. Yet if we distinguish humanitarian action generally, and not just that which reacts to the most extreme cases of repression, from action to secure a group's supposed right of self-determination it is not clear why the mere fact that humanitarian action interferes in the self-determinative process should disqualify it. For external powers can claim to be acting in support of a group whose authority stems simply from their attempt to restore justice in their part of the state's territory - something which can only be done by detaching it from the established state. The authority of the external powers must derive from that. They are allied, that is to say, with those who have such authority internally, namely the rebel group who, whatever their other aims, are defending people against repression. This has nothing to do with the upshot of self-determination understood in terms of the group's strength of will to be a separate political community, though it may, of course, coincide with it.[24]

We may notice here that there is a serious ambiguity in Walzer's general opposition to intervention as interfering with the processes of self-determination. He speaks for the most part of interference in the affairs of a political community, for example when people are involved in a revolutionary struggle against a comprehensively repressive regime. But the situation is very different when there is civil strife arising from a nationalist uprising, as in our present scenario. For then the question to be decided is what political community or communities there are. We cannot speak, therefore, when the outcome is as yet undecided, of the self-determination of a political community needing to be safeguarded against external interference. All we can say is that *people's* self-determination - their capacity as individuals to determine of what community they are to be part - is what may need protecting by a principle of non-intervention.

There is something very distasteful in Walzer's idea that the process of self-determination needs to be worked out through an armed conflict which tests the wills of its participants. Certainly it seems to underrate the superiority that an established state is likely to have in such a context, which will skew the outcome away from what the product of an uncoerced procedure would have been. But in the situation where a group is being repressed *qua* national minority it is evident that its group identity is being determined by the repressive state, quite irrespective of whether its members would wish to so identify themselves in any act of self-determination. Humanitarian action on their behalf stands in stark contrast to action to secure a national group's supposed right of self-determination precisely because it does not involve the external powers in employing their own criteria of what sort of group possesses such a right. The group whose circumstantial right of secession is recognized is one whose identity is determined by the repressive state itself. This group's organizations acquire authority not because they are legitimated by self-determinative procedures but just because they must defend their members over whom the state has forfeited authority.

In allying with a repressed group humanitarian actors are not intentionally interfering in self-determinative procedures, precisely because they are making no judgement on what the proper outcome of such procedures should be. It is not, as we have seen that Walzer claims, because in the absence of a real political community when shocking atrocities occur the idea of self-determination finds no application. It is that the idea of self-determination as conferring a systemic right of secession becomes irrelevant when a minority is repressed just in virtue of being the minority that it is. Then the circumstantial right of secession which they possess, if that is the only way in which their rights can be protected, trumps any systemic right of territorial integrity the repressive state may have originally possessed. By its behaviour it forfeits the exercise of such a right and the authority which would normally be associated with it in a part of its territory.

6.

Even if all this is true analytically, so that humanitarian actors may, on a statist conception, derive their authority from allying with circumstantially entitled secessionists, the situation on the ground in the scenario we envisage is much less clear cut. The established state will claim that its actions against the minority, even if repressive, are a reaction to a rebellion which it has a right to suppress: they are, that is to say, directed against the minority *qua* rebels, not *qua* their constituting the national group they supposedly do. It may be very hard to judge where the truth lies, though a history of official repression, or even mere serious discrimination, antedating nationalist insurgency will tilt the scales against the state's story. It is important, however, that external powers should not find themselves manipulated by nationalists who provoke repression in order to generate a humanitarian case for support. Conversely, some repressive reactions are so massively disproportionate to the threat posed that they can only be interpreted as directed against the minority *per se*, not against it as a rebellious group. It is in these sorts of circumstance, I am suggesting, that humanitarian action may be rightfully undertaken.

We have in this situation a straightforward case of a minority group engaged in armed conflict with the forces of the established state and which possesses proper authority on account of that state's forfeiture of it through repressive behaviour - behaviour which cannot be explained simply as a reaction to a rebellion for which the rebels lack any authority. Then military action by external powers may involve an alliance with rebels strictly for humanitarian ends and irrespective of the rebels' wider goals. In this case those giving military assistance are engaged in a just war because the self-defence of the national minority is a just cause. But it is a just cause because what is being defended are the individual members of the minority themselves. No reliance is placed, as it would be if systemic rights were involved, on the kind of group the minority constitutes and whether as such it has a claim to be defended.[25]

In such an alliance external powers are fighting a war, the point of which, like that of interstate war, is to secure a space within which jurisdictional rule can be maintained by those who represent the people there. It is not, unless incidentally, their job to do anything that could properly be called law enforcement or policing to protect human rights. For if those violating rights are the forces of the state then these need to be beaten back militarily. If, by contrast, they are armed gangs under no proper authority then it is the rebel government's responsibility to deal with them, and external forces can only assist in this. They are not, as on cosmopolitan principles, doing some police work on their own authority. Indeed, they would be infringing the authority of their allies were they to do so by operating in accordance with their own conceptions of justice, not those of their allies.

The resistance of cosmopolitans to this statist story is based on the idea that there is no theoretical need for such an internal group to mediate the authority of external agents to protect individual human rights. On just war principles I believe that there is, if only because to go to war justly one must have a just cause. But if the state offering external assistance has not been wronged then it itself lacks such a cause. It is those on whose behalf it acts who have a just cause, and the assisting state acquires one by allying with them. But it can associate itself with the rebels' cause only if the rebels have authority to fight for it.[26]

Furthermore, the just war account of justifiable military support for a repressed minority seems to me to be much more realistic than the cosmopolitan defence. It grants that external powers will have their own interests and will choose to enter or not to enter alliances accordingly. It presupposes, though this raises larger questions than the present paper can address, that humanitarian action is a political option for particular states, rather than the general duty that cosmopolitans take it to be. In exercising this option external powers will, if successful, effect constitutional changes internationally. These affect the shape of political communities, not just the lives of individuals. Inevitably these changes will alter the relationships of relative amity or enmity between states and hence the balance of power. States will intervene on behalf of potential friends, not enemies. They will also be cautious, so as not to provoke counter-intervention, for the fear of alliance with internal groups is always that of internationalizing a domestic conflict and turn what is ugly but limited into something ultimately bloodier even if better regulated. Conversely, however, the fear of external action on behalf of secessionists should deter an established state from repressing a minority more than if it could be confident that following any intervention its territorial integrity would be retained.

The cosmopolitan preference, other things being equal, for changing regimes rather than borders depends on its fundamental assumption that human rights can be grasped quite independently of their embedding in any particular type of jurisdiction. As such it requires, in principle, only an enlightened regime to put them into effect. The statist conception, by contrast, goes naturally with a view of human rights as differently understood in the different jurisdictions from which they arise.[27] The moral significance of boundaries is to protect such particular jurisdictions as what make possible a tolerably happy life for those within them. But not just any boundaries can create viable jurisdictions, and that for a whole variety of quite contingent reasons. One reason is the unwillingness of members of some dominant group to treat their fellows as equal citizens, which may, notoriously, have ideological underpinnings in the belief that they are, indeed, not equal. In these circumstances jurisdictional rule for both groups within the same boundaries may not be consistently applied, so that the system does not embed anything that we could think of as human rights. It is such circumstances, I have argued, on statist principles, that may give rise to a justified secession and humanitarian action in support of it.

Notes

1   For a discussion of what I mean by repression see Paul Gilbert, *Terrorism, Security and Nationality* (London: Routledge, 1994), p.156.

2   See A.C. Arend and R.J. Beck, *International Law and the Use of Force* (London: Routledge, 1993), ch.8.

3   Nigel Dower, *World Ethics* (Edinburgh: Edinburgh University Press, 1998), p.20. Compare the thinking in Onora O'Neill, *Bounds of Justice* (Cambridge: Cambridge

University Press, 2000), Part II. This is, I think, what Samuel Scheffler would call an extreme cosmopolitanism about justice: *Boundaries and Allegiances* (Oxford: Oxford University Press, 2001), ch.7.

4   Cp. Andrew Mason, *Community, Solidarity and Belonging* (Cambridge: Cambridge University Press, 2000), pp.194-200.

5   Cp. F.X. de Lima, *Intervention in International Law* (Den Haag: Uitgeverig Pax, 1971), p.16.

6   *Second Treatise of Civil Government*, § 226.

7   See Gilbert, *Terrorism, Security and Nationality*, pp.28-33. Gordon Graham, who adopts a just war theory approach to intervention, maintains that 'the precise determination of this idea of authority is unclear ... and we could not conclude therefore that this ... principle would set any very substantial restrictions on intervention'. *Ethics and International Relations* (Oxford: Blackwell, 1997), p.109.

8   Cp. Hegel, *Philosophy of Right*, 349, quoted and discussed by Mervyn Frost, *Ethics in International Relations* (Cambridge: Cambridge University Press, 1996),p.152.

9   Whom, of course, he contrasted with barbarians, whom he thought of as natural slaves.

10   That this bald answer is possible, though not mandatory, for statists indicates that the statist conception I have outlined differs from the picture Michael Walzer draws of the state's right to non-intervention as deriving from the political community's right of self-determination, which is reflected in, among other things, its specific sort of jurisdiction. As we shall see in more detail later, no such principle is appealed to in the statist objection to intervention as I reconstruct it here (*Just and Unjust Wars* (New York: Basic, 1977), ch.6).

11   I do not discuss the issue here. Suffice it to say that some such interventions can seem imperialistic, for few would wish to follow J.S. Mill in defending intervention among 'barbarous people' ('A Few Words on Non-Intervention', *Collected Works Vol. XXI* (Toronto: Toronto University Press, 1984), pp.111-124).

12   This is a point that is easily seen from a statist viewpoint but may be lost sight of from a cosmopolitan one, when the almost inevitable violation of human rights involved may seem to reflect a failure on the part of the state. International law does, however, recognize a distinction between cases which fall short of civil war and those - belligerency - which cross the line into it. (See A.V.W. and A.J. Thomas *Non-Intervention* (Dallas: Southern Methodist Press, 1956), pp.215-221.) In these latter cases the state really has lost authority in a part of its territory because in that part the rebels have taken control so that it is now up to them to exercise jurisdiction, pending its possible recapture by state forces.

13   This is not to deny that constitutional change may be accepted for administrative reasons, or to further self-determination on the liberal principles that generally accompany cosmopolitanism.

14   See David George 'Distinguishing Classical Tyrannicide from Modern Terrorism', *Review of Politics* 50 (1988).

15   See Thomas. loc. cit. So the position described may require some change to international law. What it does *not* require is a change which permits intervention within a state - 'qualified sovereigntism', as Charles Jones calls it (*Global Justice*, Oxford: Oxford University Press, 1999, p.214). For it allows us to preserve the principle of sovereignty while still permitting military assistance to repressed groups, thus escaping between the horns of the dilemma that we either recognize state sovereignty or protect people from injustice. It is true that the principle of territorial integrity of existing states would be breached.

16   In the circumstances described this would exemplify what Alan Buchanan calls a *remedial* right of secession, in *Secession* (Boulder: Westview, 1991), pp.27-81.

Buchanan regards it as the least problematic of such possible rights. But while he goes on to deny any systemic right of secession in pursuit of self-determination, I am not here committed to such a view. Rather, I am inclined to deny a right of military assistance to procure successful secession for self-determination, while I allow it as a means of self-defence. For assisting a repressed group to defend itself by seceding is quite different from assisting in the defence of a group that has seceded for other reasons.

17   It may be said in either of the circumstantial or systemic right cases that the established state lacks legitimacy or no longer has legitimate authority with respect to the repressed minority. But it is, to my mind, important to keep the notion of legitimacy and proper authority apart. There are a number of reasons for this. First, if consent to a state or its being 'a vehicle for self-determination' (Mason, *Community, Solidarity and Belonging*, p.198) is the measure of its legitimacy then many established states lack legitimacy with respect to most or some of their population whom they are not repressing; while if the authority of a state depends upon its just treatment of citizens then even an illegitimate state could maintain its authority. Second, by the same criteria, a rebel group that organized to resist oppression might, at least as yet, lack legitimacy but possess authority. Conversely, what is likely to lie behind the view that a repressive state only temporarily forfeits authority is the assumption that, by some independent criterion, it retains legitimacy, and this is what allows a distinction to be drawn between state and regime such that authority can be brought back into line with presumed legitimacy.

18   There is a case for describing what occurs as *partition*, which implies an externally imposed separation, rather than *secession*, which may be taken to imply an act of self-determination. But I insist that the separation is actively sought, though not necessarily for the systemic reasons that are associated with self-determination.

19   Brian Orend, *Michael Walzer on War and Justice* (Cardiff: University of Wales Press, 2000), pp.96-97.

20   Walzer, *Just and Unjust Wars*, p.93.

21   Orend, *Michael Walzer*, p.105.

22   Walzer, *Just and Unjust Wars*, p.107.

23   Ibid., p.101.

24   We can see this by comparing the grounds on which humanitarian actors would recognise a group to ally with against a repressive state from the grounds on which acting to promote self-determination would dictate recognition. In the latter case external powers would employ their own criteria of what constitutes a group with a right of self-determination, that is to say, of what sort of group it is whose collective will should determine what state they have. (The problem is famously captured in Ivor Jennings' comment on self-determination: 'on the surface it seemed reasonable: let the people decide. It was in fact ridiculous because the people cannot decide until somebody decides who the people are' (*The Approach to Self-Government* (Cambridge: Cambridge University Press, 1956), p.56). In all probability the criteria employed will reflect the conditions which supposedly legitimate the power's own state – a group occupying an historic territory if that state is so constituted, an ethnic group if it is ethnically constituted, and so forth. Now we may very well wish to use this fact to cast doubt on Walzer's permission for intervention on behalf of a separate political community with popular consent, since recognizing a group as such a community will inevitably involve deploying some more specific criteria of what sort of group does have a systemic right of secession. Typically, the established state and the *soi disant* national minority will differ on what this criterion should be. But if the people in the territory are to be genuinely self-determining then what the criterion is should itself be

something they must themselves decide. It should not be imposed from without as a result of external action that favours one criterion rather than another.

25 So Richard Norman's objection to Walzer, in *Ethics, Killing and War* (Cambridge: Cambridge University Press, 1995), pp.132-139, does not apply here. For it is the lives of the minority, not some abstract political community, that are being defended.

26 Nor are these just war principles idle. For if military action is undertaken on behalf of a group of people then they must have some control over it, which the terms of an alliance provide. 'One cannot', as Walzer puts it, 'intervene on their behalf and against their ends' (*Just and Unjust Wars*, p.104). But this is a demand for which the cosmopolitan conception has no place.

27 See Richard Bellamy, 'Citizenship and Rights' in R. Bellamy (ed.) *Theories and Concepts of Politics* (Manchester: Manchester University Press, 1993) for a republican development of this picture.

PART V
THE NEW INTERNATIONAL
ORDER

Chapter 12

Global Village, Global *Polis*

Iain Brassington

Introduction

Sometimes we hear or talk about international order or international community in a loose sense; sometimes we talk about *an* - or *the* - 'International Order' much more specifically. Every so often, we hear talk about a *'new* International Order' - for example, as mentioned by President Bush in the early 1990s. But implicit in the idea of the international, capitalized or not, there must be the national. Indeed, relations between nations, *inter nationes*, are constitutive of the international; but this simply means that a reasonably clear idea of the national is necessary. Trivially, if we are to consider the relation between *A* and *B*, we have to be able to *distinguish* between the two; we have to be prepared to mark where one stops and the other begins. Therefore to attempt to talk about 'International Order' implicitly brings with it questions of the delineation of domestic and foreign, questions of sovereignty, and questions of the integrity of borders.

What I want to do here is to open up these questions by exploring the notion of the border itself. While there *are* pressing debates about the normative status of relationships between political entities, the intention is to look at what it is that allows a 'between nations' in the first place. From this, hopefully, some contribution will have been made to answering questions concerning the moral cogency of national boundaries, the ethical position of (an) 'international order', and the relationship of moral concern to concepts such as the nation, the foreign and the international.

Are political borders morally problematic at all, though? I think that they can be. On an everyday level, we tend to accept that there *is* a moral difference between the domestic and the foreign, suggesting a correlation of some sort between moral concern and political borders. The thought here is that, while the presence of troops on the streets of Freetown certainly *has* a moral dimension, the sorts of questions we would be asking would be different according to whether they were under UN or Sierra

Leonean command. If troops were necessary to quell civil unrest on the streets of Britain, British people presumably would prefer that they be British rather than Swedish. Part of the moral problem with an *international* order, by contrast, is that it seems to go beyond what is indicated by the prefix '*inter-*', between. It allows an intervention by certain political entities in the business of others in a manner that is contrary to this intuitive preference.

International intervention looks rather as though it razes political borders and thereby levels the intuitive moral differences between the domestic and the foreign. But this means that it cannot be *inter*national at all, since, as I have already indicated, for the word 'international' to be meaningful, there must be a recognition of the borders between nations. Such a recognition *does*, at the very least, seem to play an important part in the international arena, and inform the idea of sovereignty and political integrity. The UN Charter's talk of states' obligation to 'refrain... from the threat or use of force *against the territorial integrity* or political independence of any [other] state', for example, seems to be in keeping with this.[1] And so there is a tension that becomes apparent in the manner in which we choose to conceptualize international intervention. If we stress the 'international', we are committed to a system of national borders and political integrities; but if we stress the 'intervention', there is the implication either of the dissolution of borders between political entities, or else the subordination of those entities to an International Order, with the attendant intuitive problems in terms of sovereignty and integrity.

On this basis, perhaps the commitments implied by 'international order' are too incoherent for the concept to survive; there is an apparent paradox involved in crossing a border while still recognizing its validity *as* a border. Along similar lines, the idea of an international order apparently pays lip-service to sovereignty - it has been suggested, for example, that international intervention 'should not be viewed as an affront to sovereignty, but as a necessary tool to preserve it'[2] - but ignores it in practice: this would make it difficult for order or intervention *inter nationes* to be possible in good faith. And this thought can easily lead us to the further, related point that the international order may simply be hegemony in a badly-fitting disguise.

So there are very different problems presented by something like an intervention for the sake of human rights (which, though it might take all kinds of forms, including military occupation, I shall refer to as simply an 'intervention'), and an invasion in the more 'traditional' sense - for example, for the sake of annexation. In an important sense, the latter is morally fairly straightforward. Invasion for a motive such as territorial gain may be abhorred or condemned, but there is no reason to suppose that it repudiates the principle of sovereignty as inviolable - it simply refuses to recognize sovereignty in a certain case. This lack of recognition may be nefarious or mistaken, but it is not morally *complicated* for that. An invasion is not concerned with the foreign *as* foreign. Intervention, on the other hand, makes no explicit claim about sovereignty, and appears, problematically, to want to *retain* the foreign as foreign. Oddly, this potentially means that an annexation of one state by another might still be able to pay more respect to the *principle* of the sovereign inviolability of states than would an intervention in the name of restoring an elected government.

Boundaries, Borders and Congruence

The problem with squaring an international order with states' integrity might lie with either the order or the border. Briefly, I want to sketch out a few arguments for thinking that it is the international order, and its propensity to overrun the state, that needs rejecting or re-evaluating. These arguments revolve around the claim that moral and political borders are congruent, and that therefore sovereign integrity morally trumps internationalism. I shall look at an Aristotelian viewpoint which would plausibly reject internationalism as contrary to justice, and a Hobbesian view that would simply deny that terms like justice and injustice work internationally. Both views concentrate on the entity doing the intervening, rather than the intervened-upon. An argument that could be presented from the standpoint of the intervened-upon to the effect that internal issues are no business of the outside will be dealt with - albeit a little less directly - later.

According to Aristotle, states are conglomerations of people who have come together for the sake of some 'good purpose', which involves self-sufficiency at the very least.[3] The *polis* is considered to be more important than the individual; 'even if the good of the community coincides with that of the individual, it is clearly a greater and more perfect thing to achieve and preserve that of the community',[4] not least because it is the *polis* that provides the framework through which the individual is best able to flourish and so fulfil his very individuality; to be a fully-developed human implies a 'need to participate in a community of a certain sort'.[5] As Yack puts it, the *polis* 'serves to *complete* a... set of human capacities. Aristotle is thus willing to say that the polis exists for the sake of the *good* human life, just as animals and plants exist for the sake of *mere* human life'.[6] Each individual's concern for his own essential wellbeing commits him to the *polis*, the factor which guarantees a certain standard of life.[7]

Insofar as the *polis* supports and nurtures its members towards the completion of human capacities, there are certain manners in which the population is the concern of the wider *polis*: 'what is to the common advantage is just';[8] and so there will be an extent to which there is a teleological commitment from the *polis* to the citizenry. Nevertheless, there is no commitment from the *polis* to a generalized humanity or the world as a whole; one's commitments to others depend on one's relationship with them - the closely related will outweigh the more distantly so,[9] and foreigners are not part of the political association by definition. The *polis* nurtures *its* members, but need not concern itself with those outside its borders. Hence the *polis* defines the limits of concern.[10]

If this is so, it may be *prima facie* wrong to get involved with overseas issues. Governments often have much better things to do for the benefit of their people than go galumphing off around the world at vast public expense; and this sort of expense, if it curtails the function of the *polis* in relation to its people, defeats what was the object of the association in the first place (especially if this vast public expense could be better spent nurturing the citizenry through the provision of schools, health and so on). So there is no prospect of internationalism: the closest we get is pan-Hellenism; but even with this concession, it remains the case that generally states should look after their constituent members rather than foreigners, which means that intervention in foreign affairs is something that the state should avoid as anti-constitutional if at all possible. (The constitution is not a legal system: it is what constitutes the *polis* - that is, the citizens themselves. They live *in*, not *under*, a constitution.[11]) The priority rests with the local.

Of course, the pragmatics of scarcity mean that states' responsibilities owed to their constituencies *not* to get involved with each other may be reversed, so that involvement is not only *right*, but *required*. But even here, it is still the nurturing concern of the *polis* rather than any suprapolitical motives that is at work; the justice of a state's actions outside its borders is defined by the manner in which those actions forward the state's ends. A tax rise to fund humanitarian intervention across the world would be, for the Aristotelian, unjust, since embarking on such a policy would commit one to reversing the natural order of political concerns - but perhaps a tax rise to fund an expedition to secure mineral resources *would* be just. Either way, though, the point remains that justice demands the *avoidance* of commitments to those outside the *polis* unless these commitments secure some good *for* the *polis* in return.

However, we need not be this strong in our arguments against an international order. It might not be the case that internationalism is *un*just - it might simply *lack* justice. This would be a Hobbesian picture. What is important here is that in the Hobbesian world there is *nil crimen sine lege*: hence the moral status of foreign, rival states is not of real concern.[12] Therefore, because there is simply no international standard of justice by which we might assess invasions or interventions (going to war being neither just nor unjust, on the basis that '[w]here there is no common Power, there is no Law: where no Law, no Injustice'[13]), the concern of an international order for the principle of sovereignty or for human rights would be nonsensical. The only standard would be utility to the domestic: an international action could be just if, but only if, it was in some way defensive or secured the *internal* interests of a given Commonwealth.[14] A state arbitrates *within* its borders, but this is where justice, and so its moral responsibilities, stops. States are, obviously, stateless actors; action outside political borders is analogous to action in a State of Nature, and 'notions of Right and Wrong, Justice and Injustice have there no place'.[15]

So there is an element of coherence between Aristotle and Hobbes insofar as both would claim that any activity of a state beyond its legally-established borders would have nothing to commend it morally. For both, justice lies in the State and not in any wider framework. There is never scope for international order; there is no justice involved in intervention in *foreign* affairs simply because, for both writers, they *are* foreign and so beyond justice. And this could, potentially, be stretched to a point where we need not lose too much sleep over, say, the carpet-bombing of areas of rural South America in the name of drug enforcement policies. But this would not be on the basis of narcotic enforcement within an *inter*national order so much as the preservation of the national. In a world run according to these non-international principles, there would arguably not be *foreign*, so much as extended domestic, concerns. We would not have any concern in the moral status of our foreign neighbours at all; all the concern we *would* have would be based on the extent to which they get in the way of our meeting our concerns for ourselves. Whatever order there might be, then, is certainly not based in consideration of the *international*.

I do not think that this sort of worldview can be right, though; it is intuitively disquieting, and I do not think that it is empirically supportable. Such a worldview as that which I have attributed to Hobbes cannot accommodate the idea that states should respect each others' sovereignty. Insofar as one of the *problems* with international orders is that they *do* seem to ignore sovereignty, the suggestion must be that we think that sovereignty is worth protecting, and this is *irrespective* of any other views we may have on the international system.[16] We think that it is wrong for *A* to invade *B*, and also that there is something morally special about *foreign* intervention. This latter niggle is not just because of narrow, parochial concerns such as the risk to 'our boys out there', but also because we might well have, for example, worries about neo-imperialism. All this is obviously incompatible with a thought that the scope of moral concerns stops at the next customs point.

Meanwhile, there is more disquiet, I think, about leaving other areas of the world entirely to get on with life. We are not, I think, generally uncomfortable with the idea that there might be a moral demand to do *something* to ensure that food supplies reach a refugee population in *C* or to suture interethnic bloodletting in *D*; often we *are* uncomfortable with the thought of indolence in these circumstances. It is not obvious that there is any national interest to be served here. Admittedly, we *might* intervene simply because we prefer not to be aware of this sort of thing - but it is not clear why a navel-gazing population would send news crews to grim areas of the world in the first place if this was so. No one *forces* us to feel bad about genocide in Southeast Asia. Equally, I suppose that there might be an incentive to intervene so as not to be bothered by refugees - but again, this end could be met in other ways (for example, shooting the starving or dissidents on behalf of the prevailing forces in the trouble spot in question). Why dress up self-concern as humanitarianism or compassion if we are *genuinely* morally unconcerned about others?

If moral horizons were congruent with our political boundaries, it would never occur to anyone to raise questions about the rights and wrongs of foreign intervention. So I think that questions of foreign intervention and international orders are morally disquieting because our moral horizons are *not* congruent with our political borders. What seems to be missing from arguments that would either deny that there is any justice outside of the state, or that moral concerns stop, or even simply diminish, at political boundaries, is an account of why it is that questions about international orders and the value of the sovereignty of states other than our own get raised at all.

Boundaries, Frontiers and Incongruence

I have made no bones about the fact that I think that a good portion of the problems associated with questions of international orders comes from the fact that they involve the word 'international': because one cannot have 'international' without 'national', the scope of moral concern is subordinated to questions about *national* interest, *national* sovereignty and so on. I want to argue that this ordering is incomplete: that there is scope to see the national not as the *fundamental* aspect of international relations, but as something which itself comes from other, *more* basic premises. I want to do this with the argument that the notion of a moral *boundary* or *border* is, after all, pretty incoherent – we would be better off talking about a moral *frontier*; a frontier can always be extended, while a boundary remains static. If this is successful, to talk about the congruence of moral and political borders is to miss the point.

The argument begins with a return to Aristotle and his contention that man is *politikon zoon*, the 'political animal'.[17] This means that man is an animal both with a propensity to form associations, but also whose humanity is fully realized in those associations.[18] The *polis* is a reification of an association which is itself ultimately derived from community of concern among the associates for the fulfilment of their human ends (keeping, with Yack, the distinction between the basic ends necessary for brute life and the higher ends constitutive of humanity as a moral creature). Hence this concern foundationally determines and constitutes the concerns of the political community at large as manifested and reified in the *polis*. Clearly, then, when association is *based* on concern, this concern cannot be limited to that which is within extant political boundaries or to citizenship. The teleologically formative concerns of the state can only be a reflection of the concerns of its members and the concerns they had *before* the foundation of the *polis*. This means that questions of insider, outsider, citizen and foreigner can only arise *after* the reification of the *polis*; the epithet 'citizen' can only be applied *after* the foundation of a state of which one *can* be citizen. This is implied by the claim that 'we say a citizen is a member of an association, just as a sailor is':[19] being a sailor depends on there being something to sail; being a citizen depends on there being a city. Citizenship, then, cannot be all that is involved in political concern.

So what is the nature of the political community and the concerns that underpin it? Aristotle notes in many places that there are many animals which are gregarious.[20] What marks out human political existence from that of other animals and makes it possible to live in *poleis* is the faculty of speech:

> Speech is something different from voice, which is possessed by other animals... [It] serves to indicate what is useful and what is harmful, and so also what is just and what is unjust... *It is the sharing of a common view in these matters that makes a household and a state.*[21]

While speech takes different forms, the fact remains that it is present in all humans (another Aristotelian definition of the human, *zoon logon ekhon*, I understand in this context as the animal with *speech*) and indicates things which are the same for all humans.[22] So if the *polis'* primordial concern is with citizens *qua* humans, rather than with citizens *qua* citizens, it is also the case that in the human faculty of speech lies the basis of the *polis*: commun*ication* begets commun*ity*.

If speech allows the *polis*, and the *polis* is crucial to the human *telos*, then it follows that the possibility of the fulfilment of human ends must lie alongside the possibility of speech. Obviously, speech itself has certain demands - possibly the most obvious being that of proximity. At its most basic, then, the *polis* demands some sort of nearness between individuals. It is on the basis of this nearness that the similar teleological concerns *of* human animals for the human essence are *found*, but not found*ed*. There is, then, an inevitable local bias to concern - one cannot find without encounter. However, what is important is that the priority is of the local because it is *near*, rather than because it is part of an extant association.

If membership of a political community, and so moral concern, does not extend to the foreigner, as Hobbes and the isolationist reading of Aristotle would have it, it turns out that this is simply because he is distant: beyond commun*ication*, so beyond, but not *excluded* from, commun*ity*. Location is important, but it is not constitutive (*solely* constitutive, anyway) of political communities. All location does is facilitate the *possibility* of community. This claim seems to be borne out by the existence of nomadic or diaspora groups, which may well have a sense of community as strong as, or stronger than, that within more geographically specific communities: indeed, this is what marks them out as groups in their own right in the first place. Hence the irony of Leopold Bloom, Joyce's wandering Jew, suggesting that 'a nation is the same people living in the same place'. For what is it that makes a people 'the same' - or, for that matter, the place it occupies - if not the recognition that there is something that unites them as such?

> — By God, then, says Ned, laughing, if that's so I'm a nation for I'm living in the same place for the past five years.
> So of course everyone had a laugh at Bloom and says he, trying to muck out of it:
> — Or also living in different places.
> — That covers my case, says Joe.[23]

In this sense, the foreigner is the stranger - the parallel is preserved, for example, in the French *étranger* - and is so because he is, as the German

Ausländer suggests, the outsider, or distant-dweller. The concern of the community stops at the borders of the *polis* simply because these borders represent the range of association - not because there is anything special about these borders themselves. It is only diachronically that the community attains (or *believes* that it attains[24]) a commonality of history, lineage and law that augments this. Synchronically, though, the limits of moral concern are congruent with the outside edges of the *polis* largely because there is no one beyond there with whom it is possible to associate. This is where I think Aristotelian chauvinism and international isolationism go wrong - they think *too late*. Simply by recognising the other as being human, one recognizes a community - a holding-in-common. This does not seem much, but given that it is concern for human flourishing that bases the Aristotelian *polis* in the first place, an isolationist or chauvinist turning away from the affairs of other humans in other communities cannot be sustainable. Certainly one may be a member of a certain *polis*; but this membership represents, and does not exhaust, community.

To continue along this line, we know that Aristotle says that 'every state is an association'[25] - for which he uses the word *koinos*: shared. To associate, according to the *Shorter Oxford*, is to join with or to keep company with someone or something. The word and its cognates derive from the prefix *ad-* and the stem *socius*, relating to what is shared. Political association, then, is a making-shared of what is already held in common by humans - putting it in the public, rather than the private domain. The *polis* is the public manifestation of a shared concern. Given that, as Alexander Bickel points out, the Aristotelian state is *constituted* and characterized *by* the citizenry,[26] to be a member of the *polis* is a matter of 'sharing in the constitution':[27] that is to say, both *being* a part of the community and *having* a part of what is communal.

The shared and public nature of the concerns that base the *polis* means that, within a state, a certain institutional interest can be taken in those individual affairs which constitute a part of the community in the name of the nurturing function of the *polis* towards the citizens (which is what underlies the association in the first place). So, for example, one citizen's assaulting another runs contrary to the principle basing the *polis*; therefore, it falls to these institutions to deal with the situation. Similarly, if another citizen falls ill and cannot support or be supported by his family, then the association has certain responsibilities of aid,[28] since the nurture of members of the community is part of the *telos* of the *polis*. A *polis* can intervene or play a role in its constituents' lives - but this is not the paternalism of a separate and superior entity so much as a reflection of the manner in which the *polis* is a manifestation of concern: the *polis* does not have interventionary *rights* so much as *duties*. This is not to contradict the principle that the *polis* is superior to the individual: remember that it is only within the *polis* that one becomes a fully human individual at all.

Political boundaries, in essence, indicate the frontiers of concern and community; however, it does not follow that concern and community are *limited* by political boundaries. This argument appears to complement that highlighted by Phil Ross in this volume: that '[t]he contours of [the] polity are defined by [a] shared morality'. If this is right, then it looks as though the association that forms the *polis* could, at least theoretically, be infinite. And, by the same token, it is not at all obvious why one should not be a part of several communities at the same time, each representing a particular 'sharing' of a certain concern or experience. It is possible for any single person to have multiple communities - be they in terms of language, history, occupation, an intense dislike of football, whatever.[29] The relative importance of each commun*ity* need not be fixed; and sometimes there will be conflict between communities - Parekh points out that it is perfectly possible to support the English cricket team against Australia, but the West Indian team at other times, and to be no less a member of the community (or 'community of communities') entitled 'British' for that.[30]

Two suggestions, I think, would be forthcoming from such a picture. One is that, if association is prior to, and is the foundation of, the *polis*, then the relationships that pertain between individuals *within* the *polis* also pertain *without* it. Our relationships with one another would be determined by the process rather than the reification of association. The other suggestion would be that, if states are constituted by associating individuals, then there is nothing special about relationships between *states* that cannot be reduced to that which pertains to relationships between individuals. Correspondingly, if it is legitimate for the affairs of the people of Newcastle to be, at least partially, the concern of the people of Newhaven - that is, *within* national boundaries - then it would seem to follow that such concerns could be found which ignore national boundaries - especially if it is easier for the people of Newhaven to associate across the Channel. The notion of sovereignty would be shown *not* to represent an impermeable associative horizon.

Phenomenal Politics

What I have argued so far might still support a reinterpreted priority of the local. Once the demands of concern which drive the *polis* have been met, it would be perfectly coherent for the barriers to go up. I would have commitments to, from and with my community, but not to foreigners, even if I conceded their humanity as a concern like mine. Once a *polis* has achieved the self-sufficiency that is so important to Aristotle ('self-sufficiency [of the *polis*] is both end *and perfection*'[31]), it can support the human flourishing within it adequately. So it is no longer clear why the process of association should continue. Why go beyond perfection? Even if there *is* an initial situation in which concerns are nothing to do with international boundaries, why should it be the case that a reified *polis* would feel any responsibility towards another? It looks as though there still might be no moral pull on a given community from outside if it would no longer serve the concerns of the community to continue the process of association demanded by political teleology.

Admittedly, I think that it is uncertain that any state ever *is* so self-reliant as to be able to isolate itself from others. And, of course, *poleis do* associate with those 'superfluous' members of their own population who are not contributory to self-sufficiency. This suggests that association *does* go beyond necessity. But this is not sufficient to provide us with any normative guidelines as to why it *should*. The Aristotelian *polis* is not an altruistic institution; it does not demand that *all* humans be supported, even though mutual support and *philia* that extend beyond the strictly necessary are praised as virtuous.[32]

Frankly, I cannot presently suggest a solution to this problem. However, I do not think that I need to dwell on it for my present purposes. I am not trying to argue for or against an international system or international altruism: what I am trying to do is to argue that the non-congruence of our moral concerns with political borders is because political borders are based on, and therefore do not define, communities of concern. Concern, then, can *easily* become international because it is *pre*national. 'Foreign' describes, at most, that which lies within another state's boundaries - but I think that this is an accident of geography, and not something that can be relevant morally.

So to question things like *why* one should associate with the foreign is to beg the question: the association comes before the word 'foreign' becomes appropriate. Even Aristotle admits that 'there would be a community and therefore a sort of justice *even if there were no* polis' as its guarantor.[33] Pre-political association is already a minimal community.[34] I am even willing to allow a priority of the local to remain as an important feature of international relations and therefore of any international order. What is questionable, though, is not so much the nature of relationships with the *foreign* as what it is that 'local' is taken to mean. I do not think that it can be seen as a term that is wholly topological. This suggests, I think, that there is scope for a questioning of what we mean when we talk about political borders.

I have argued above that central to the communities of concern that define the concerns of the *polis* is the matter of the scope of speech: concern does not extend to the foreigner because he is an *Ausländer*, and therefore a stranger. One cannot base public concern on privately held concerns, even if these concerns are common to all humans, if they are simply out of reach and unknown. However, if Aristotle were defining his politics today, I think that he would have to accommodate in the idea that man is *zōon logon ekhon* the recognition that speech is not limited by distance. 'Speed... has made distance meaningless,' notes Hannah Arendt, 'for no significant part of human life - years, months, or even weeks - is any longer necessary to reach any point on the earth.'[35] Phenomenally, I think that we might well argue that 'the local' might today be anything but a term that covers how far, for example, one can walk in a day, or the amount of land necessary for self-sufficiency. What does it mean to prioritize the interests of the nearby over the distant, the familiar over the foreign, when we can quite easily know more about the politics of Peru than the people living across the road, and when a household in Birmingham, England could easily be less familiar than one in Birmingham, Alabama? (Obviously, reverse this if you spend more time in the deep South than the West Midlands.)

It no longer follows, in fact, that there is a correlation between *l'étranger*, the unfamiliar stranger, and *der Ausländer*, the distant dweller. The phenomen*on* and the phenomen*ology* of the 'global village' mean that the *polis* can be an entity that exists atopically; *der Ausländer* is no longer (necessarily) the unencountered, *l'étranger*. What counts is encounter, not place. Place certainly remains an arena for encounter, but so too is mass communication (think about the famous footage of starving Ethiopian children in 1984: TV pictures brought the reality to us, and so facilitated an encounter irrespective of distance). Within this atopical encounter, there is the potential for community, or, more radically (but in a spirit truer, I think, to Aristotle's), the *recognition* of community. (Whatever the merits and problems with the rest of his book, this squares with Peter Unger's quick and easy demonstration that it is encounter *simpliciter* that is at the centre of our moral responses, and that it is incoherent to give weight either to its *typos* or *topos*.[36]) The topological *limits* of the *polis* having been abandoned, then, there is no reason why the *polis* should not be global. Justice might still reside in the community, but there is no reason why this community should be limited to a particular national *polis*.[37] And given that we *do* show concern across the world, and *want* news from there, I think that it is empirically clear that our parameters for association are expansive, not limited by the borders of a state.

I noted above that internationalism seems to be in conflict with the intuitive feelings many of us have about the invulnerability of sovereignty. However, I seem now to be suggesting that international borders are an irrelevance, and so not invulnerable after all. Morally, I think that this is so. However, politically, it need not be. Community of concern above and beyond political borders is no more of a threat to states' integrity than is the manner in which community of concern *within* the *polis* is a threat to, say, a household's integrity. So the principled argument against an international order to the effect that a state's affairs are no one else's concern is, I think, fallacious: it assumes a priority of the political border over the moral frontier that I have tried to refute. It assumes also that just because the political boundary is a moral irrelevance, there will be a constant threat of unwelcome interference: but I do not think that this follows either. My argument, in fact, *obviates* the idea that national sovereignty is squashed beneath an international order. An international order based on a global *polis* would, I think, guarantee the political integrity and sovereignty of states just as a traditional *polis* guarantees the integrity of the citizenry or household.

It would deny, however, that respect for political boundaries is the entirety of international decency. Non-intervention is important, but not the *most* important principle.[38] If we think it is right to stop a fight in the street, this is not because we think that the fighters are subordinate to certain laws: we think that people should not fight and that laws, there to regulate the relations between people, should reflect this. We are entitled to intervene if, and because, it is right: it is not right to intervene only because of entitlement. In this way, no state or order is *entitled* to intervene within another's boundaries: but this does not mean that it may not or should not.

Summary and Conclusions

What I have tried to argue can be summarized, roughly, as follows. Traditionally, the concept of international order, or *a* or *the* international order, new or otherwise, implies the laying down of certain rules about the relationships between states which concentrate on the nation. The possibility of such rules, though, must presuppose that the principle of sovereignty is the *sine qua non*: '[t]he most fundamental pillar of international society is state sovereignty.'[39] Without such a condition, it would simply be incoherent to try to bring some sort of order to transactions between states. As such, moral boundaries are defined by national boundaries. Further, the prioritizing of national and political boundaries diffuses the notion that states have any responsibilities to each other beyond a respect for sovereignty. There is no place in an international order for invasion; but nor is there any case for intervention, military or otherwise (for example, in the form of economic sanctions), on humanitarian grounds.

My point has been, though, that an international system based on the prioritization of political boundaries ignores how those political boundaries came to be there in the first place. This sort of system is not only relatively new,[40] but also has little suggestion of *a priori* validity.[41] The boundaries of the *polis* are, rather, informed by communities of concern, which are all but unlimited in the 'global village'. As such, the relationships that underpin the *polis* - community of concern, aims, ends and interest - stretch outside the boundaries of the *polis*.

Beitz makes a claim that '[i]ntervention, colonialism, imperialism and dependence are not morally objectionable because they offend a right of [national] autonomy, but rather because they are unjust'.[42] *If* there is no possibility for establishing a law beyond states, then this is false, and for Hobbesian reasons. But the stance I have been advocating here is that there *is* a basis for an international justice beyond states, and that it grows out of pre-political association. This association does not overwhelm individual states, although it does demand that we re-evaluate their genesis. This associative understanding of the nature of relationships between nations is, I hope, truly *inter-*, rather than *supra-*, national, because these relationships are inter-personal before they are political; and they can easily be interpersonal between established *poleis*. Laws might need an association like a *polis*, but I think that, internationally, there is plenty of scope for something *like* a *polis* to exist which is compatible with states' integrity.

I do not see why there is an enormous difference between these organizations being formally based in states, or less formally in the global village. It is the *association* rather than the *polis* that counts; associations base, and are not based *on*, political borders. International intervention *can* be at odds with the notion of sovereignty;[43] but an international order that is drawing from roots similar to those which sustain an Aristotelian *polis* need not be. So while I broadly agree with Kresock's sentiment, mentioned at the start of this piece, that internationalism can preserve sovereignty, I think it is for different reasons: I think that sovereignty is Kresock's starting-point (and bearing in mind that he is writing as a lawyer, this is reasonable), whereas for me it is relatively low down in the list of considerations. It is *not* all-important, or even supremely important.

Justice can be established in a global village which is seen as a nascent global *polis*. Indeed, an order *inter nationes* is the only possible guarantor of the integrity of states. The associative model which I am advocating does not imply a systematic trampling on political boundaries - it is *anti*-systematic. Any systems that there may be spring from association, rather than base it. Worries about UN troops on the streets of Freetown, therefore, have their place - but their place is moral, not topological.

Notes

1   Charter of the United Nations, §I, Art. 2, 4. Emphasis mine.
2   Kresock, D., ' "Ethnic Cleansing" in the Balkans: The Legal Foundations of Foreign Intervention', *Cornell International Law Journal*, vol.27 no.1, 1994, p.235.
3   Aristotle, *The Politics* (Harmondsworth: Penguin, 1992), I, i, 1252a1 – I, ii, 1253a34. See also Aristotle, *Ethics* (Harmondsworth: Penguin, 1976), VIII, ix, 1160a11 ff.
4   *The Politics*, I, ii, 1094b10.
5   Miller, F., *Nature, Justice and Rights in Aristotle's Politics* (Oxford: Clarendon Press, 1997), p.375.
6   Yack, B., *The Problems of a Political Animal* (Berkeley: University of California Press, 1993), p.101. Emphasis mine.
7   Aristotle, *Oeconomica* (London: Heinemann, 1935), I, i, 1343a10-11.
8   *Ethics*, VIII, ix, 1160a11 ff.
9   Ibid., 1160a5 ff.
10   *The Politics*, I, ii, 1252b6 ff: 'So, as the poets say, "It is proper that Greeks should rule non-Greeks".'
11   Ibid., III, iii, 1276b1 ff.
12   Hobbes, T., *Leviathan* (Cambridge: Cambridge University Press, 1999), ch.XIII.
13   Ibid.
14   Cf Hobbes, T., 'Human Nature', *The Elements of Law Natural and Politic* (Oxford: Oxford University Press, 1994), XIV, §13.
15   Hobbes, *Leviathan*, ch.XIII.
16   Cf. inter alia, Beitz, C., *Political Theory and International Relations* (Chichester: Princeton University Press, 1979), pp.92-93.
17   *The Politics*, I, ii, 1253a3.
18   Ibid., 1253a4-5.
19   Ibid., III, iv, 1276b21.
20   See, for example, Aristotle, *Parts of Animals* (London: Heinemann, 1937) in addition to the more obvious comment in *The Politics*.
21   Ibid., I, ii, 1253a7 ff. Emphasis mine.
22   Aristotle, *On Interpretation* (Oxford: Clarendon Press, 1974), 16a6-10.
23   Joyce, J., *Ulysses* (Oxford: Oxford World's Classics, 1998), p.317.
24   Cf Seymour, M., 'On Redefining the Nation', *The Monist*, vol.82 no.3, 1999, p.412.
25   *The Politics*, I, i, 1252a1.
26   Bickel, A., *The Morality of Consent* (New Haven: Yale University Press, 1975). For further discussion of this, see, *inter alia*, Schofield, 1996, who claims that for Aristotle,

citizenship is not a matter of possessing rights, but one of sharing the constitution; pertinent points are also raised by Johnson (Johnson, C., 'The Hobbesian Conception of Sovereignty and Aristotle's Politics', *Journal of the History of Ideas*, vol.46 no.3, 1985), and by Schall (Schall, J., 'Aristotle on Friendship', *Classical Bulletin*, vol.65 no.3/4, 1989).

27 Schofield, M., 'Sharing the Constitution', *Review of Metaphysics*, vol.49 no.4, 1996.

28 Cf Locke, J., 'An Essay Concerning the True Original, Extent and End of Civil Government' in Barker, E, *Social Contract* (London: Oxford University Press, 1960), VII-VIII, §§94-97.

29 Cf Parekh, B., et al., *The Future of Multi-Ethnic Britain* (London: Profile Books, 2000), esp. §§2-4.

30 Ibid., §3.24.

31 *The Politics*, I, ii, 1253a27 ff.

32 See, for example, *Ethics*, VIII, iii.

33 Aristotle, *Eudemian Ethics* (London: Heinemann, 1934), VII, x, 1242a19-28.

34 Derrida, J., 'The Politics of Friendship', *Journal of Philosophy*, 1988, vol.85 no.4, p.636.

35 Arendt, H., *The Human Condition* (Chicago: University of Chicago Press, 1998), p.250.

36 Unger, P., *Living High and Letting Die: Our Illusion of Innocence* (New York: Oxford University Press, 1996), chap.2, §3.

37 Cf Miller, op. cit., p.84f.

38 Amsutz, M., *International Ethics* (Lanham: Rowman & Littlefield, 1999), p.142.

39 Ibid., p.120.

40 Dower, N., *World Ethics* (Edinburgh: Edinburgh University Press, 1998), p.50.

41 Ibid., p.64.

42 Beitz, op. cit., p.69.

43 Cf Hoffman, J., *Beyond the State* (Cambridge: Polity Press, 1995), p.184.

Chapter 13

A Non-Liberal Approach to the Concept of an 'International Order'

Philip Ross

International Order or Global Polity?

With the end of the Cold War, and the advance of what some call 'globalization', the concept of an international order, or *new* international order (if not an embryonic global polity), seems to be a fashionable topic of debate. Thus, former US President George Bush, in a State of the Union address in January of 1991, declared that there is a new 'big idea', that of a 'New World Order... to achieve the universal aspirations of mankind - peace and security, freedom and the rule of law'.[1] His successor, Bill Clinton, declared, according to Zygmunt Bauman, that 'for the first time there is no difference between domestic and foreign policies'.[2] Bauman himself, whilst suggesting that it is grossly premature to talk, as Francis Fukuyama does, of 'an end to history', does argue, quoting Paul Virilio, that one can, 'with growing confidence', talk of an 'end of geography'.[3]

Such notions are of course not entirely new ones. Kant, for example, discusses both the concept of an international order and the notion of a global polity or state in his *Perpetual Peace*. Indeed, Kant distinguishes what he calls a '*pacific federation*' from both a '*peace treaty*' and an '*international state*' or '*world republic*'. For Kant, writing at the end of the eighteenth century, the prospects for world government were remote. The 'positive idea of a *world republic* cannot be realised', he writes, since 'this is not the will of nations, according to their present conception of international right'. Yet, if 'all is not to be lost', this world republic 'can at best find a negative substitute in the shape of an enduring and gradually expanding *federation* likely to prevent war'. This *pacific federation*, Kant argues, differs from a mere *peace treaty* in that whereas the latter may terminate '*one* war', the former 'would seek to end *all* wars for good'.[4]

> Peoples who have grouped themselves into nation states may be judged in the same way as individual men living in a state of nature, independent of external laws; for they are a standing offence to one another by the very fact that they are neighbours. Each nation, for the sake of its own security, can and ought to demand of the others that they should enter along with it into a constitution, similar to the civil one, within which the rights of each can be secured.[5]

For Kant this agreement or constitution, securing perpetual peace between sovereign peoples or nation states, consists in a set of rules or conditions governing both the internal constitution of states and their mutual relations. These include the outlawing of the practice of acquiring independent states by 'inheritance, exchange, purchase or gift', the gradual abolition of 'standing armies' and of national debts contracted in the course of 'external affairs', the outlawing of the practice of forcible intervention in the 'constitution and government' of other states and of such 'acts of hostility' as 'would make mutual confidence [between states] impossible during a future time of peace'.[6] Further, every state within this pacific federation of states, Kant maintains, ought to have a 'republican' civil constitution. This domestic constitution includes the principle of '*freedom* for all members of a society (as men)', the principle of the '*dependence* of everyone upon a single common legislation (as subjects)', and, thirdly, the principle of 'legal *equality* for everyone (as citizens)'.[7]

Kant justifies his insistence that all states in the pacific federation be 'republican' on two grounds: Firstly, the republican constitution is, Kant claims, 'pure in its origin (since it springs from the pure concept of right)'. Secondly, Kant claims that the adoption of a 'republican' constitution by all states in the federation conduces to the 'desired result', that is, 'a perpetual peace'. This is so, Kant argues, because in the 'republican' polity the consent of the citizens will 'inevitably' be required to 'decide whether or not war is to be declared' and these citizens, Kant claims, 'will have great hesitation in embarking on so dangerous an enterprise'. By contrast, in a state where the head of state is not a 'fellow citizen' but the 'owner of the state', the ruler of such a state is more likely to go to war as he or she incurs no real personal sacrifices. Such a ruler is, Kant argues, likely to view war 'as a kind of amusement'.[8]

Lastly, there is to be a condition of 'universal hospitality' in this pacific federation, by which Kant means the 'right of a stranger not to be treated with hostility when he arrives on someone else's territory'.[9] Kant also adds a 'secret article' to the conditions for perpetual peace where, perhaps hopefully, if not self-servingly, he requires that the 'maxims of the philosophers on the conditions under which public peace is possible shall be consulted by states which are armed for war'.[10]

John Rawls, rather more recently, and in what he regards as explicitly Kantian vein, has also argued for an international order. Rawls calls this a 'Law of Peoples', by which he means a 'particular political conception of right and justice that applies to the principles and norms of international law and practice'.[11] Rawls rejects the notion of world government: 'I follow Kant's lead', he says, 'in thinking that a world government would either be a global despotism', or make for a 'fragile empire torn by frequent civil strife as various regimes and peoples tried to gain their political freedom and autonomy'.[12] I will return to detailed consideration of Rawls' work in the next section.

Kant does seem to me to be ambivalent as regards the idea of world government. He does refer to the 'positive idea' of a world republic, as noted above. He does, however, say that laws 'progressively lose their impact as the government increases its range, and a soulless despotism, after crushing the germs of goodness, will finally lapse into anarchy'. 'It is', however, Kant concludes, the 'desire of every state (or its ruler) to achieve lasting peace by thus dominating the whole world, if at all possible', but '*nature* wills it otherwise, and uses two means to separate the nations and prevent them from intermingling - *linguistic* and *religious* differences'. These differences, Kant states, may 'certainly occasion mutual hatred and provide pretexts for wars'. But, perhaps in classic Enlightenment vein, Kant maintains that as 'culture grows and men gradually move towards greater agreement over their principles, they lead to mutual understanding and peace'. 'And', he adds, 'unlike that universal despotism which saps all man's energies and ends in the graveyard of freedom, this peace is created and guaranteed by an equilibrium of forces and a most vigorous rivalry.'[13]

Global 'governance', if not global government, also features in the 'third way' ideology of Anthony Giddens, the topic of much discussion of late. The 'third way', Giddens maintains, is a 'globalizing political philosophy' looking to 'promote further global integration'.[14] There are, he maintains, five areas where global institutions need to be strengthened, these being, 'the governance of the world economy, global ecological management, the regulation of corporate power, the control of warfare and the fostering of transnational democracy'.[15] Giddens, whilst welcoming economic globalization, which he claims to be 'by and large... a success',[16] envisages the creation of a 'world financial authority' and even, ultimately, a 'global central bank'.[17]

A Modern Liberal International Order

Modern liberal political theory offers an obvious way of conceptualizing an international order. Assuming that a global polity is not on the agenda of modern liberalism, an international order can be conceived as a 'neutral' framework of fundamental rights or norms to which all peoples or political communities subscribe but, within the limits of which, individuals, peoples or nations can pursue their own conceptions of the good life. This does seem to be the upshot of Rawls' *The Law of Peoples*, a work already mentioned above.

Rawls conceives in this work of a 'Society of Peoples', which he takes to mean all those peoples 'who follow the ideals and principles of the Law of Peoples in their mutual relations'.[18] Rawls adds that these peoples have their own internal governments which, in his words, may be 'constitutional liberal democratic' or 'non-liberal but decent governments'.[19] Indeed, Rawls identifies five types of domestic societies in the contemporary world: 'reasonable liberal peoples', 'decent peoples', 'outlaw states', societies 'burdened by unfavorable conditions' and, finally, 'benevolent absolutisms'.[20] Rawls seems to be principally concerned with the relations between liberal and what he calls non-liberal but decent peoples.

Rawls distinguishes between what he calls the 'ideal' and 'non-ideal' in his formulation of a right or just international order. In the first part of the former, Rawls' substantive theory of justice, justice as fairness, as outlined, for example, in his *A Theory of Justice*,[21] is extended to the 'society of liberal democratic peoples'. In the second part of this 'ideal' theory, justice as fairness is extended to the 'society of decent peoples'. 'Decent' societies, Rawls argues, are not liberal democratic, but they have 'certain features making them acceptable as members in good standing in a reasonable Society of Peoples'. The ideal theory is completed when liberal and decent peoples agree to the same Law of Peoples. 'A Society of Peoples is reasonably just in that its members follow the reasonably just Law of Peoples in their mutual relations.'[22] Rawls adds that the aim of his 'Law of Peoples' would be fully achieved when 'all societies have been able to establish either a liberal or a decent regime, however unlikely that may be'.[23] Rawls writes:

> Our hope for the future of our society rests on the belief that the nature of the social world would allow reasonably just constitutional democratic societies existing as members of the Society of Peoples. In such a social world peace and justice would be achieved between liberal and decent peoples both at home and abroad. The idea of this society is realistically utopian in that it depicts an

achievable social world [providing] political right and justice for all liberal and decent peoples in a society of Peoples.[24]

Both *A Theory of Justice* and Rawls' later major work, *Political Liberalism*,[25] in Rawls' words, 'try to say how a liberal society might be possible'. *The Law of Peoples* 'hopes to say how a world society of liberal and decent Peoples might be possible'.[26] Rawls' fundamental ideas of the 'social contract', the 'original position' and the 'veil of ignorance',[27] as developed in *A Theory of Justice*, are thus extended in *The Law of Peoples* to this international society of liberal and 'decent' but 'non-liberal' peoples. Rawls conceives of a 'second original position', paralleling his original original position. In this second original position, 'representatives of liberal peoples make an agreement with other liberal peoples... and again later with nonliberal though decent peoples'. Each of these agreements is 'understood as hypothetical and nonhistorical, and entered into by equal peoples symmetrically situated in the original position behind an appropriate veil of ignorance'[28] - this latter construct designed to ensure impartiality in the choice of principles regulating relations, in this case, between peoples. 'Hence', Rawls concludes, 'the undertaking between peoples is fair.'[29]

Rawls also sees a parallel between the arrangements for a domestic society and the society of peoples with regard to his 'difference principle'. With the difference principle in the context of a domestic society, one is concerned with a baseline of equality in the distribution of social values or what Rawls calls 'social and economic primary goods'.[30] With the society of peoples, Rawls argues, one begins with the baseline of 'equality of and the equal rights of all peoples'.[31] Departures from simple equality in the case of a domestic society are legitimated, according to Rawls' theory of social justice, if such inequalities are 'to the benefit of all citizens of [the] society', and, in particular, the 'least advantaged'. With the Law of Peoples, however, 'persons are not under one but many governments, and the representatives of peoples will want to preserve the equality and independence of their own society... [agreed] inequalities [in this context] are designed to secure the many ends that peoples share'.[32]

Rawls also seeks to extend the fundamental ideas of his *Political Liberalism* to this 'Law of Peoples', ideas such as 'reasonable pluralism', the 'overlapping consensus' and the concept of justice as 'political' rather than 'metaphysical'.[33] In the 'Society of Peoples', Rawls argues, the 'parallel to reasonable pluralism [in a reasonably just democratic society] is the diversity among reasonable peoples with their different cultures and traditions of thought, both religious and nonreligious... A (reasonable) Law of Peoples must be acceptable to reasonable peoples who are thus diverse; and it must be fair between them....'[34]

Rawls, in conclusion, lists eight principles for his conception of international right, his law of peoples. Peoples, he insists, are free and independent and this fact is to be respected by (all) other peoples; peoples are to observe treaties and undertakings; peoples are equal; peoples are to observe a duty of non-intervention; peoples have the right of self-defence but no right to instigate war for reasons other than self-defence; peoples are to honour human rights; peoples are to observe specific restrictions in the conduct of war; peoples have a duty to assist peoples living under what Rawls calls 'unfavourable conditions' that prevent such peoples having a 'just or a decent political and social regime'.[35] Rawls contends that these eight principles of the Law of Peoples are 'superior to any others'.[36]

One should note, consistent with Rawls' conception of *political* liberalism, that the 'Law of Peoples' does not require all societies to be liberal. Such an insistence, Rawls argues, 'would fail to express due toleration for other acceptable ways (if such there are, as I assume) of ordering society'.[37] A liberal domestic society, Rawls argues, respects its citizens' 'comprehensive doctrines'[38] provided that these doctrines are 'pursued in ways compatible with a reasonable political conception of justice'.[39] Similarly, Rawls maintains, 'provided a nonliberal society's basic institutions meet certain specified conditions of political right and justice and lead its people to honor a reasonable and just law for the Society of Peoples, a liberal people is to tolerate and accept that society'.[40]

Modern Liberal Conceptions of an International Order: Commentary and Critique

I take Rawls' *Law of Peoples* to be an exemplar of a modern liberal approach to the concept of an international order (although this does not preclude the possibility of a non-Rawlsian version - perhaps one dispensing with Rawlsian constructions such as the 'original position'). I aim here to outline an alternative conception of an international political order which might broadly, but non-conventionally, be described as communitarian, neo-republican or neo-Aristotelian. The fundamental idea behind this alternative conceptualization, as implied by the last of these terms, is derived from Aristotle:

> The real difference between man and other animals is that humans alone have perception of good and evil, right and wrong, just and unjust. And it is a sharing of a common view in these matters that makes a household or a city.[41]

I am not here concerned with whether or not Aristotle was right to suggest that humans alone are subjects of moral consciousness. (The point has been contested by some.[42]) Nor am I concerned here with the proper relations between human and non-human beings, or between 'citizens' and 'non-citizens', although of course these are all important and related issues. Rather, my concern here is with a conception of the nature of the polity, which I interpret as Aristotelian, as defined by the shared morality of its citizenry.

This I take to be in contrast to Weber's classic definition of the modern state as a 'human community which (successfully) lays claim to the *monopoly of legitimate physical violence* within a given territory', where both 'territory' and the use of 'physical violence', as a 'specific means', are seen as 'defining characteristics of the state'.[43] Admittedly, Weber is only concerned here with defining the state 'sociologically'.[44] In this one may have an anticipation of Habermas' point concerning the conflict between 'facticity' and 'validity' in legal and political theory, between what he calls the 'objectivating viewpoint' of the social sciences, and the essentially normative approach of moral philosophers and philosophers of law.[45] This chapter, in line with the other chapters in this book, is principally concerned with normative questions and not the relation between a normative and an 'objectivating' viewpoint, nor with the alleged problem of normative approaches being 'constantly in danger of losing contact with social reality',[46] central though these questions are. For Habermas, the normative approach 'starts with the socially integrating force of rationally motivating, hence noncoercive processes of reaching understanding', processes 'providing a space for distance and recognised differences within a sustained commonality of convictions'.[47] I shall return to these ideas shortly.

Habermas does note that from the 'objectivating viewpoint of the social sciences, a philosophical approach that still operates with the alternatives of *forcibly* stabilized versus *rationally* legitimated orders belongs to the transitional semantics of early modernity'.[48] At the risk of appearing to want to revive modern, if not pre-modern, perspectives, I am here concerned to advocate a moralistic conception of the polity and indeed of citizenship. In this conception neither the use of physical violence nor territory is essential, nor is the distinction between an 'order' and a 'state' since the conception is compatible, in principle anyway, with the anarchist notion of moral force replacing physical force.[49] The contours of this polity are defined by the shared morality of its members - its citizenry. It extends as far as its morality does, where the function of the citizen *qua* citizen may not, given considerations of realistic practicality in a large and complex society or order, be actually to share in governing, as Aristotle insisted,[50] or administration in the absence of government, but rather to uphold and debate the shared morality. This morality, I contend, is concerned with both the Right and the Good, to use Rawls' terminology,[51] and is designed to answer, in the round, the classical Greek question of how one should live.[52]

I classify this alternative conception of the polity and, for the purposes of this chapter, the *global* polity, as non-liberal. Non-liberalism needs to be contrasted with both illiberalism, where illiberalism might be understood, for example, as the kind of moral conservatism advocated by Devlin in his *The Enforcement of Morals*,[53] and anti-liberalism, for example, the conception of the fascist state propounded by, among others, Gentile.[54] This said, given the term non-liberal, the contrast with modern liberalism is conceptually central. Ironically, however, this non-liberal polity can, I suggest, be understood in much the same terms as Rawls defines what he calls a 'well-ordered society', namely a society or polity 'designed to advance the good of its members' and, 'effectively regulated by a public conception of justice'.[55]

Rawls' fundamental philosophical starting point, at least in his *A Theory of Justice*, is to provide, in his words, 'an alternative systematic account of justice that is superior... to... utilitarianism'.[56] For Michael Sandel, Rawls' work, at least in *A Theory of Justice*, is a prime example of what he calls 'Kantian liberalism'.[57] For Sandel, Kantian liberals 'avoid affirming a conception of the good by affirming instead the priority of right, which depends in turn on a picture of the self prior to its ends'.[58] Kantian liberals, Sandel argues, are opposed not only to utilitarianism (given that utilitarianism, according to Rawls, for example, 'does not take seriously the distinction between persons'[59] - it is only concerned with aggregating persons' interests or preferences, or more crudely, pleasures and pains, in pursuit of the greatest happiness of the greatest number), but 'also to any view that regards us as obligated to fulfil ends we have not chosen - ends given by nature or God, for example, or by our identities as members of families, peoples, cultures or traditions'.[60] For Kantian liberals, Sandel maintains, 'it is precisely because we are freely choosing, independent selves that we need a neutral framework, a framework of rights that refuses to choose among competing values and ends'.[61]

Of course Rawls does appear to insist on unity as regards the conception of Right or justice in the domestic society or the society of peoples, that is the framework of rights, which does imply some political choice between competing values - justice is itself a value, but, Rawls argues, 'there is no urgency to reach a publicly accepted judgment as to what is the good of particular individuals. The reasons that make such an agreement necessary in questions of justice do not obtain for judgements of value.'[62] I think, personally, that there may be grounds here for generating confusion with regard to some of Rawls' later work, specifically *Political Liberalism*, with its contrast between a 'moral' and a 'political' conception of justice. Rawls states in *Political Liberalism* that the idea of a well-ordered society as justice as fairness, as explicated in *A Theory of Justice*, is 'unrealistic'. This is because 'it is inconsistent with realizing its own principles under the best foreseeable conditions'. Rawls says that this 'ambiguity' is removed in *Political Liberalism* and the theory of justice as fairness is 'presented from the outset as a political conception of justice'.[63] 'Which moral judgements are true', Rawls says in *Political Liberalism*, including, presumably, the moral judgment as to the nature of social justice, 'is not a matter for political liberalism'; political liberalism 'rather than referring to its political conception as true, refers to it as reasonable instead', it articulates 'political and not all values'.[64] It is political and not 'comprehensive' liberalism.[65] The 'general problems of moral philosophy are not the concern of political liberalism'; political liberalism sees its form of political philosophy as 'having its own subject matter' which is 'how... a just and free society [is] possible under conditions of deep doctrinal conflict with no possibility of resolution'.[66]

Whether the view of justice as fairness as a 'freestanding view',[67] impartial between comprehensive doctrines, is coherent or continuous with Rawls' earlier work in *A Theory of Justice*, is not my concern here. Rawls himself views *Political Liberalism* as continuous with *A Theory of Justice*.[68] Given the above, Rawls presumably sees *The Law of Peoples* as continuous with both *A Theory of Justice* and *Political Liberalism*. Sandel, for one, refers to Rawls' liberalism in *Political Liberalism* as 'minimalist liberalism' (as contrasted with Kantian liberalism) which is not 'the application to politics of Kantian moral philosophy, but a practical response to the familiar fact that people in modern democratic societies typically disagree about the good'.[69]

Sandel opposes to liberalism, whether 'Kantian' or 'minimalist', his version of 'republican theory': He writes: 'Instead of defining rights according to principles that are neutral among conceptions of the good, republican theory interprets rights in the light of a particular conception of the good society - the self-governing republic.' He notes that, 'in contrast to the liberal claim that the right is prior to the good, republicanism thus affirms a politics of the common good'.[70]

I do not personally wish to contest what Rawls calls the 'priority of the right over the good'.[71] One has a duty to be just; there is no parallel duty, I suggest, to pursue the good life (tentatively defined as that life which allows one to flourish as a human being and the particular kind of human being one is,[72] or to develop certain qualities of character or virtues (unless so doing is necessary in fulfilling one's obligations mandated by considerations of justice). However, it seems to me logically possible, and I would argue both philosophically and politically appropriate, both to affirm a politics of the common good and to assert the priority of right as justice. The 'rights secured by justice',[73] to use Rawls' phrase, do not, I would argue, follow from a particular conception of the good life or the good society, nor are they merely instrumental to active participation in the republican polity - they are requirements of justice - of acting in accordance with the Right incumbent upon all subjects of moral consciousness. However, it is perfectly plausible, I suggest, to imagine a (global) polity united on a common conception of justice and a common conception of the good (including the virtues). This would entail a polity which upholds justice and the common pursuit of excellence. It would require of its citizens those virtues necessary for the maintenance of the polity ('the qualities of character necessary to the common good of self-government', as Sandel puts it[74]), the ecological preservation of what Paul Taylor calls 'earth's community of life',[75] and the individual and collective pursuit of human excellence or perfection, a democratic perfectionism.[76]

Of course, it may be a good thing, at least for modern individuals, that persons be allowed, within limits, to pursue their own conception of the good. However, if it is a good thing that individuals, or perhaps whole cultures, societies or peoples, pursue their own conception of the good life, this necessarily implies a common, unitary conception of the good - a unitary conception which in the modern liberal mind (but not the non-liberal) may have only one element or claim, namely that it is a good thing that individuals or peoples pursue their own conception of the good.[77]

Conclusion: A Rationalist Communitarianism

One might conclude that what I am advocating here is a version of what Gray[78] calls the 'Enlightenment project' of a 'universal civilization', a civilization or order informed by shared values discoverable by reason, as opposed to being distilled from a particular tradition, and that this project is both unrealistic given present levels of cultural, moral and social diversity (where diversity, at least in some societies, is increasing according to some social theorists[79]), and inadequately pluralistic, if pluralism is indeed desirable as Rawls and Gray, for example, argue.[80] It may be that modern liberalism is a more suitable vehicle for conceptualizing an international order from the point of view of accommodating diversity in the world. One might, for example, argue that in accommodating diversity we should adopt what Barry[81] calls 'justice as impartiality', a 'crucial task' of which is to 'mediate between conflicting conceptions of the good', where, Barry argues, 'a fatal objection to the idea of a duty to pursue the good is the existence of unresolvable dispute about what the good consists in'. Impartial justice, Barry maintains, 'is fair between conflicting conceptions of the good in virtue of its maintaining a certain kind of neutrality between them', where rules of justice become 'rules of the kind that any society requires if it is to avoid conflict'.

I would agree, as already noted above, that there is no strict duty to pursue the good life, whereas there is such a duty where justice is concerned. However, the idea that unresolvable dispute about the nature of the good undermines the assumption that one has a duty to pursue the good could equally well be made about justice itself, if the theory of justice is to have any content at all. The reason why one has no duty to pursue the good, other things being equal, has nothing to do with the existence or non-existence of agreement as to the nature of the good life. There would be no *duty* to pursue the good even in circumstances of complete agreement as to the nature of the good life. Rather, the good, unlike justice, is simply not the kind of value to which strict duties are attached. Barry seems to imply that it is easier to agree on questions of justice than it is on questions of the good, justice being, in the modern liberal mind, narrower in scope. However, justice is just as much an evaluative term as the good life, and there is, in existing human society, specifically modern liberal-individualistic society, deep division as to exactly what justice mandates, as MacIntyre, for one, points out.[82]

The main objection to modern liberalism and a modern liberal international order is, I think, succinctly put by Sandel - namely that the effect of a modern liberal political culture, whether national or international, is to impoverish political discourse and to erode the 'moral and civic resources necessary to self-government'.[83] The adequately self-directed community is one united on a common morality, one that is rationally acceptable and subject to rational discourse and criticism. It is, in this sense, well-ordered.

As to the fact of diversity, I suggest that Aristotelian pluralism[84] is, at least in principle, capable of accommodating modern or, as some would have it, postmodern diversity. We need not, as Hilary Putnam[85] suggests, be entirely monistic as to the nature of human flourishing, different human beings may flourish in different ways consistent with a general notion of what human flourishing consists in. Whether this amounts to what Rawls calls a 'thin' theory of the good[86] I do not consider. I do think it amounts to a form of perfectionism as a political principle which Rawls appears explicitly to reject.[87]

I suggest, counter to the prevailing social theory of late or post-modernity, that the world is not becoming more diverse, at least in the sense of the radical conceptual diversity or disagreement noted, for example, by MacIntyre,[88] in his description of relations between the Spanish *conquistadores* and the natives of the 'New World' in the sixteenth century, or between the colonial English and the native Irish of the early eighteenth century. That kind of radical conceptual diversity is such as to make communication and mutual understanding impossible, and it is the kind of diversity which might be seen as typical of the pre-modern or early modern world. I suggest that the kind of capitalist modernization which Marx and Engels describe as remaking the world in its own image, in the *Communist Manifesto* of 1848,[89] has all but done its work, and has put paid to actual examples of diversity in what Wittgenstein called, and later Wittgensteinians call, (diversity in) 'forms of life'.[90] One might call this 'globalization', 'modernization' or 'westernization'.[91] We all increasingly, I suspect, by and large, speak the same language today, even if we still use different languages. This agreement in 'form of life' (that is, conceptual framework) makes logically possible substantive agreement (and disagreement) over the values that ought to govern our collective order. (We need to agree on the meaning and use of the term 'justice', for example, in order to meaningfully agree or disagree about the nature of the just social order.) The diversity noted by the theorists of late and/or post-modernity is not of this kind, I suggest, and does not, in principle, militate against the kind of unity in values suggested here. Diversity in (individual) styles of life or living, the 'expansion of choice in consumption, lifestyle and sexuality', characteristic of the alleged 'New Times' of late-modernity,[92] for example, is not comparable to diversity in 'forms of life'.

Finally, I should note that what is entertained here is what Habermas, for one, argues to be an outdated notion - namely the idea of the 'macrosubject of a communal whole'. This is in contrast to what he calls 'anonymously intermeshing discourses' extending in principle globally in 'worldwide political communications' giving form to an embryonic '*world citizenship*',[93] which latter Habermas sees as a realistic, present-day alternative to that of the communal whole. Nor, relatedly, is the shared morality of this communal whole a discourse ethic, the attractions of this latter concept aside.[94] It has not been my purpose here to try and spell out what that ethic might be. Whether the notion of a global, rationalist communitarianism amounts to an example of what Bauman[95] calls the 'dream/consolation' of a 'globalized intellectual', vainly searching for a sense of global community in the face of a rampant global individualism, I do not feel qualified to answer.

For Cooper we 'have grown up with the legacy of the Enlightenment. We want to believe in a single global order, in universal rights and universal law. These are desirable goals, but we must deal with the world as it is, not as we want it to be.'[96] Cooper's point hints at an ancient question, the relation between the ideal and the actual. Minimally, one should note that dealing with the world 'as it is' does not necessarily imply abandoning one's values, nor adapting one's values to suit the particular contingencies of time or place. In this sense being realistic in politics does not imply the adoption of realism or indeed relativism as a guide to political action.[97]

My concern here has been with the notion of an international order or global polity. Other chapters in this book specifically focus on the ethics of military intervention. These issues are plainly connected, as Brassington's discussion in this volume demonstrates. Kant, as above, outlaws forcible intervention by states in the constitution and government of other states, Rawls talks of a duty of non-intervention, but both also insist on states adopting certain principles in their domestic affairs and in their relations with other states. Walzer,[98] too, outlaws military intervention except in cases of assisting a legitimate state to defend itself against aggression (the assistance given to Kuwait in the Gulf War, for example), or, in exceptional cases, to uphold basic human rights, which might cover, for example, military intervention by NATO in the wars in former Yugoslavia. The notion that states are justified in interfering in the affairs of other states to prevent human rights violations, prosecute 'war criminals', or, indeed, paradoxically, to repel aggression, implies adherence to, and enforcement of, international or global norms. A modern liberal international order, of a kind, may indeed be in the making. Alternatively, actions such as the Gulf War, and the recent bombing of Belgrade, may be taken as evidence of a resurgent neo-realism, and the collapse of global order.

I suggest, in conclusion, that economic and cultural globalization, and indeed the problem of ecological management, incline in the direction of a global order, if not a global polity. It has been my purpose to outline, broadly speaking, what a non-liberal, 'republican' conception of such an order might look like.

Notes

1 Cited in G. Esler, *The United States of Anger* (Harmondsworth, Penguin, 1998), p.35.
2 Z. Bauman, *Globalization: The Human Consequences* (New York, Columbia University Press, 1998), p.13.
3 Bauman op. cit., p.12.
4 Kant, *Political Writings*, ed. H. Reiss (Cambridge, Cambridge University Press, 1991), pp.104-105.
5 Kant, op. cit., p.102.
6 Kant, op. cit., pp.93-96.
7 Kant, op. cit., p.99.
8 Kant, op. cit., p.100.
9 Kant, op. cit., p.105.
10 Kant, op. cit., pp.114-115.
11 J. Rawls, *The Law of Peoples with The Idea of Public Reason Revisited* (hereafter *LP*) (Cambridge Mass., Harvard University Press, 1999), p.3.
12 Rawls, *LP*, p.36.
13 Kant, op. cit., pp.113-114.
14 A. Giddens, *The Third Way and Its Critics* (Cambridge, Polity Press, 2000), p.122.
15 Giddens op. cit., p.124.
16 Giddens, ibid.
17 Giddens, op. cit., pp.126, 127.
18 Rawls, *LP*, p.3.
19 Rawls, ibid.
20 Rawls, *LP*, p.4.
21 J. Rawls, *A Theory of Justice* (hereafter *TJ*), revised second edition (Oxford, Oxford University Press, 1999).
22 Rawls, *LP*, pp.4-5.
23 Rawls, *LP*, p.5.
24 Rawls, *LP*, p.6.
25 J. Rawls, *Political Liberalism* (hereafter *PL*) (New York, Columbia University Press, 1993).
26 Rawls, *LP*, p.6.
27 See Rawls, *TJ*, pp.14-19, 118-123.
28 Rawls, *LP*, p.10.
29 Ibid.
30 Rawls, *LP*, p.41. For a definition of 'primary goods' see Rawls, *TJ*, pp.54-55, 78-81 and Rawls, *PL*, pp.178-189.
31 Rawls, *LP*, p.41.
32 Rawls, *LP*, p.41.
33 Rawls, *PL*, pp.11-15, 36-37, 131-172.
34 Rawls, *LP*, pp.11-12.
35 Rawls, *LP*, p.37.
36 Rawls, *LP*, p.41.
37 Rawls, *LP*, p.59.
38 For a definition of this term see Rawls, *PL*, p.175.
39 Rawls, *LP*, pp.59-60.
40 Ibid.
41 Aristotle, *The Politics*, trans. T.A. Sinclair (Harmondsworth, Penguin, 1962), pp.28-29.

42 L.E. Johnson, *A Morally Deep World: An Essay on Moral Significance and Environmental Ethics* (Cambridge, Cambridge University Press, 1991) pp.61-75.

43 M. Weber, *Political Writings*, ed. P. Lassman and R. Spiers (Cambridge, Cambridge University Press, 1991), pp.310-311.

44 Ibid., p.310.

45 J. Habermas, *Between Facts and Norms* (Cambridge, Polity Press, 1996), p.6.

46 Habermas, ibid.

47 Habermas, ibid.

48 Habermas, ibid.

49 Thus Tolstoy, for example, writes, that 'if men are rational beings, then their relations should be based on reason, and not on the violence of those who happen to have seized power... [the violence implicit in the idea of government] has no justification' (L. Tolstoy, 'The slavery of our times' in G. Woodcock, *The Anarchist Reader* (Glasgow, Collins, 1977), p.309).

50 Aristotle, op. cit., p.102.

51 See, for example, Rawls, *TJ*, pp.392-396.

52 For an analysis of the nature of this question see J. Habermas, 'On the pragmatic, the ethical, and the moral employments of practical reason' in J. Habermas, *Justification and Application: Remarks on Discourse Ethics*, trans. C. Cronin (Cambridge, Polity Press, 1993, pp.1-18.

53 P. Devlin, *The Enforcement of Morals* (Oxford, Oxford University Press, 1965).

54 Z. Sternhell, 'Fascist ideology' in W. Laquer (ed.) *Fascism: A Reader's Guide* (Harmondsworth, Penguin, 1979), pp.325-408, on p.366.

55 Rawls, *TJ*, p.4.

56 Rawls, *TJ*, xviii.

57 M. Sandel, *Democracy's Discontent: America In Search of a Public Philosophy* (Cambridge, Mass., Harvard University Press, 1996), pp.8-17.

58 Sandel, op. cit., p.13.

59 Rawls, *TJ*, p.24.

60 Sandel, op. cit, p.12.

61 Sandel, ibid.

62 Rawls, *TJ*, p.393.

63 Rawls, *PL*, xvii.

64 Rawls, *PL*, xx.

65 Rawls, *PL*, xvii.

66 Rawls, *PL*, xxviii.

67 Rawls, *PL*, xxx.

68 See Rawls, *PL*, p.7n.

69 Sandel, op. cit., p.18.

70 Sandel, op. cit., p.25.

71 Rawls, *TJ*, p.28.

72 C. Pateman in her introduction to her edited collection *Feminist Challenges* suggests that human beings are fundamentally 'feminine and masculine, that individuality is not a unitary abstraction but an embodied and sexually differentiated expression of the unity of humankind' (C. Pateman and E. Gross, eds., *Feminist Challenges: Social and Political Theory* (Sydney, Allen and Unwin, 1986), p.9). If this is true, then the nature of the good may differ, for example, between women and men.

73 Rawls, *TJ*, p.4.

74 Sandel, op. cit., p.25.

75 P. Taylor, *Respect for Nature* (Princeton, Princeton University Press, 1986), pp.101-115.

262 Human Rights and Military Intervention

76   Rawls seems to imply, in his discussion of perfectionism (*TJ* pp.285-292), that this notion is inherently elitist, requiring that some persons should sacrifice their projects and aspirations, and an equal claim on material resources to realize such aspirations, in order that 'higher' persons can realize theirs. I can see no necessary connection here.

77   Rawls' account of the good seems to be somewhat fuller than this. See, for example, *TJ*, p.376. Yet Rawls concludes that, in a 'well-ordered society', the 'plans of life of individuals are different...', and persons are left free to determine the good, the views of others being counted as merely advisory'. Further, this 'variety in conceptions of the good is itself a good thing' (Rawls, *TJ*, p.393).

78   J. Gray, *False Dawn: The Delusions of Global Capitalism* (London, Granta, 1998), p.2.

79   See, for example, A. Giddens, *The Third Way: The Renewal of Social Democracy* (Cambridge, Polity Press, 1998), p.34.

80   Gray himself puts forward what he calls a 'communitarian-liberal' perspective (J. Gray, 'After social democracy' in G. Mulgan (ed.) *Life After Politics* (Glasgow, Fontana, 1997), pp.325-338). In this perspective, the liberal value of individual autonomy is not to be understood in terms of universal rights or principles, but, rather, 'local understandings, grounded in particular forms of common life and liberty' (p.330).

81   B. Barry, *Justice as Impartiality* (Oxford, Oxford University Press, 1998), p.12.

82   A. MacIntyre, *After Virtue: a study in moral theory* (London, Duckworth, 1985), pp. 244-255. For Rawls (*PL*, pp.156-157), a liberal view of justice 'removes from the political agenda the most divisive issues'. Yet his liberal-egalitarian conception of justice, which 'protects... basic rights... assigns them a special priority' and 'includes measures to insure that all citizens have sufficient material means to make effective use of those... rights', invites contention as MacIntyre (ibid.) indicates.

83   Sandel, op. cit., p.23.

84   See, for example, J. O'Neill, 'Polity, economy, neutrality', in *Political Studies*, 43, 3 (1995), pp.414-431. O'Neill writes (p.425) that, within Aristotelian pluralism, diversity can be encouraged but only within the bounds of a specific account of the good.

85   H. Putnam, *Reason, Truth and History* (Cambridge, Cambridge University Press, 1981), p.148.

86   Rawls, *TJ*, pp.347-350.

87   Rawls, *TJ*, p.289. See, also, note 76.

88   A. MacIntyre, 'Relativism, power, and philosophy' in K. Baynes et al. (eds.) *After Philosophy: End or Transformation* (Cambridge Mass., MIT Press, 1987), pp.385-411, on p.390.

89   K. Marx and F. Engels, *The Communist Manifesto*, A.J.P. Taylor (intro.) (Harmondsworth, Penguin, 1967), pp.82-83.

90   L. Wittgenstein, *Philosophical Investigations*, trans. G.E.M. Anscombe (Oxford, Blackwell, 1967), para.241.

91   I refer here to globalization rather than neo-liberal globalism (see Gray, *False Dawn*, op. cit., p.3).

92   Giddens, *The Third Way and its Critics*, op. cit., pp.27-28.

93   Habermas, *Between Facts and Norms*, op. cit., pp.505, 514.

94   See Habermas, *Justification and Application*, op. cit., pp.19-112.

95   Bauman, op. cit, p.3. Giddens (*The Third Way and its Critics*, pp.63-64) suggests that communitarianism as a political theory 'has its problems'; the term 'community' does 'too much work in communitarian theory'. Further, communities, 'if they become too strong', breed 'identity politics, and with it the potential for social division, or even disintegration'. I suggest that the form of communitarianism entertained in this chapter does not suffer from these faults. The principal emphasis is not on community *per se* but polity and citizenship, moralistically conceived.

96 R. Cooper, 'Is there a new world order?', in G. Mulgan (ed.), *Life After Politics*, op. cit., pp.312-324, on pp.322-323.

97 The truth in relativism, as against universalism, is I think simply this: There may be social/cultural preconditions for recognizing the 'truth' regarding matters of value. It may, for example, be unreasonable to have expected Aristotle not to have defended slavery in his *Politics* (op. cit., pp.32-37). It does not follow, however, that Aristotle was right to defend slavery, nor that slavery is not objectively morally wrong (as I, for one, would argue). O'Reardon, in this volume, advocates what he calls a 'contextualist' over a 'universalist' approach, citing Charles Taylor (a name often connected with communitarianism) as an example of the former, against Rawls as an example of the latter. There may be specific goods which are internal to particular cultures, as O'Reardon suggests. However, I would argue in rationalist, universalist vein that we can extract a sense of the Right and the Good independently of such contextualist claims.

98 M. Walzer, *Just and Unjust Wars* (New York, HarperCollins, 1992). For Walzer there is such a thing as international society composed of 'independent states'. Further, this international society 'has a law that establishes the rights of its members - above all, the rights of territorial integrity and political sovereignty' (op. cit., p.61). Independent states have a moral right to resist aggression and to enlist the help of others states in resisting aggression, aggression being the 'name we give to the crime of war' (op. cit., p.51). Of the Gulf War, following the Iraqi invasion of Kuwait in August of 1990, Walzer says, 'acts of aggression like the Iraqi invasion *ought to be resisted* - not necessarily by military means, but by some means' (op. cit., xvi). As to the fate of persecuted minorities within independent states, Walzer states that the 'radical mistreatment of such people may justify military intervention' (op. cit., p.55).

PART VI
WIDER VALUES

Chapter 14

Stretching Humanitarianisms: Cultural and Aesthetic Values and Military Intervention

Alexander Moseley and Heather Eisenhut

'Who kills a man kills a reasonable creature, God's image; but he who destroys a good book, kills reason itself, kills the image of God, as it were, in the eye.'[1] John Milton

We begin by agreeing that military intervention to stop genocidal campaigns is justifiable, but what we also wish to establish in this paper is that intervention to halt the destruction of a culture and its artefacts warrants a similar justification on the grounds that a violation of humanity's cultural artefacts is a violation of humanity's right to self-expression, a right that is not born of dependency or of subsidy, but which intimately and ultimately expresses an individual's conscience, mind, and aesthetic values.

To establish this stretching of military intervention to include works of art, we shall outline the vital relationship that exists between art and man. We shall also outline why the threat to art is as pernicious as the threat of aggression towards men. Art, we argue, should possess a moral and political sanctity deserving our utmost measures to protect it: as Milton says, to kill a work of art is to destroy man. Nonetheless, a *realist* vision of war, values and life is defended, if such an expression is pertinent when expressing a thoroughly ethically idealist viewpoint: realism in this instance requires looking hard at human life and realizing that some things are worth fighting for: life is more than the proliferation of numbers.

The Legal Situation

In 1954 the UN passed the Hague Convention for the Protection of Cultural Property in the Event of Armed Conflict. This is an excellent convention that seeks to remove places and items of man's cultural heritage out of war's reach, unless military necessity requires otherwise (Article 11.2). The law accords a strong duty of responsibility to those in charge of art to protect it and to remove it from potential destruction. The Article does not emanate from an intellectual or legal vacuum, but stems from the grand tradition of the just war theory that stipulates the moral boundaries of war and warfare. The just war theory acknowledges moral sanctuaries for 'innocents' or, in modern parlance, 'civilians'; the tradition of protecting women, children, and priests from warfare forms a persistent moral code throughout the ages.[2] The stretching of the tradition to include places is also not new, for churches, monasteries, indeed, the holy groves of pagans were deemed sacred places that should not experience the brutal invasion of war. But to defend an ancient practice in the modern world requires a modern tongue: the meaning of 'sacred' has been all but lost in the secular West and so, like many moral precepts that do not translate well into economically and socially complicated societies, new forms of distinguishing the good life from the bad should be deployed.

The starting position for any ethical discussion of art's moral status cannot begin with what the law, national or international, states on the matter. Legislation reflects moral arguments rather than the other way round; but more importantly the enforcement of legislation requires a moral motivation, and where that motivation is lacking, or is subject to debilitating ambivalence, the law is not likely to be enforced. This we have seen most dramatically with the recent destruction of Buddhist statues in Afghanistan, which directly contravened the Hague Convention Article 4,[3] and, we can add, the destruction of the World Trade Towers in September 2001 by terrorists in which the twin towers could be seen as standing as secular symbols representing global capitalism, America, and the free world. We believe that the case for cultural protection should also seek to enthuse the moral motive for art's protection and, if necessary, for intervention to secure important art works for posterity.

Defining Art

The greatest difficulty for the position we are advancing in establishing a sacrosanct moral status for art is defining what constitutes art. To some extent a work of art is not something that is mass produced: works of art are unique objects and the creations of single minds inhabiting specific cultures. For ease of exposition, we will refer to the Hague Convention for a brief summary on what defines art: 'movable or immovable property of great importance to the cultural heritage of every people, such as monuments of architecture, art or history, whether religious or secular; archaeological sites; groups of buildings which, as a whole, are of historical or artistic interest; works of art; manuscripts, books and other objects of artistic, historical or archaeological interest; as well as scientific collections and important collections of books or archives or of reproductions of the property defined above.'[4]

To avoid slipping into a discussion and elaboration of aesthetics and an evaluation of the terms 'great importance', 'interest', 'important collections' and so on, we must presume that we can establish what is a work of art and what is not. This is an unfortunate leap to make, especially when the mind's appetite is so whetted, but a necessary one if we are to justify active intervention to save or to secure works of art from destruction. We would agree that distinguishing art from non-art is an objective assessment, but not one for this paper. The path that we must take is to first of all justify art's moral status. We shall then establish why we ought to protect art.

A work of art is the culmination of a person's powers of intellect and creativity - the better the work of art, the higher the faculties that are engaged by the artist and the viewer. A work of art, an artificial creation of the artist's hands, presents a unique and human vision. This vision captures, or attempts to capture, the ineffable, that which persists beyond our capacity to evoke in normal everyday communication. Our spiritual being is manifested in art works; or, metaphorically speaking, human beings give birth to art, and it is not amiss to assimilate its status to that of a child deserving our respect and our moral consideration.

The best of art taps into the eternally developing and evolving human spirit - what may be termed the cultural legacy of each generation, grounding it in a distinct locality and context which yet transcends the particular moment for the eternal path along which humanity proceeds. It is a path that artists may forge, lament, criticize, or deny, but in so doing they add their voices, music, painting, poetry, sculpture to humanity's cultural heritage.

Art is thus sacred in a formal sense and thereby demands moral consideration. By the formal sense of 'sacred', we mean that art demands our moral reverence, even if we do not personally like a particular work of art, because, again reverting to Milton, art is 'God's image' to the human eye, or in more secular terms, art attempts to gain the perspective of human perfection, of humanity's highest capacities thrown into creative acts. To revere something is to value it highly, more highly than the transient preferences that ebb and flow with daily life. It is to recognize that art's value persists not just in the present but into the future as well, and accordingly to recognize that its existence requires a sustained maintenance beyond that offered by the present generation. As Jacob Burkhardt puts it: 'All human knowledge is accompanied by the history of the ancient world as music is by a bass chord heard again and again; the history, that is, of all those peoples whose life has flowed together into our own.'[5]

Art is thus something that the artist often seeks to preserve beyond the present moment. To produce a work of art, the artist implicitly or explicitly (consciously or sub-consciously) is seeking immortality through words, paint, or music. Unsurprisingly few artists are ever contented with their completed works, especially if they are able to surpass them as their skills develop, just as a society is never wholly satisfied with itself but is constantly straining for improvement and perfection, even if the guiding ideal is prelapsarian.

Once finished, a work of art enters the human heritage, capturing firstly the artist's vision, secondly the vision of his or her culture and epoch as substantiated by the individual artist, and thirdly, capturing something uniquely human - something which the higher, cultured faculties of any person can recognize as peculiarly human in origin and in vision. Even the earliest renditions of men and women, seen on cave walls or in Neolithic carvings, provide the viewer with a glimpse into an aesthetic vision that is recognizably individual and human. But since individuals belong to cultures, the carvings provide the viewer with an invaluable insight into the values and visions of that culture. Art substantiates the personal and social; it is thoroughly the product of an individual, but it carries with it cultural echoes, and whether that person is a dissenting voice or an apologist he or she cannot thoroughly separate themselves from their culture; but the product stands as a manifestation of their freedom to express themselves and their beliefs and ideals.

Thus when a work of art is attacked, the attack is not merely on the physical object - the painting, book, composition, or building - but on the human mind and human culture: to attack art is to attack humanity's intellectual roots.

Destroying Works of Art

The destruction of a human life is an act that warrants complex justifications or, in the absence of any justification, an ensuing punishment. The concept of human rights, or of human dignity, accords the individual a morally *sacred* status, which we today recognize as deserving protection from aggression. Yet the destruction of a work of art is arguably just as heinous an act, for it destroys not only the culmination of a person's highest efforts, it also destroys the highest capacities that humanity can reach. Byron writes 'On the Bust of Helen by Canova':

> In this beloved marble view,
> Above the works and thoughts of man,
> What nature *could*, but *would not*, do
> And beauty and Canova *can!*

To which Byron adds a footnote: 'The Helen of Canova is without exception, to my mind, the most perfectly beautiful of human conceptions, and far beyond my ideas of human execution.'[6] To rip up Byron's poem after he penned it, or to break the Bust of Helen destroys the vision that the artist presents and the vision that the viewer enjoys: it would not just be an irrelevant aggression against an inanimate object, but an aggression against the manifestation of a person's mind and hence against his or her mind.

To look at the moral status of art from a different perspective, we need to compare it to the so-called basic or necessary values for life. Food and shelter are rightly deemed requisites for life, but so they are for most animals. Humanity is of a much more complex and spiritual nature, and since the dawn of our consciousness, we have created cultural artefacts from cave paintings to temples that seek to reflect the inner vision that we sometimes hold of ourselves and of the world. These visions constitute not only ephemeral, fleeting attempts to give meaning to human life, but they constitute additions to the great cultural stock of humanity's aesthetic heritage. Art is not just for present audiences, private or public, but also for future audiences. As such it attempts to transcend time and place.[7] It is generated from the particular circumstances of the artist but it becomes a reflection of a universal human consciousness, a set of symbols and sounds which all humans can recognize as uniquely human, whatever their aesthetic quality.

Only the proverbial philistine holds that life requires only visible and mundane values such as food and shelter *and no more besides*, as if human beings were cattle that seek nothing but indolent grazing. Art reflects our convictions, our image of ourselves, of others, and of the world we inhabit, and these values are indispensable for human life, for guiding our thoughts and most importantly, as philosophers should recognize, of providing an image of the goal or end of our actions. That is, to assist in providing answers to the questions: what ought I to do, what kind of person or society should we be and so on. (That is, to engage in philosophy.) Now, the production of any value requires effort and thought - means and ends, and in the production of art, especially good art, a person deploys the highest skills he or she can offer.

Art is accordingly not the achievement of the ordinary or mundane mind. It is a product of greatness and insight that is at once rare and rarefied. In the words of Vaclav Havel:

> Art constitutes a distinctive way of seeking truth - truth in the broadest sense of the word, that is, chiefly the truth of the artist's inner experience - then there is only one art, whose sole criterion is the power, the authenticity, the revelatory insight, the courage and suggestiveness with which it seeks its truth, or perhaps the urgency and profundity of this truth.[8]

And from Keats' *Ode On A Grecian Urn*: 'Beauty is truth, truth beauty - that is all ye know on earth, and all ye need to know.' To destroy art is of course to destroy value and truth. But arguably the destruction of art is akin to the destruction of food or shelter, yet even more disastrous: art gives life its meanings, without which life becomes pointless, animalistic, barbaric, habitual. It is this kind of narrow life - the life of Kant's *unmündigkeit* (intellectual immaturity) - that the iconoclast wishes to reproduce or impose, a life that is simplistic, with one particular viewpoint, one that eschews art or its pluralistic possibilities, for art presents alternatives and subtleties the iconoclast cannot conceive. To the philistine who says, 'Life's not like that,' the philosopher must reply, 'Who's life?'

Iconoclastic policies and the belief structures that support them are thoroughly anti-élitist, seeking to rein in the higher reaches of the human mind and to substitute a bland sameness, a homogeneity that brooks no dissent. Accordingly, iconoclasm is the violence of the egalitarian against the élite, of the mindless against the mind, of the envious and of the nihilist against those who seek to revere or exalt values and use their talents to express them. Iconoclasm is the boot of totalitarian authority smashing down onto the face of individuality in George Orwell's *1984*. It is also, of course, about control - about removing the individual search for meanings, of eradicating meanings that have been hitherto produced that still can provide us with the instrument - the image, the sound, the words - to think beyond or deeper than before, to remind us what we have been, what we have achieved, and what we still may recall and struggle for.

The essence of the iconoclast is captured by what Adam Smith refers to as 'a man of system', a man who believes he possesses a complete and exhaustive intellectual theory, and of course, who also believes that his system is true and all other systems or attempts at philosophy are false. Visions of life presented by different philosophical conceptions are thus subject to his condemnation and his desire to rid the world of such unnecessary distractions. Icons of competing systems of thought are thus to be waged war upon and destroyed. But it is not just physical entities (books, museums, compositions) that are destroyed in iconoclasms, but the underlying subjective and cultural vision that produced it. Hence Chairman Mao desired to erase the past from China, to start with a fresh slate, without any icons, intellectual, or behavioural echoes of the past. Hence the Protestants following Luther desired to rid the Church of Catholic symbolism (Luther: 'the external world is of no consequence!'), and hence the Taliban sought to remove vestiges of Buddhism from Afghanistan in 2001.

The philosophical fault in iconoclasm lies in the monistic system in which the truth is both attainable and attained by members or leaders of the sect. Those who disagree, dangerously become heretics to be either converted or killed. Artists of course are often targeted for their past or present potential threat to a monistic vision. A few heroic artists have survived threats to their work (Shostakovich, Kundera, Vaclav Havel, etc), or have been employed by the authorities to celebrate their own vision of humanity: and how wonderful it is to enjoy the subtle parodies such artists employ to mock their masters!

But ironically, the very people who seek to destroy their competitors' monuments present an aesthetic vision of humanity. Even when, like the Taliban, they seek to destroy all images, they simultaneously present an alternative. Their vision is often couched in political or theological terms which may denounce alternative or even all art, icons, poetry, or music; but any vision depends on a trick of the imagination to consider what life would be like without promiscuity, without guns, without alcohol, without violence, without other religions, without certain ethnic minorities, without others' icons, without annoying questions, without thinkers, and so on.

Utopian systems are thus works of art in themselves even when they deride art. Yet even those that do not mention the art world, logically imply that art should be destroyed, for works of art may undermine the particular utopian vision presented. Each artistic endeavour presents a threat to any closed system (Plato was very concerned to control the forms that art and music may take in his 'republic'). Artists often seek to abandon traditions, customs, and formulations in their drive to express their inner vision, hence they are such dangerous persons for totalitarian regimes. Even though they may have previously assisted to bring about the regime through their artwork, their minds continually seek the new, and they cannot abide regulation and constraint, and soon they turn against those who wish to trap their thoughts.

Protecting Art

To protect art therefore is to protect freedom and the symbol of freedom that human beings require to unleash all aspects of their talents - in literature, philosophy, art, technology, music, mathematics, and so on. Those who seek to destroy art works are knowingly or unknowingly destroying the pinnacle of human capacities, and are undermining people's freedom to think, to define themselves, and to expound their particular vision of life. Art is symbolic of that licence, of that freedom, and to attack the symbol is, in art's case, to extinguish that freedom. The brighter forces behind iconoclasm of course know what they seek: the monopolization of the world's thoughts and with it the imposition of their own particular creed. But the production of art requires some freedom or licence to create, it cannot be forced - when it is forced with the complicity of the artist, art suffers. Creativity cannot flow where there is no freedom, and it flows best when human beings have created the capacity for some leisure, and when they know what to do with that leisure. Art is an effect but also a symbol of freedom. Both art and freedom are fragile entities that flourish together and an attack on art is an attack on freedom. When freedom is attacked art declines both in quantity and quality; yet it also declines when concepts of sacred and sacrosanct are undermined, for both flow from the higher faculties that any person or civilization can attain. The relationship between the sacred and the freedom is 'as two twins cleaving together, [leaping] forth into the world' (Milton, *Areopagitica*).

We can also understand the importance of securing the moral status of art from present notions of political freedom. Political freedom, as we presently understand it in the modern world, suggests rights and duties and social contracts between political equals; yet while the language of present expositions is drawn to a legalistic, positivist language devoid of metaphor, the language of rights cannot help but invoke echoes of the sacred and the reverential.

For example, those who argue for protecting minority cultures are requesting the protection of a people's right to define their own vision - often in a hostile world - and to provide the freedom to form their own path. But self-determination does not exist in a vacuum - as dictatorships of various hues have recognized when they have sought to destroy minority cultures. Self-determination rests on a cultural legacy imbued in language and in art. Their cultural legacy - the art that they have produced - is the greatest source of their present identity and the means by which their identity continues to evolve. Sometimes that art may be in the form of songs or folk tales, in more complex societies it is manifested in literature, compositions, architecture and paintings. An attack on a culture's artistic heritage is thus an attack on its identity but also on its potential for the future reproduction of its values.

Individuals are forged in the cultures that nurture them, and as Hayek postulated: 'It may well be asked whether an individual who did not have the opportunity to tap into such a cultural tradition could be said even to have a mind.'[9] To undermine cultural traditions is to remove crucial psychological and sociological building structures that provide for the maturation of the mind, many of which are not thoroughly obvious to observation. Such structures are ultimately the source of any individual's talents, and provide for the mental growth of the individual; yet when customs or rules constrain the mind, imposing on its fragility absolute doctrines of obedience or the smothering mediocrity of the masses, then the mind withers and crumbles. 'Capacity for the nobler feelings', writes John Stuart Mill, 'is in most natures a very tender plant, easily killed, not only by hostile influences, but by mere want of sustenance; and in the majority of young persons it speedily dies away if the occupations to which their position in life has devoted them, are not favourable to keeping that higher capacity in exercise.' Art works obviously are the first cultural manifestations dictators desire to censor and eliminate.

Intervening for Art's Sake

Such barbarism seeks the dissolution of civilization, which ranges from the vast division and specialization of labour that corresponds with civil society to the effects and products of civil existence: notably freedom, learning, and art - the need for a cultured population is vital for the sustenance of any society that deigns to call itself civilized. But cultural icons can only be preserved where there is the moral force that sufficiently abhors attacks on art so much, that it prompts men to defend and to protect it. Iconoclasm is an evil that should betoken such intervention. The UN Hague Convention presents responsibilities on protecting but not intervening to defend cultural sites, hence it offers no motive or justification for the defence of humanity's most precious works. Iconoclasm is seen as destructive but not so destructive as to warrant preventative action.

That art should be protected from the ravages of warfare - as established in the Hague Convention - is uncontroversial. But to actively defend art from attack - or to punish aggressors - is apparently too controversial to admit into law. Yet it is as small a moral step as that of moving from the protection of refugees to waging defensive war on their behalf. Intervening to save lives is readily justifiable, but human *life* is not mere sustenance: human beings need art, they need to have the freedom to express the spirit of a culture to the maximum. Indeed, the destruction of the World Trade Towers in September 2001 shows how rapid is the moral response to the destruction of American icons as well as to the lives lost. Had the buildings been empty, or had the attack been on Mount Rushmore, the response would have been only marginally less.

Freedom of expression should be an inalienable facet of human life, but whereas we can readily accept - or at least acknowledge - that such freedoms ought to be protected against censorship, rarely do we leap to the active protection of a manuscript or temple about to be destroyed.

Partly this is because as physical entities and not sentient beings, works of art cannot be said to possess rights. A work of art is a reconstituted, artificial entity, not a living being. For most ethicists deliberating on the choice between saving a person and saving a work of art, the person would triumph without a second thought. But a person lives a mortal life, whereas his vision represented in his works strains for immortality. Plato died, his genes dissipating within four generations, but his works - his vision of humanity - live on. John Stuart Mill famously asks whether it would be better to be a dissatisfied Socrates than a satisfied fool, but arguably it is better to secure the ideas of Socrates for posterity than to let them perish and save the fool.

But beyond securing their protection, is it justifiable to militarily intervene to stop the destruction of irreplaceable works of art? Yes.

Art is irreplaceable by its very nature, but what it represents, as we have been arguing, is deserving much greater consideration than the mere physical instantiation it takes. Works of art certainly require the protection that the Hague Convention seeks, but they deserve more than that. The violence meted against art is violence meted against a people's cultural identity. When that culture dies, living individual members lose their cultural heritage and therefore lose a part of themselves. If they lose that heritage through the voluntary abandonment of old traditions, then nothing is lost for that people - and they should not be condemned for changing their ways, for they gain new ways of living. But the artefacts of their history ought to be protected. If they are lost through aggression, then everything is lost. The culture is terminated.

We come to the final problem in our argument: who is to secure the heritage of humanity and who is to intervene to protect it? Some of the authors in this collection refer to the concomitant obligations that arise from rights, especially positive rights to something such as health care. In a sense we cannot avoid the implication that obligations are thoroughly imperfect, falling on those who are close and who possess the wherewithal to fulfil the obligation. But we also want to emphasize a strong moral conviction that certainly has its roots deeply embedded in both our cultural structures and in our humanity. That is, some things are certainly worth fighting for.

Some Things Are Worth Fighting For

We need to distinguish the positive and the normative aspects of what we are asserting. Empirically, do human beings fight for values worth fighting for? Of course they do. But do they fight for aesthetic values? Of course: the Jews have fought for their Promised Land, an aesthetic vision hardly distinguishable from the theological status of God's chosen; the Greeks fought for Helen of Troy, the most beautiful woman abducted by the Trojans; the English soldiers in the trenches of World War One were infused with visions of their home - rural landscapes and placid villages of merry ol' England; American soldiers in various Twentieth Century conflicts have fought for democracy, which is not just a political theory, but an aesthetic vision of humanity deploying images of stable and accountable government, the society of contract rather than status, and so on. The same is true of fighting for Heimat, Communism, or for 'Harry, England, and St George'.

But asking whether people *should* fight for values is to pose an absurd question, if it implies that a person could live without fighting for values and still be said to be a moral person. We are not quibbling over whether human beings could exist without some struggle or some fight to defend their interests against aggressors, for we are more interested in what values constitute morally appropriate values to fight for. We can understand fighting for a vision - a vision of a world without poverty or without ignorance; but we can also understand fighting for a temple, a woman, a book, a painting. And it is certainly not because these things are commodities, for trading commodities is much more conducive to mutual satisfaction than fighting for them, but it is because these represent *visions of life* that subsume the plurality of values of a culture.

The particular issue that we can finally raise is who should defend art from iconoclasts. The answer can only be: those who are close to it and who possess the wherewithal, and accordingly for whom those values mean something.

This paper was written before the destruction of the Buddhist statues by the Taliban in March 2001, it was also written before the terrorist attacks on America on 11 September 2001. These barbaric attacks have underlined the philosophical differences between those who support civilization and those who seek its demise. Civilization requires a pluralism in all aspects of life, a pluralism that escapes the mentality of the 'man of system' or the controlling totalitarian, and art in all of its aspects, agreeable and disagreeable, is a manifestation of both that cultural depth and complexity that civilizations produce as well as the internal vision made concrete by the individual. The individual's right to freedom of expression is quickly becoming a universally held principle deserving military protection and even intervention from aggression, and in this paper we have argued that that should be extended to include the products of his expression. To destroy art is to destroy humanity.

Notes

1   Milton, *Areopagitica*, Dover, New York, 1981, p.6
2   However, the just war tradition is more often applied between groups that share many things in common and hence which are accepting of each other's humanity. Wars between widely differing cultures generally disregard the conventions. Cf. F.J.P. Veale, *Advance to Barbarism: the Development of Total Warfare from Sarajevo to Hiroshima*, The Mitre Press, London, 1968.
3   Perhaps Article 5.2, depending on the status of the Taliban regime.
4   Article 1. Definition of Cultural Property.
5   Burkhardt, *The Greeks and Greek Civilisation*, Faber, London, 1999, p.364.
6   Byron, *Poetical Works*, Oxford University Press, Oxford, 1970, p.92.
7   As noted by Giambatista Vico in *New Science*.
8   Vaclev Havel, 'Six Asides About Culture', in *Open Letters: Selected Prose 1965-1990*, Faber and Faber, London, 1991, p.280.
9   Friedrich Hayek, *Fatal Conceit: The Errors of Socialism*, Routledge, London, 1990, p.23.

Index